artWORK

Protest, Media and Culture

Series Editors:

Ruth Sanz Sabido is Lecturer in Media and Communications at Canterbury Christ Church University.

Stuart Price is Professor of Media and Political Discourse, and Chair of the Media Discourse Group, at De Montfort University.

Protest, Media and Culture publishes edited collections and monographs dedicated to the study and analysis of an irrepressible phenomenon: the worldwide resurgence of social, cultural, political and economic discontent.

Sites of Protest, edited by Stuart Price and Ruth Sanz Sabido
Protest Campaigns, Media and Political Opportunities, Jonathan Cable
The Pink Tide: Media Access and Political Power in Latin America, edited by Lee Artz
artWORK: Art, Labour and Activism, edited by Paula Serafini, Jessica Holtaway and Alberto Cossu
Songs of Social Protest: International Perspectives, edited by Aileen Dillane, Martin J Power, Eoin Devereux and Amanda Haynes

artWORK

Art, Labour and Activism

Edited by Paula Serafini, Jessica Holtaway
and Alberto Cossu

London • New York

Published by Rowman & Littlefield International, Ltd.
6 Tinworth Street, London SE11 5AL, United Kingdom
www.rowmaninternational.com

Rowman & Littlefield International, Ltd., is an affiliate of Rowman & Littlefield
4501 Forbes Boulevard, Suite 200, Lanham, Maryland 20706, USA
With additional offices in Boulder, New York, Toronto (Canada), and Plymouth (UK)
www.rowman.com

Selection and editorial matter © 2018 Paula Serafini, Jessica Holtaway and Alberto Cossu

Copyright in individual chapters is held by the respective chapter authors.

All rights reserved. No part of this book may be reproduced in any form or by any electronic or mechanical means, including information storage and retrieval systems, without written permission from the publisher, except by a reviewer who may quote passages in a review.

British Library Cataloguing-in-Publication Data
A catalogue record for this book is available from the British Library

ISBN: HB 978-1-78660-188-9
       PB 978-1-78660-189-6

Library of Congress Cataloguing-in-Publication Data Is Available
ISBN 978-1-78660-188-9 (cloth: alk. paper)
ISBN 978-1-78660-189-6 (pbk.: alk. paper)
ISBN 978-1-78660-190-2 (electronic)

∞™ The paper used in this publication meets the minimum requirements of American National Standard for Information Sciences – Permanence of Paper for Printed Library Materials, ANSI/NISO Z39.48–1992.

Contents

List of Figures — vii

About the Authors — ix

Preface — xiii

   Introduction — 1
   Paula Serafini, Alberto Cossu and Jessica Holtaway

1. Reimaging, Reimagining or Reimagineering: Rebranding Ulster — 25
   Sheelagh Colclough and Sarah Feinstein

2. Art, Activism and Addressing Sexual Assault in the UK: A Case Study — 45
   Winnie M. Li

3. Macao before and beyond Social Media: The Creation of the Unexpected as a Mobilisation Logic — 65
   Alberto Cossu and Maria Francesca Murru

4. The Political Value of Techno-Future — 87
   Emanuele Braga

5. Changing the Narrative: Highlighting Workers' Rights in Environmental Art Activism — 105
   Paula Serafini

6. Working Dancers: Contemporary Dance Activism in Argentina — 127
   Konstantina Bousmpoura and Julia Martinez Heimann

7	Making Art Relevant in the Aftermath of the Egyptian Uprising *Rounwah Adly Riyadh Bseiso*	147
8	Collective Art-Making to Agitate for Social Change: In and between Theatre, Live Art, Community Art and Protest Camps *Mel Evans*	167
9	Embracing Failure, Educating Hope: Some Arts Activist Educators' Concerns in Their Work for Social Justice *Jane Trowell*	189
10	In Case of Emergency Make Art: Exploring the (Non)function of Art in Response to Humanitarian Disasters *Jessica Holtaway*	209
11	Post-Autonomous Art and Common People in Barcelona *Roger Sansi*	225
	Conclusion *Jessica Holtaway, Alberto Cossu and Paula Serafini*	237
Acknowledgements		249
Index		251

List of Figures

1.1 *Royal Heavies*, 2007, Sheelagh Colclough (mixed media). Image credit: Sheelagh Colclough. 32
1.2 *Bill*, 2014, Sheelagh Colclough (mixed media). Image credit: Sheelagh Colclough. 34
1.3 *Francis*, 2014, Sheelagh Colclough (mixed media). Image credit: Sheelagh Colclough. 35
3.1 Total of tweets created by Macao or directed to Macao (from 1 April 2012 to 30 June 2012). Image credit: Alberto Cossu. 73
3.2 Macao aphorism from the launching campaign. Image credit: Macao. 78
5.1 Gilberto Torres holds a picture of kidnapped trade union activist Aury Sará Marrugo while standing outside the British Museum with two BP or not BP? performers, 11 October 2015. Image credit: Paula Serafini. 111
5.2 Image of the *Arpillera* being displayed by members of London Mexico Solidarity and The Wretched of the Earth at the *History of BP* exhibition. Image credit: Paula Serafini 116
6.1 CNDC, Ode to Ourselves, the One We All Know, 2010. Image credit: Marcelo Raggone. 132
6.2 CNDC, *Small Patchworks of Our Most Recent History*, 2010. An allegorical scene to celebrate the approval of the same-sex marriage law in Argentina. Image credit: Marcelo Raggone. 138

6.3	Street performance in the Congress Square of Buenos Aires in defence of the National Dance Law, 29 April 2014. Image credit: Javier Fuentes.	141
10.1	Image from *Portrait in Mask*, 2012. Image credit: Kaya Hanasaki.	211
10.2	Film still from *Do Not Enter*, 2013. Image credit: Kyun-Chome.	214
10.3	*Moving the Mountain*, a film still from Komori and Seo's documentary film series *under the wave, on the ground*, 2014. Image credit: Haruka Komori and Natsumi Seo.	218
12.1	Four coordinates for the study of art activism and labour.	246

About the Authors

Konstantina Bousmpoura is an independent researcher, filmmaker and dancer. She has worked in filmic ethnography, direction and production of documentaries and dance projects in Buenos Aires, Seville and Athens. Her latest feature-length documentary *Working Dancers* focuses on contemporary dance, labour rights and politics and was released in 2016.

Emanuele Braga is an artist, researcher and activist. He is the cofounder of the dance and theatre company Balletto Civile (2003), the contemporary art project Rhaze (2011), cofounder and developer of MACAO, new centre for art and culture (2012) and cofounder of Landscape Choreography (2012), an art platform questioning the role of the body under capitalism. Emanuele's research focuses on models of cultural production and processes of social transformation, and theoretical issue of political economy, institution of the commons and labour rights (*La moneta del comune*, published with Andrea Fumagalli in 2015).

Rounwah Adly Riyadh Bseiso is a final-year PhD candidate at the Centre for Media & Film Studies at the School of Oriental and African Studies (SOAS). She currently has a forthcoming journal article in *Comparative Studies of South Asia, Africa and the Middle East* and has published a chapter in the edited book *Narrating Conflict in the Middle East: Discourse, Image and Communications Practices in Lebanon and Palestine*.

Sheelagh Colclough is a Belfast-based multidisciplinary artist who has sixteen years of experience in collaborative arts practice: arts education and engagement, production, programming and research. In recent years, she has exhibited with Golden Thread and PS² galleries in Belfast and has programmed and participated in a series of collaborative practice events for Ulster University. She completed a collaborative artists' residency at the Tyrone Guthrie Centre with The Performance Corporation, Ireland, in 2015 and was artist in residence with IZOLYATSIA, Ukraine, in July 2016. Sheelagh is currently a board member of Blue Drum, a Dublin-based community arts and cultural rights organisation. Much of her work examines the hierarchies of state-sanctioned social interventions present in many community and collaborative art projects.

Alberto Cossu is a Lecturer in New Media and Digital Culture in the Department of Media Studies at the University of Amsterdam. He conducted research on the mobilisation of knowledge and art workers in Italy, on peer-to-peer models of organisation and production in Italy and France (within the EU Project P2PValue), on digital economy and co-working spaces in Italy and Thailand. He has published articles in *City, Culture & Society, Social Media + Society* and *Studi Culturali*. Alberto is a cofounder of PLANK (Politically Led Art and Networked Knowledge).

Mel Evans is an artist and campaigner part of Liberate Tate. Her book *Artwash: Big Oil and the Arts* was published by Pluto Press in 2015. Her play "Oil City" was produced by Platform and presented as part of the Two Degrees Festival in 2013. Her writing has been published in Contemporary Theatre Review, Performance Research Journal, Internationale Online, The Guardian, The Independent, New Internationalist, Dissent!, Red Pepper and others. She regularly speaks about art and politics at events, which have included Economic Exceptionalism at the Institute of Contemporary Arts London, D&AD President's Lecture, Performing Protest Conference Leuven University, Artwash Book Tour UK and Ireland, Curating Conflict at the V&A Gallery London, and Question Everything at the Cambridge Festival of Ideas.

Sarah Feinstein has worked in the cultural sector for over eighteen years, acquiring skills in collections management and arts administration. Most recently, she worked as a researcher at the Pankhurst Center Heritage Museum (Manchester) and the Prisons Memory Archive (Belfast). She holds a BA in Liberal Arts from The Evergreen State College, an MA in Arts Administration and Policy from the School of the Art Institute of Chicago and an MA in Creative and Critical Analysis from Goldsmiths University London. She is currently a doctoral candidate at the Institute for Cultural Practices at the University of Manchester and serves as a trustee for the Manchester District Music Archive.

Julia Martinez Heimann is an independent researcher, filmmaker and educator. She has worked in direction and production of documentaries and cultural series for cinema and television in Buenos Aires since 2009. Her latest feature-length documentary *Working Dancers* focuses on contemporary dance, labour rights and politics and was released in 2016.

Jessica Holtaway is a PhD candidate in the Department of Visual Cultures at Goldsmiths College, University of London. Her research explores themes of globalisation, energy politics, politicised art practices, institutional practices and political theory, with a core focus on the writings of Jean-Luc Nancy. She has published a paper on institutional ethics in the peer-reviewed journal *Museological Review*. Jessica is a cofounder of PLANK (Politically Led Art and Networked Knowledge).

Winnie M. Li is a writer, activist, rape survivor and PhD researcher in Media and Communications at the London School of Economics. She explores the uses of social media by rape survivors to narrate their experiences. She is the Co-Founder of the *Clear Lines Festival*, the UK's first-ever festival dedicated to addressing sexual assault and consent through the arts and discussion. A George Mitchell Scholar, she holds degrees from Harvard and Goldsmiths and writes widely about rape, across a variety of formats. Her debut novel *Dark Chapter*, was published worldwide in 2017. winniemli.com.

Maria Francesca Murru, PhD, is lecturer in Sociology of Cultural Processes at Università Cattolica di Milano, Faculty of Political and Social Sciences. Her research interests are focused on online public spheres and mediated civic participation and she is currently engaged in research projects dealing with media representations and emergent publics. Recent publications include: 'The performative role of hashtags in the politicisation of Europe: 2014 European elections on Twitter', in I. Vobič, T. Deželan, *(R)evolutionizing Political Communication through Social Media*, IGI Global, Pennsylvania; 'Listening, Temporalities and Epistemology: A Hermeneutical Perspective on Mediated Civic Engagement', *Participations* 13(1).

Roger Sansi was born in Barcelona, Spain, in 1972. After studying at the Universities of Barcelona and Paris he received his PhD in Sociocultural Anthropology at the University of Chicago (2003). He has worked at Kings College and Goldsmiths College, University of London. Currently he is Professor of Social Anthropology at Universitat de Barcelona, Spain. He has worked on Afro-Brazilian culture and religion, the concept of the fetish and on contemporary art in Barcelona. His publications include the books *Fetishes and Personalism* (Berghahn, 2007), *Sorcery in the Black Atlantic* (edited with

L. Nicolau, Chicago University Press 2011), *Economies of relation: Money And Personlaism in the Lusophone World* (University of New England Press 2013) and *Art, Anthropology and the Gift* (Bloomsbury 2015).

Paula Serafini is a Research Associate at CAMEo Research Institute for Cultural and Media Economies, University of Leicester. She holds a BA in Art History and Management (Universidad del Salvador, Argentina), an MA in Anthropology and Cultural Politics (Goldsmiths) and a PhD in Social and Cultural Analysis (King's College London). Her work is concerned with the relation between aesthetics and politics, and she has conducted research on art activism, performance, museum ethics and most recently digital art and social media. Her work has been published in journals such as *Third Text* and *Anarchist Studies*, and she is currently working on her first monograph. Paula is a cofounder of PLANK (Politically Led Art and Networked Knowledge).

Jane Trowell is an arts educator, based in London. She works on the relationship between art, education, social and ecological justice. In 1991, Jane started working with social justice and arts group *Platform*. Here she cocreated the arts and activism course for adults 'The Body Politic' (2004–2009) and co-initiated the current youth programme 'Shake! Young Voices in Arts, Media, Race & Power'. She curated Platform's fifty-day season of teach-ins and arts activist commissions 'C Words: Carbon, Climate, Capital, Culture' at Arnolfini, Bristol, in 2009, and co-led the campaign 'Action Saro-Wiwa' during 2014–2015. In the formal sector, Jane taught for many years at Birkbeck College, Chelsea College of Art & Design and on the PGCE and MA in Art & Design Education at the Institute of Education (UCL). Jane is currently a doctoral student at the School of Education, University of Lincoln.

Preface

artWORK: Art, Labour and Activism explores contemporary practices at the intersections of art, labour and activism, with the intention of generating interdisciplinary approaches to social engagement within culture and the arts. This collection of chapters developed over a period of eighteen months. The formative discussions began at a conference at King's College London on 18 September 2015: *Techniques of Art and Protest*, organised by PLANK research (Politically Led Art and Networked Knowledge), a network founded by what was then a group of PhD students from Goldsmiths Visual Cultures and Cultural Studies Departments, the Department of Culture, Media & Creative Industries at King's College London, and the Department of Social and Political Studies, Università degli Studi di Milano.

Techniques of Art and Protest was an interdisciplinary conference, featuring talks and workshops that aimed to bridge institutional, non-institutional and disciplinary practices. The conference explored how the singular demands of academic, artistic and activist forms affect the overall proximity of political horizons. Among wider discussions on art and social change, it addressed the possibility of unionising in the arts. It reflected on the complexities of mutual aid organising. It began to consider how we might create alternative economic models to rethink artistic and cultural production. And it reflected on how we might influence changes in the rights and conditions of migrant workers.

These discussions and reflections highlighted the importance of sustaining an interdisciplinary approach to labour issues in the arts and creative industries, as well as in art activist practices that take place outside of institutional frameworks. The conference created an intersection where practitioners and researchers from different fields met to discuss shared experiences and alternative approaches to key issues. *artWORK* aims to continue these conversations; to create wider discussions on the themes of art, labour and activism; and perhaps to spark new approaches to creative activism and to social practices within art and the creative industries.

Introduction

Paula Serafini, Alberto Cossu
and Jessica Holtaway

While the relationship between art and politics is hardly new, we are currently in the crest of a global wave of artists and creative workers increasingly engaged in the social and political space. They take part in national and global social movements (e.g. Occupy, Tahrir Square, Umbrella Revolution), they create movements of their own (e.g. Network of Occupied Theatres in Italy and Greece), they protest the structures and dynamics of cultural institutions (e.g. Liberate Tate), they experiment with alternative economic models and currencies (e.g. Macao and D-CENT), they do social research and radical education (e.g. Platform and Iconoclasistas), they support neighbourhoods and fill the void left by the state's retreat from the social space, they confront the exploitative dynamics of an art system subjected to the market and they host and co-produce art at a time when the budget for arts and culture is being diminished in numerous countries across the world. Parallel to this, activists are engaging in different forms of art-making as a form of political action – from the art exhibitions of National Gallery workers fighting privatisation of their contracts in the UK to the artistic interventions of environmental groups from around the world at the COP21 meetings in Paris.

As a result, the debate on the social and political role of art has recently been revamped. Political, cultural, economic, philosophical, sociological and anthropological interventions have been disseminated on this nouvelle vague of 'engaged art(ists)' in the past decade and more specifically in the past five years. But the specialisation of academic work makes it difficult to capture the sheer complexity of this phenomenon.[1] This volume contributes to the debate by acknowledging the nuances and particularities of this emerging scene of socially and politically engaged artists and tackling it by including contributions from different academic domains and from the actors themselves, in an attempt to thread together different facets and understandings of this phenomenon. By bringing in the perspective of labour in art activism to the debate – considering how art (and) activism spaces allow forms of labour that are 'distinct from the "work" of possessive individualism' (Kester, 2011: 112) – this volume looks to make a specific contribution to the field, focusing on internal processes, organisational issues and reflections from academics and practitioners on the labour of activism, artistic labour and the political function of art.

Considering this focus, the contributions in this volume explore two main questions that engage with the practicalities and politics of art activism, and with the implications of new discourses emerging from practice for theory on aesthetics and politics. First, how can the organisational structures required for collective action generate new ways of art-making and resist co-option into capitalist frameworks? And second, in what ways do practices at the intersection of art and activism reproduce or challenge ideas around the instrumentalisation of art and 'art for arts sake'? The chapters in this volume provide insights into a number of contemporary practices at the intersection of art, labour and activism, and they each address aspects of these questions, if not tackling them directly. But in order to begin constructing answers, it is necessary to think about how specific concepts and perspectives from different fields such as aesthetics, art theory, sociology and anthropology can be applied to the study of practices that stand at the intersection of art, labour and activism, considering the theoretical challenges that can arise in our attempts to study forms of protest, communication, art and organisation from different disciplinary perspectives. While each chapter in this volume adopts a particular analytical lens, this book is at the same time a call for the blurring of disciplinary boundaries and the embracement of interdisciplinary approaches, acknowledging that practices that sit across different spheres of the social, such as those explored here, benefit from transdisciplinary forms of understanding.

AESTHETICS, PERCEPTION AND THE SOCIAL

There are two dynamics that are usually at play when we think of the relationship between aesthetics and politics: the aestheticisation of politics and the politicisation of aesthetics. The first implies the process through which politics – as enacted in the institutional political field – becomes aestheticised. Examples of this are the spectacular character of coordinated marches, speeches and other political events that are conceived with attention to the visual and other sensorial qualities, but which through this emphasis generate a shift in the way politics is perceived and understood. Benjamin most famously described this in relation to the aesthetics of Fascism (2008) and the exercise of control. On the other hand we find the politicisation of aesthetics, which can be understood as a dynamic close to that described above (i.e. the instrumentalisation of art by the political apparatus) or as the complete opposite: a politicisation of what was previously an autonomous practice, now politicised, democratised both in its content and processes and put to the service of enacting social and political change (Benjamin, 1970). Boris Groys (2014) argues that art activism lies, contradictorily, somewhere in between these two dynamics.

Also relevant here is Jacques Rancière's writing on aesthetics and politics (2004, 2006, 2010). Aesthetics for Rancière is 'a delimitation of spaces and times, of the visible and the invisible, of speech and noise, that simultaneously determines the place and the stakes of politics as a form of experience' (Rancière, 2004: 13). At the same time, he equates the aesthetic act to the political act, considering them both as ways of disrupting consensus (Rancière, 2010: 140). This book seeks to explore the ways in which art and aesthetics are politicised, as well as the aestheticisation of politics. But instead of looking at the politics of the establishment and maintaining Benjamin's cautious stance on the potential dangers of this phenomenon, we look at the politicisation of art for the enactment of democratic politics, and at the non-institutional politics of the grassroots, understanding aestheticisation as a heightened awareness of the sensorial, the relational and the embodied in political work.

If in the past decade we have been witnessing a new wave of artists becoming activists, it follows that scholars should, on the one hand, acknowledge the cycles in which these phenomena took place in the past century[2] and, on the other hand, avoid overdetermining the originality of such waves by applying a rigid structural grid to them. Boris Groys's 2014 essay 'On Art Activism' sparked a wide discussion on this issue on some of the most important arenas for contemporary art debates. Here he argued that unlike previous waves in which the ambitions of art reached the social and the political (he focuses on Russian avant-gardes and other historical cases), the most prominent feature of the current art activism wave is actors' willingness to impact society in a political way 'without ceasing to be artists'. In a response to Groys's essay, artist, activist and theorist Gregory Sholette (2016) exhorts practitioners and participants to 'occupy, organise and repeat'. This constant cyclical renewal of practice means that every wave of art activism is always entirely new.

Following Sholette we consider that each single wave of art activism is not just new, it is entirely new as it is based on an event-object which discloses a future in which no given utopia is fixed to be achieved. If in previous cycles tactical protesting has deployed creative repertoires of action, the 'newness' in the current cycle of art activism lies in the double movement for which, at the start of the current wave in the early 2010s, first there is an acknowledgement and exploration of the relationality of artistic, social and political processes and second, these newly articulated social relations are linked to processes of economic production. It is on this double movement that we are situating this book, at the intersection between political, creative and economic processes. These processes are also connected to the articulation of social and political forces in the global scenario, as the blurring of social and economic impact is reshaping business organisation and social movements alike. It is for these reasons that we argue for a more encompassing notion of 'movement' – in addition to a broader understanding of art – that is capable of including a range of subjects displaying a variable degree of political subjectivation linking political and economic stances. We can understand this as a process of hybridisation that mirrors what happened in the field of business organisations when they shifted their mission to maximise social impact (Hoffman et al., 2012).[3]

A reconsideration of the notion of movement invites a rethinking of the notion of art, and what its limits, if any, are. As Whybrow (2011, 6) recalls, one of the most compelling interrogatives posed within the 2006 Frieze talks was 'Is art still art when art is everywhere?' This question arises from a process of aestheticisation which invested the whole society through practices which have been defined by Nicolas Bourriaud as *relational aesthetics*. Bourriaud's expression 'relational aesthetics' – the title of his 2002 book, originally published in French in 1998 – has become an influential term in discourses on contemporary art, and often frames analyses of participatory practices. In simple terms, 'relational aesthetics' describes art that is characterised more by its dynamism and social significance than by its final aesthetic 'product'. In recent years the writings of Claire Bishop, in particular her book *Artificial Hells,* have continued to contextualise this expression, referencing the term with relation to themes of spectatorship and emancipation. These writings, through a focused critique of the *aesthetics* of relational practices, emphasise a perceived 'clash' between artistic and social critiques, and have opened up debates on the role of art in social change and the social value of creative practices. These debates have triggered alternative expressions, such as Grant Kester's use of the term 'dialogical art', which develops a focus on the dynamism and multiple layers of significance in participatory and collaborative art. They have also sparked opposition from certain socially engaged and activist artists, as scholars of relational aesthetics often dismiss art that falls too much on the activist side as being non-autonomous and doomed to be purely representational of any given social movement (Kester, 2011: 31–32).[4]

In his conception of relational aesthetics, Bourriaud understands artistic gestures as 'an angelic programme' that can 'patiently restitch the relational fabric' (Bourriaud, 2002: 36). Here, for Bourriaud, artworks are divine interventions and have an uncanny potential to generate a social impact. However, this assumption ultimately fails to address and critically evaluate the foundations of this apparent divide between the aesthetic and the social. As a result, art practices are framed as practices that *serve* social requirements, practices that are separate from, and instrumental to, larger social programmes. In particular, participatory practices are framed as participating in a pre-defined social programme, rather than as creative gestures that work within a social framework and that can change and move beyond the structures of those frameworks.

To address how participatory practices alter and transcend social paradigms, and open up new ways of communicating, requires a close look at, and perhaps deconstruction of, the perceived divide between aesthetics and social bonds. Responding to Bourriaud's claim that art can 'patiently restitch the relational fabric' (Bourriaud, 2002: 60), we might ask: if art is also part of this fabric, how can it 'self-repair' and continue to weave new social ties and narratives? By situating creative practices, in particular art activism, as *part of* our social fabric, we no longer visualise it as 'at our service', but it becomes a way of creating radically new social paradigms – paradigms that do not have a prescribed outcome, but that allow for collaborative participation. Here, art is instrumental, not just in 'restitching' social fabric, but in creating new connections and sustaining creative freedom. It is this dynamism that we hope to spotlight in this collection of chapters.

Returning to Kester's concept of 'dialogical art', explored in his 2011 book *The One and the Many* (and introduced in his earlier text, *Conversation Pieces*) might be of use here. For art to be dialogical means it cannot be reduced to one particular meaning, but that it is incalculable. Rather than acting as set of fixed signifiers, this visual language is dynamic and demands that we perpetually 'unlearn' and learn through praxis (Kester, 2011: 226). The increasing prominence of participatory art indicates an increased emphasis on the sociality at the heart of aesthetics. Consequently, this volume of chapters approaches themes of activism and labour through an understanding that visual and performance-based practices are part of an unfolding dialogue. We are approaching discussions of art, labour and activism through the understanding that art is communicative and that it necessarily invites participation. Even the act of spectatorship can be a form of engagement-with and participation.

Awareness of the inherent sociality of aesthetics increasingly defines emergent discussions of art, in particular practices that fall under the umbrella of art activism. However, this does not indicate a uniformity of approaches to art, activism and labour. As this book will highlight, there are many differing approaches to these themes but, based as they are on this common understanding that art has open-ended discursive potential, we believe that any emergent conflicts are 'agonistic', in that they recognise 'difference' as a shared condition of being, and aim to sustain creative freedom (Mouffe, 2013).

An example of this agonistic relation is the exchange between Boris Groys and Gregory Sholette alluded to earlier. Both theorists recognise the inherent sociality of aesthetics and both move beyond the binary differentiation between 'art' and 'politics'. But when Groys argues that artistic aestheticisation has a deconstructive impact that necessarily concerns the political (Groys, 2014), Sholette responds, critiquing Groys's analysis of art activism for being too 'clean'. He argues instead that aestheticisation also allows for increased visibility of right-wing ideologies (Sholette, 2016). This discussion and the conflicts within the two approaches presented expose the complexities of aestheticisation and contribute to a deeper understanding of the temporal affectivity of creative practices. They invite us to look at the ways in which creative practices can easily become absorbed into the status quo and emphasise the need to develop responsive approaches to the intersections of art, labour and activism. This intersection can be addressed through discussions on the 'processuality' of art and the impact this has within capitalist systems of exchange (Holmes, 2013). To move beyond a perceived divide between art and politics, and to look at the communicative significance of creative practices, leads to analyses of the *processes* of both art making and art viewing. It is through these processes that artists and art viewers can embody the potential for new social bonds and networks.

These shifts in focus from a perceived divide between aesthetics and politics to an acknowledgement of their interaction and on occasion, synonymy, call for closer attention to the intersections of practice in which the concepts of art, labour and activism noticeably converge. The idea of an intersection carries with it a sense of 'cutting between' that paradoxically creates a connection. To identify intersections is to cut between these imbricated concepts of art, labour and activism. In doing so, we hope to reveal ways in which these concepts coalesce to become affective (in this context, affectivity might take the form of a shift in a group's consciousness or sense of their practice, opening up new opportunities for renewal and development). Extending the metaphor of the intersection as a conceptual convergence, increased affectivity might include practitioners altering the course of particular projects, collaborating with others or perhaps just slowing down and reflecting upon the direction of a project – a process that can itself be transformative. This collection draws from a range of creative practices: street art, dance, protest, theatre, performance, institutional practices, curatorial practices, media and technology, arts education and evolving forms of exchange.

ART IN AND OF SOCIAL MOVEMENTS AND THE IMAGINARY OF ARTISTS AS WORKERS

Artists are (again) at the frontlines of political mobilisation, as a response to the social and economic circumstances that affect them in both direct and indirect ways. They mobilise themselves and try to aggregate fellow citizens around ideas of radical citizenship and self-governance; but they do so in their own peculiar way. What is needed then is to investigate what happens when artists' own tools are deployed in mobilisation, in both physical spaces and in digitally-mediated environments. The contributions we host in this book offer a situated and microphysical point of view that we deem useful to account for the specific role played by art in mobilisation and to avoid the risk of overlooking the elemental components of political action. We argue that a more thorough consideration of such components can contribute to a deeper understanding of the aesthetic, affective, cultural, political and ethical stances that are responsible for the existence and the shaping of the 'stitching mechanisms' (Bennett et al., 2014) at work in large-scale digitally mediated movements. As a result of its intense reliance on cultural, social and affective dynamics, the mobilisation of artists offers a vantage point from which to both reassess the assumptions that have guided the understanding of the recent wave of mobilisations in terms of connective action (Bennett and Segerberg, 2012) and update our understanding of the linkages between art and political action.

A consideration of the components of art in political mobilisation calls first for an identification of the object of analysis. A fundamental task when seeking to understand art *in* mobilisation concerns its framing as a 'productive field'. This means that, although performances, chants, choreographies, puppets and other creative or artistic performances have been somewhat taken into account in the scholarly literature in at least three different fields (social movement studies, sociology of art and sociology of culture), the problem is that often these works, although inspiring, reveal a conceptualisation of art in mobilisation which is limited for two fundamental reasons: objectivation and instrumentalisation (Tucker, 2012). The first problem lies in the arbitrary segmentation operated only when the perceivable expression of creative acts that, by definition, are the product of complex processes is analysed.[5] From this point of view, what is investigated is mostly the effects of the visible presence of a creative product in its context of reception, which is often a protest context. This leads to the second problem. As social movement scholars explain (della Porta and Diani, 2006, chapter 7), protest is one of the many ways in which political mobilisation takes place. But marches, rallies, demonstrations and parades undoubtedly constitute some of the key arenas in which creative performances are publicly staged in an attempt to attain visibility and recognition for the movements and the causes that they advocate.

Furthermore, protests have traditionally been organised by social movements or coalitions (Diani, 1992), or, according to Bennett and Castells, by crowds themselves, the most fundamental unit of which is the *activist*. Accordingly, the main question which scholars – in particular the few who explicitly deal with art and social movements – have posed can typically be rephrased as: how are activists using art in mobilisation? In a nutshell, the underlying assumption is that art, performances and creativity can be assimilated to a kind of 'colourful magic hat' out of which activists can draw innovative tactics for successful protest. Using a more formalised language, art and aesthetics constitute a sub-group of a wider repertoire of action that a given social movement is able to activate.[6] This perspective is still viable, and what is being questioned here is not the capacity of such a perspective to explain what has happened in the past decades or in the contemporary occurrences in which art and protest are linked instrumentally (or are understood as such). Indeed, as Calhoun argues, 'Instrumental thinking is dominant in the field because of the specific post-1960s struggles that have defined it, but it exists and has the intellectual power it has because of a much longer history linking reason to control (including control over emotions), (Calhoun, 2001: 49). In empirical terms, we can apply this analytical lens for instance in the case of a non-professional artist-activist using his or her creativity in protest or co-opting professional artists for the production of protest artefacts.[7] As one activist puts it, looking back at protest tactics in the late 1990s and the playful approach of certain demonstration blocs: 'For me . . . the Pink and Silver was tactical frivolity . . . so you are using frivolousness . . . tactically in a situation where everyone is geared up for confrontation'.[8] The interviewed activist sees frivolousness as a tactic to be deployed in effective protesting, for example to draw police attention to herself and to divert it from something going on elsewhere. However, such an approach shows its limits when the only people involved are artists themselves, mobilising on their own. Sociological cleavages are to be put back into the frame to properly address the differences and mergers in art, protest and activism. As we will address in the conclusion of this book, it is crucial to assess *who* the actors engaging with creative repertoires are and what the arenas in which they are engaging are, and to identify the intended outcome of their mobilising, if any.

The politics of aesthetics and the aesthetics of politics, politicised artists and avant-gardes have all produced, and have themselves been, widely debated topics in Western thought. Of course, it is not just in speculation that the two realms have crossed paths. As Mathieu Grégoire (2013) highlights, a specific category of French art workers[9] have engaged for the whole past century in a struggle for their rights. But a history of artists organising does not mean that there is nothing new in contemporary artists' mobilisations. In fact, Grégoire's main argument is that, starting from reasons and desires that appear consistent throughout the twentieth century, art workers have constructed distinct emancipatory horizons over time.[10] What is revealing is that through these different lenses it is possible to reconstruct the underlying logic of the global social conflict in a given context.

Indeed, while largely unknown today outside certain circles, there is a strong history of artists organising as workers against an unequal art world and its system and for a more inclusive and accessible cultural realm. Contrary to the common belief that artists are individualistic and incapable of organising, the United States, for instance, offers 'a substantial history of non-governmental guilds, unions, associations, and collectives organized by artists' (Sholette, 2011, 124). A prominent example of this is the Art Workers' Coalition (1969–1971) in New York, which fought to change the structure of the art world (McKee, 2016: 142–43). It challenged the lack of representation of women and people of colour as exhibiting artists in museums, but also campaigned for the accessibility of art and culture, succeeding, for instance in getting the Museum of Modern Art (MoMA) to implement a free admission day. There were, in addition, a number of calls for artists to strike in the 1970s, which positioned artists as workers armed with the refusal of labour as their weapon (Sholette, 2011, 56). More recently, the city of New York also saw the emergence of W.A.G.E. (Working Artists and the Greater Economy), a network organising for the regulation of the payment to artists by cultural organisation and the building of sustainable labour relations.[11] Also recently the exhibition *Art Work: A National Conversation about Art, Labour and Economics* and the accompanying paper by the same name emerged as a space for artists and cultural workers to reflect on their status as workers and catalyse action across the country (McKee, 2016, 141). On the other side of the pond, the volunteer-run Artists' Union England was created with the aim of organising and representing the previously unrepresented voices of professional artists. And in the Global South, chapter 6 in this volume looks at the recent high-profile case of dancers organising as workers in Argentina.

But it is also necessary to situate the struggles of artists in contemporary political and economic contexts. In this regard, it might be useful to broaden the category of artist to cultural worker, in order to encompass the different kinds of labour carried out by artists and creatives within the cultural and creative industries today. The cultural industries can be defined as 'those involved in the production of "aesthetic" or "symbolic" goods and services; that is, commodities whose core value is derived from their function as carriers of *meaning*' (Banks, 2007: 2); this production of meaning is deliberate and self-conscious. Banks lays out what he argues are 'fundamental features of the political organization and practice of cultural work': The 'art-commerce' relation (the tension between the cultural and the economic as separate spheres, but also their increased overlapping); the creative cultural worker (the primary makers of text in the industry, but those whose working lives we know less of as they are often not recognised as workers) and ordinary workplaces (the daily spaces of cultural production) (Banks, 2007: 6).

While the cultural and creative industries 'are perceived to be generating seductive new models for work and industrial organization' (Banks, 2007: 4), and workers are encouraged to regard themselves as autonomous and celebrate the flexible and individualised aspects of their work, creative work has become increasingly entrenched in the neoliberal model and tendencies towards individualism have weakened workplace democracy (McRobbie, 2002) and the collective bargaining power of workers.

In his book by the same name, Sholette (2011) describes the *dark matter* of the art world as the body of often exploited, undervalued and invisible art workers that make up the structures and foundations of the hierarchical and extremely unequal art world. He argues that there has been an increasing amount of informal non-parliamentary organisations that have emerged in response to these conditions in the field of the arts in a context of neoliberal globalisation. In a slightly optimistic manner, he adds: 'We appear to be far from witnessing some general art strike today. Still, conditions for unprecedented self-organisation are readily available to artists as an increasing number of professional cultural producers turn to social networking sites, online art galleries, and individual webpages as a way of directly distributing images and information about their work' (Sholette, 2011: 117).

When examining the mobilisation of artists, it is important to note that there are two ways in which they are reacting to the state of the art world: the first is demanding regulation and better rights, and the second is exiting the sphere altogether and operating outside of the frame of cultural institutions (Holmes, 2004). The latter was the case of many artists who were crucial to the alterglobalisation movement in the late 1990s and early 2000s, as well as more recently in the global wave of protests that emerged after the 2008 economic crisis. In his account of the Occupy movement, Yates McKee argues that Occupy allowed artists to adopt the identity of workers, and soon after the identity of debtors that would define the movement. McKee speaks of how Occupy saw the emergence (in the United States we might add) of 'the artist as an organizer' (2016: 26).

In order to better frame the context that these artists as organisers are part of, we must also take into account the prominent role that digital media have come to play. The diffusion of information and communications technology (ICT) has attracted growing attention within the interdisciplinary field of contentious politics (Tilly and Tarrow, 2007). Contributions in this field have stressed the question of whether, and to what extent, ICT has reshaped modes and practices of political mobilisation. In particular, along with technological developments from the 1990s onwards, questions around 'whether organizations still have a role in grassroots mobilization, whether dense face-to-face community networks are still necessary to support collective action, and whether identity bonds still need some kind of shared direct experience and/or 'real' interaction to develop' (della Porta and Diani, 2006: 132) started to emerge. From the outset, the social movement debate seems to frame the articulation of media and mobilisation by privileging an organisational point of view.

More recently, uprisings in North Africa (the Arab Spring), in Spain (Indignados) and in the United States (Occupy Wall Street, which then globally spread as a 'protest brand') have renewed the debate on the role of social media in the organisation, recruitment and life of these mobilisations. In this context, Lance Bennett and Alexandra Segerberg (2013) propose a typology that differentiates between movements based on a more traditional collective logic from the emerging connective logic in which digital media are the organising agents. Dealing with the same wave of mobilisation, Manuel Castells (2012) identifies a fundamental common feature among them: their being inextricably linked to the creation of autonomous communication networks, supported by the Internet and, in particular, by wireless services. This feature separates them from previous experiences, so that they are not just social movements anymore: they are networked social movements.[12] Within this overarching framework, what we propose in this book and through the chapters it hosts is to shed some light on the multiplicity of linkages between artists and political mobilisation processes, examining not only internal organisational processes but also the role of art and new media in facilitating the organisation, production and communication of political action.

SOCIAL MOVEMENTS, ORGANISATION AND THE LABOUR OF ACTIVISM

'Organisation' and 'relation' are two terms that relate to different schemes and political sensibilities. Whereas organising entails a structured and structuring activity aimed at efficacy and goal-attainment, relation constitutes a looser and wider concept that embraces both general human relations and the abstract ideas that shape groups, communities and organisations. In this sense, the concept of relation allows room for a political stance, room that is often used by social movements, whose aims tend to include a struggle to define new modes of relations and, ultimately, to search for a different (and better) life.

Within the art activism 'scene', the issue of organisation is rarely worded in these terms; rather, it is framed in relational terms, implying such topics as care, conflict, embodiment and power distribution – this is comparable on both a theoretical and practical level to the understanding of relations employed in the theory of relational aesthetics described earlier. Relation, in other words, represents a discursive device through which it is possible to deal with the multiple empirical options that are available, in terms of configuration of participation and, most importantly, through which one can tackle, reflexively, the political and ethical issues connected to organisation. The theme of relation is crucial for the life of movements, in terms of both their internal and external dynamics. Concerning the internal point of view, relations are fundamental to the extent that they constitute a field in which struggles are fought in order to establish a hierarchy among the other core areas of the movements' activities. In particular, relations are deeply interconnected with both the logic of action and the models of cultural production. Concerning the latter, the design and the implementation of alternative models of cultural production are often conducted with relations in mind, as both oppositional and supportive elements. Relations, therefore, do not only operate on two separate realms, but they also act as a hinge between the inside and the outside of movements.

When looking at art, labour and activism from a social movement perspective, theories emerging from and inspired by New Social Movement theory can also offer a valuable framework, given that they place the importance of culture not only on the 'content' of political actions – for example, values, message – but also on its capacity to shape a set of skills, tools and habits from which to construct 'strategies of action' (Swidler, 1986). The issue of collective identity in particular remains key for activists and researchers alike, 'one which is decisive to understand the emergence, persistence, and decline of protest movements' (Gerbaudo and Treré, 2015).

The collective identity that we find in the context of collective action can be based on a number of elements, such as belonging to the same organisations, shared experiences or values and lifestyle, among others. Identity plays a key role in an individual's construction of the meaning they give to their actions (Melucci, 1996: 39). It is also an essential aspect of movements, argue Klandermans et al. (2002) because it creates a shortcut to participation. People are more inclined to participate due to their identification with others. Considering collective identity is important because it can help us better understand actors' positioning in collective art-making, labour struggles and collective action; it is a useful lens for an analysis of collective subjectivities, which is enhanced when considered alongside organisational or relational processes. The analysis of collective identities and subjectivities is also complemented by looking at the development of the individual, political subjectivity of actors, given that 'the study of individual subjectivity as both a strategy of existence and a material and means of governance helps to recast assumptions about the workings of collectivities and institutions' (Biehl et al., 2007: 5). Questions on the nature of the political act and the potential of art as a vehicle for disruption and political openings – examined for instance, as stated earlier, by philosophers like Jacques Rancière (2010) – are of relevance here and explored in different ways along this volume, considered for instance alongside the identity of the artist as worker and their becoming into political actor (Bousmpoura and Martinez Heimann, chapter six) and the politicisation of survivors of sexual assault as creative subjects with political agency (Li, chapter 2).

In the past decade we have witnessed the emergence of a body of literature from the fields of organisation and social movements, proposing a convergence of these two fields (Davis et al., 2005). As noted by Clemens (2005), however, social movement scholars demonstrate a deep discomfort with the concept of organisation. Conceived as a system of order and authority, it seems incapable of taking into account processes of social change. Growing attention has been dedicated to how activists are able to avoid structures and processes of institutionalisation, with new media playing an important role in providing a non-hierarchical environment. It is the case of connective action (Bennett and Segerberg, 2012) in which social mechanisms characterised by weak ties have allegedly made it possible to overcome the rigidity of collective action, the latter conceived as a super structural process that endangers freedom and fluidity.

Another process – and we might also say, political stance – that has dominated several recent analyses of social movements and that is at the core of many of the practices addressed in this volume is prefiguration: the attempt to build a practice in the now that is based on the model future society we aspire to (Maeckelbergh, 2011). Prefiguration, while not a new practice, has been both an important exercise and a popular analytical lens of alter-globalisation movements, Occupy and other groups and movements from across the world that emerged thereafter. Prefigurative politics can be a conscious approach to politics and a commitment to creating, testing and implementing in the now new and more democratic structures, forms of organising and decision-making, new economies and new ways of relating to each other. It can also be found in the values upheld by a group, in the small, unconscious acts that 'prefigure' alternative practices, structures and relations. As Yates argues, prefiguration can be understood as one of two things: 'The building of movement "alternatives" or "institutions" or a 'way in which protest is performed' (Yates, 2015: 2). Prefiguration is a key issue in the study of art, labour and activism because it is an approach and a stance adopted by artists finding new ways of working and of organising themselves politically (see, for instance, Evans's exploration of the processes of art activist collectives in chapter 8, and Braga's study of artists mobilising and creating their own forms of currency in chapter 4). But also, through the use of art as a form of action, activists can find new ways of prefiguring social relations, using art as a language and as a space for rethinking political action and organising (Serafini, 2015, and Bseiso, chapter 7, this volume).

While prefiguration was – and to an extent, still is – in vogue, on the other hand in the past decade issues of power and leadership in movements have been relatively neglected. In fact, only recently has a renewed interest in these dynamics reemerged, countering the overwhelming quantity of contributions that have emphasised the flat and distributed nature of the new forms of mobilisation, marginalising the role of leadership and hierarchy. An indicator of this trend is the latest work of Manuel Castells (2012), which deals with the wave of mobilisation that has sparked globally since 2010. In previous work Castells (2009) had dealt extensively with the issue of power. In his most recent book he conceives of the autonomy of 'third spaces' – the spaces resulting from the interconnection between occupied urban spaces and digital networks – as being based on the intrinsically free nature of the online space (Castells, 2012: 222). Other studies highlight, however, how digital networks are deeply influenced by mechanisms of verticality, authority and exclusion (Gonzalez-Bailon and Wang, 2016; Nunes, 2014). And certain voices (Arvidsson et al., 2016; Gerbaudo, 2015) state that we need to overcome the network paradigm in order to better understand the crowd dynamics that are emerging in social media as well as in processes of mobilisation.

Looking at the literature that attempts to return attention to issues of leadership and power within the field of social movements, the contribution of Simon Western (2015) helps us to remember how anarchists like Bakunin, Proudhon and Kropotkin did not have particular taboos regarding dealing with leadership. For them 'individuals and groups take temporary leadership autonomously and on behalf of the wider collective, without assuming a formal position of power or authority over others' (Western, 2015: 676). In this respect interesting connections emerge between the issues of leadership, entrepreneurship and processes of political mobilisation. Critical management studies have recently brought together these three areas (Swann and Stoborod, 2014) from an anarchist point of view – similarly to what Sholette (2011) has proposed in the field of art criticism in his analysis of the art world facing enterprise culture. Particularly relevant is Sholette's understanding of the subsumption (and the mirroring, we might add) of artistic organisational models by enterprises: 'It's not the artist's seemingly transgressive, risk-taking non-conformity, but exactly a mode of distributed risk and social cooperation denied by neoliberalism that leads certain CEOs and business thinkers to see artistic methods as near-miraculous models of 'just-in-time creativity"' (Sholette, 2011: 43). This issue was previously addressed by Boltanski and Chiapello (2005) in their analysis of post-Fordist work structures and the recuperation of artistic forms of critique into capitalist modes of organisation.

From a different angle social movement scholars interrogate the same nexus that brings together cultural innovation, artistic radicalism and forms of disruption to existing capitalist forms. Davis, in particular, focuses on topological similarities among social movements and enterprises:

> Internally formal organizations would seem to exhibit emergent features and mobilization processes very similar to those we see in social movement groups. Similarly, in their external relations, formal organizations also would seem to

mirror their movement counterparts, participating, as they do, in fluid relationships with other organizations, joining in coalitions, and engaging in political action to affect state policy. (Davis et al., 2005: xiv)

What, then, are these contemporary, creative movements? Are they still movements as we used to know them – with the same recruitment and organisational mechanics? In the international context growing attention has been paid to cultural and social entrepreneurship, to social innovation and to peer-to-peer forms of production and organisation (Arvidsson and Peitersen, 2013). At the same time, social movements and squatting centres have radically changed (Moore, 2015; Pruijt, 2013) – increasingly becoming hubs of cultural production and experimentation rather than spaces of social healing and inclusion. One thing should be noted: we are not proposing here the creation of a new label, but rather calling for a new, interdisciplinary perspective. Social movement studies have provided extremely valuable insights into political mobilisation; however, they forgot to include capitalism in the equation (Barker et al., 2013). In an attempt to capture the specificity of movements that embody the heritage of artistic avant-gardes, workers' movements and start-ups, a multiplicity of perspectives must be interwoven.[13]

PERSPECTIVES AND EPISTEMOLOGIES

Moving away from issues of organisation and structure, in the study of social movements as in the study of art, we can identify an increasing interest in bodies, and in the embodied aspect of experience. McDonald (2006), for instance, calls for a turn in social movement theory towards the embodied experience, as opposed to the predominant focus on collective identity. This turn towards embodiment fits within a wider current interest in the body coming from phenomenological perspectives in philosophy as well as sociology (Cregan, 2006; Crossley, 2001; Merleau-Ponty, 1962s), and it is important to consider it not only as a feature of art, labour and collective action as embodied practices, but also as an epistemological approach that centres the body and experience. In the first place, as McDonald points out, this focus is needed because movements are increasingly breaking with the concept of 'we-ness' and challenging the notion of collective identity as the main basis for collective action. This is not to say that there is no sense of collective identity within these movements or that embodied experiences cannot be shared and collective. It means, rather, that personal experience and individuality have gained new roles in the sphere of political action. Looking at embodiment, argues McDonald, is the right approach for studying this kind of experiences.

A focus on embodiment is also relevant here because many aspects of collective political activity are deeply embodied. Marches, for instance, are highly symbolic rituals, but at the same time they are embodied practices. Embracing the embodied aspect of political action not only allows the individual to connect with others through embodied forms of communication; it also allows them to claim a certain control over their body, in the sense of making use of the body as a political tool. This is observable in the case of political actions such as occupations, sit-ins and 'die-ins', in which the body is politicised by its materiality and presence in a space. Embodiment is a common thread among several chapters in this volume as they follow the political performances of activists and cultural workers and the politicisation of personal, embodied experiences. It is also an important perspective for analysing issues of race, gender, sexuality and disability in art, labour and activism, as it allows us to move away from the discursive aspects of identity politics and towards an understanding of the different experiences of artists and political actors in a contemporary global arena marked by racism, institutional violence, gender inequality and ableism.

A different yet related epistemological perspective represented in this volume is that of decoloniality. Decoloniality is employed here in two ways. First, as the challenge to the idea that knowledge is disembodied and universal, a belief rooted in Western epistemology and one of the bases of colonialism (Escobar and Mignolo, 2010; Mignolo, 2011). And second, as the process of applying this challenge to practices and institutions of society. The decolonial perspective is adopted in this volume, for instance, in the positioning of radical arts educators attempting to transform educational practices (Trowell, chapter 9), as well as in the work of environmental activists aiming to decolonise both cultural institutions and the environmental movement in the UK (Serafini, chapter 5).

CONCLUSION

The chapters in this volume provide a variety of perspectives from the UK, Italy, Argentina, Egypt and Spain that respond to the theme of art, labour and activism, and contribute to mapping contemporary practices that interrogate issues of creative and political labour, the instrumentality/uselessness of art and the politics of the art world. The emergent practices outlined in this collection spotlight intersections where devising new working processes and technologies is central to the making of art, and where activism is realised through 'perception of the senses'. These intersections reveal not only the ways in which art, labour and activism are conjoined, but also how new networks and affiliations can develop. The chapters in this volume have been arranged in a way that aims to sketch out an analytical trajectory – a pathway that provides different entry points onto these overarching themes. *artWORK* begins through critical engagement with established cultural programmes and the opening up of democratic cultural spaces. It highlights interventions into established paradigms and the possibility of generating new cultural practices and relations. It then looks at how new possibilities can be created through grassroots community projects, and how cultural models can be modified and developed. At the same time, each chapter illuminates issues and challenges faced by practitioners. As such the orientation of the book encourages readers to reflect closely on the lived experiences and the challenges of sustaining these cultural spaces. In a sense, *artWORK* offers a cyclical pathway that traces the development, decline and renewal of practice, emphasising the processual significance of art, labour and activism.

Chapter 1 by Sheelagh Colclough and Sarah Feinstein offers an analysis of the politics of public art and cultural policy in Ulster, focusing on the tensions between traditional community cultural forms and the emergent expressions of a 'reimaged' Ulster. In chapter 2, Winnie M Li presents a case study of Clear Lines, a festival against sexual assault, and explores the role and value of social media in grassroots initiatives, as well as issues of political, emotional and creative labour. In chapter 3, Alberto Cossu and Maria Francesca Murru offer a study of the role of social media in the emergence and mobilisation of Italian artist centre Macao. Chapter 4 by Emanuele Braga also focuses on the work of Macao and explores the potential of democratic participation and technological innovation as components for the future of culture. In chapter 5, Paula Serafini conducts a study of how performance-based activism can facilitate the production of narratives that bring together environmental issues with workers' rights. Chapter 6 by Konstantina Bousmpoura and Julia Martinez Heimann also looks at issues of workers' rights by following the case of a group of professional dancers in Argentina fighting for improved working conditions, and examining the political potential of dance. In chapter 7, Rounwah Adly Riyadh Bseiso looks at the post–Tahrir Square cultural landscape in Egypt, analysing the shift from cultural spaces towards the streets and the implications of this shift in terms of art as social practice. In chapter 8, Mel Evans also interrogates issues of art as social practice by tracing a genealogy of collective art-making in order to then reflect on the processes of art activist collective Liberate Tate. Chapter 9 by Jane Trowell explores the idea of failure as experienced by art educators, reflecting on how embracing failure can help practitioners improve their practice. Jess Holtaway's chapter, chapter 10, is a contribution to the debate on the instrumentality versus uselessness of art developed from the case study of Art Action UK; a collective that provides a 'respite residency' in London for artists living and working in East Japan following the earthquake, tsunami and nuclear meltdown in 2011. And finally, Roger Sansi's chapter reflects on the idea of the post-autonomy of art as proposed by Néstor García Canclini. Based on a historical and cultural analysis of mobilisations emerging in the past decade in Barcelona, he suggests a breakdown of boundaries between the fields of creative production, academia and politics and argues that art might now be in a 'post-autonomous' phase.

A key element of this book is its contemporary nature, as all chapters address practices that are recent and ongoing. We recognise that in communicating and addressing these emergent practices, we risk crystallising active processes. Therefore, we ask readers to approach these projects as we do, as starting points, suggestions and propositions. Each of the following chapters offers critical reflections that provide possibilities for creative developments. We hope that this critical and creative engagement will enable readers to reflect on these processes in a way that will advance their own research, activism and creative practices.

NOTES

1. To account for this impasse it is telling that different academic domains have their own labels to frame this emerging phenomenon. Sometimes the same label is used to describe so many different practices it becomes empty. It is the case of *artivism*, present in French-, Spanish- and English-speaking debates, a category which can be used to describe a plethora of different referents such as the becoming activists of artists, the becoming artists of activists, the political role of art in changing society, the single creative performance, and a global movement with very undefined common features. The term *activist art* has also been used in a similar way, but usually implies a kind of institutional art practice that engages with political issues – and not a form of political action that takes artistic form. Instead, in this volume, we favour the term *art activism* because it does not prioritise one practice or field of action in the way that activist art or artistic activism does. We believe, however, that what is at stake here is not the need for new terminology, but rather a commitment to interdisciplinary conversations that allow more holistic approaches to these kinds of practices.

2. For a link between crises and the emergence of avant-gardes see the work of Raunig for a philosophical and artistic genealogy (2007) and Grégoire (2013) for a French retrospective on art workers' struggles.

3. This is the case of several initiatives which mix entrepreneurial models, funding strategies and governance models (on this see also chapter 1, this volume). This is ever more relevant for the artistic field as it has historically been instrumental to the neoliberal turn of the once-leftists Californian ideology (Barbrook and Cameron, 1996; Boltanski and Chiapello, 2005). Indeed more recently, a growing body of publications draw on the artists' (presumed) ethos to rethink that business models achieve leadership (Sholette, 2011: 43).

4. The issue of whether art that is 'too much on the activist side' should be considered of as art or not also needs to be approached in relation to the 'end of art'

proclaimed by Danto (1997), who argued art reached its own telos when after 1965 it became an 'object of its own theoretical consciousness' (ibid., 31). In his engagement with Danto's diagnosis, Larry Shiner (2001) rather foresees a new, third phase of art (the first being one in which arts and crafts were joint before the eighteenth century, and the second a modern 'autonomous' phase which ended in the 1960s) that is yet to come. However, writing in 2001, he does not suggest which would be the most defining features of such a new phase. More recently, analysing the developments in socially engaged art (a term with which we seek to include all forms of art which engages with social, economic and political issues) we find scholars who claim that 'activism might be the first new art form of the XXI century' (Weibel, 2015: 61).

5. We are not implying that such an approach is not legitimate or is flawed. Semiotics, a fundamental branch of cultural analysis, is almost entirely based on the analysis and decodification of 'texts' (in a wide sense) detached from their empirical conditions of production and reception.

6. By this we mean a repertoire of action as a set of practices that are potentially infinite and empirically impossible to enumerate, and that are activated according to the specific circumstances that movements both face and contribute to co-creating. On this see Mattoni's elaboration of the notion proposed by Charles Tilly (della Porta and Mattoni, 2012).

7. The issue is that creativity in protest often originates from subjects relatively deprived under certain capitals while in other cases social researchers analyse highly trained artists with a high cultural capital. The question is relative to social position and professionalisation, so, in the first case we would have a popular uprising in which creativity is a tool to use to attain more visibility, while in the second it is a disguised set of practices and sensibilities.

8. Reclaim the Streets Activist (Pink & Silver Brigades) Interview, within *Tactical Frivolity*, documentary by Marcelo Exposito (2007).

9. A distinction is usually made between visual artists, performers and artists, as commonly understood, and workers, the 'maestranze' who are involved in the material aspects of the arts. This division of labour is also evident in contemporary art (artists produce ideas and artisans who specialise in metal or wood, craft artists' abstract ideas).

10. For Grégoire such emancipatory horizons represent an array of demands imagined and developed collectively by social actors, whose ambition is to escape subordination and promote institutions that are capable of advancing their collective conditions.

11. See http://www.wageforwork.com/.

12. Problems have been identified concerning the efficacy of such a conceptualisation given that social movements in their many different shapes are always, first and foremost, a network. Mario Diani, oral presentation, *EUI Summer School on Political Mobilization*, September 2013.

13. There are, of course, other perspectives and authors that are relevant to the study of the intersections between art, labour and activism, which we will not be able to expand on here. This includes much work on the politics of creative labour and the creative industries, for example, Hesmondlagh and Baker, 2011; Nixon and Crewe, 2004; Conor, Gill and Taylor, 2015; and Banks, Gill and Taylor 2013, as well as those

we were only able to briefly touch on in this introduction. Because this volume adopts a perspective that is coming from the study of social movements and the arts, issues around the creative industries and cultural policy are not as developed. These topics are, nonetheless, addressed by some of the contributors to this volume (see Li's chapter on activist festivals, Bousmpoura and Heimann's chapter on dance legislation and Colclough and Feinstein's chapter on public culture in Ulster), who offer empirical contributions on the politics and everyday practices of the creative industries, cultural institutions and cultural policy.

REFERENCES

Arvidsson, Adam and Peitersen, Nicolai. 2013. *The Ethical Economy: Rebuilding Value after Crisis*. New York: Columbia University Press.

Arvidsson, Adam, Caliandro, Alessandro, Airoldi, Massimo and Barina, Stefania. 2016. 'Crowds and Value, Italian Directioners on Twitter'. *Information, Communication and Society* 16(7): 921–39.

Banks, Mark. 2007. *The Politics of Cultural Work*. New York: Palgrave Macmillan.

Banks, Mark, Gill, Rosalind and Taylor, Stephanie. 2013. *Theorizing Cultural Work: Labour, continuity and change in the cultural and creative industries*. London and New York: Routledge.

Barbrook, Richard and Cameron, Andy. 1996. 'The Californian Ideology'. *Science as Culture* 6(1): 44–72.

Barker, Colin, Cox, Laurence, Krinsky, John and Gunvald, Alf N. (eds.). 2013. *Marxism and Social Movements*. Leiden: Brill.

Benjamin, Walter. 1970. 'The Author as Producer'. *New Left Review* I (62): 83–96.

Benjamin, Walter. 2008 [1936]. *The Work of Art in the Age of Mechanical Reproduction*, translated by J. A. Underwood. London: Penguin.

Bennett, Lance and Segerberg, Alexandra. 2012. 'The Logic of Connective Action', *Information, Communication and Society*. 15(5): 739–68.

Bennett, Lance and Segerberg, Alexandra. 2013. *The Logic of Connective Action. Digital Media and the Personalization of Contentious Politics*. New York: Cambridge University Press.

Bennett, Lance, Segerberg Alexandra and Walker, Shawn. 2014. 'Organization in the Crowd: Peer Production in Large-Scale Networked Protests'. *Information, Communication & Society* 17(2): 232–60.

Biehl, João, Good, J. Byron and Kleinman, Arthur (eds.). 2007. *Subjectivity: Ethnographic Investigations*. Oakland: University of California Press.

Bishop, Claire. 2012. *Artificial Hells: Participatory Art and the Politics of Spectatorship*. London: Verso.

Bishop, Claire. 2006. 'The Social Turn: Collaboration and Its Discontents'. *Artforum* 02: 179–185.

Boltanski, Luc and Chiapello, Eve. 2005. *The New Spirit of Capitalism*. London: Verso.

Bourriaud, Nicolas. 2002. *Relational Aesthetics*. Paris: Les Presse du Reel: 1998. English translation 2002

Butt, Gavin (ed.). 2005. *After Criticism: New Responses to Art and Performance*, Oxford: Blackwell.

Calhoun, Craig. 2001. 'Putting Emotions in Their Place', in Goodwin, Jeff, Jasper, James and Polletta, Francesca, *Passionate Politics: Emotions and Social Movements*. Chicago: University of Chicago Press, pp. 45–57.

Castells, Manuel. 2009. *Communication Power*. Oxford: Oxford University Press.

Castells, Manuel. 2012. *Networks of Outrage and Hope: Social Movements in the Internet Age*. Cambridge: Polity.

Clemens, Elizabeth. 2005. 'Two Kinds of Stuff: The Current Encounter of Social Movements and Organizations'. In Davis, Gerald et al. (eds.) *Social Movements and Organization Theory*. New York: Cambridge University Press, pp. 351–65.

Cregan, Kate. 2006. *The Sociology of the Body*, London: Sage.

Crossley, Nick. 2001. *The Social Body: Habit, Identity and Desire*, London: Sage.

Danto, C. Arthur. 1997. *After the End of Art. Contemporary Art and the Pale of History*. Princeton, NJ: Princeton University Press.

Davis, F. Gerald, McAdam, Doug, Scott, Mayer and Nathan Zald (eds.). 2005. *Social Movements and Organization Theory*. New York: Cambridge University Press.

della Porta, Donatella and Diani, Mario. 2006. *Social Movements: An Introduction* (second edition). Malden, MA: Blackwell.

Diani, M. 1992. 'The Concept of Social Movement', *Sociological Review*, 40:1–25.

Escobar, Arturo and Mignolo, Walter D. (eds.). 2010. *Globalization and the Decolonial Option*. Abingdon, Oxon: Routledge.

Gerbaudo, Paolo. 2015. 'Rousing the Facebook Crowd: Social Media Campaigning, Digital Enthusiasm and the Online Plebeian Public Sphere in the 2011 Protest Wave'. Working paper presented at the University of Milan, 31 March 2015.

Gerbaudo, Paolo and Treré, Emiliano. 2015. 'In Search of the "We" of Social Media Activism: Introduction to the Special Issue on Social Media and Protest Identities'. *Information, Communication & Society* 18(8): 865–71.

Gonzalez-Bailon, Sandra and Wang, Ning. 2016. 'Networked Discontent: The Anatomy of Protest Campaigns in Social Media'. *Social Networks* 44: 95–104.

Grégoire, Mathieu. 2013. *Les Intermittents du Spectacle*. Paris: La Dispute.

Groys, Boris. (2014). 'On Art Activism'. *E-flux journal* #56. 6/2014. Available online at: http://www.e-flux.com/journal/on-art-activism/.

Hesmondhalgh, David and Baker, Sarah. 2011. *Creative Labour: Media Work in Three Cultural Industries*. London and New York: Routledge.

Hoffman, J. Andrew, Badiane, K. Krista, Haigh, Nardia. 2012. 'Hybrid Organizations as Agent of Positive Social Change: Bridging the For-Profit & Non-Profit Divide', in Golden-Bibble, Karen and Dutton, Jane (eds.), *Using a Positive Lens to Explore Social Change and Organizations: Building a Theoretical and Research Foundation*. London: Routledge.

Holland, Dorothy, Fox, Gretchen and Daro, Vinci (2008) 'Social Movements and Collective Identity: A Decentered, Dialogic View'. *Anthropological Quarterly* 18(1): 95–126.

Holmes, Brian. 2004. 'Artistic Autonomy and the Communication Society'. *Third Text* 18(6): 547–55.

Holmes, Brian. 2013. 'Art after Capitalism' in Sholette, Gregory and Ressler, Oliver (eds.), *It's the Political Economy, Stupid: The Global Financial Crisis in Art and Theory*. Chicago: University of Chicago Press.

Kester, Grant. 2011. *The One and the Many: Contemporary Collaborative Art in a Global Context*. Durham, NC: Duke University Press.
Klandermans, Bert, Sabucedo, Jose Manuel, Rodriguez, Mauro and de Weerd, Marga. 2002. 'Identity Processes in Collective Action Participation: Farmers' Identity and Farmers'
Protest in the Netherlands and Spain'. *Political Psychology* 23(2): 235–51.
Maeckelbergh, Marianne. 2011. 'Doing Is Believing: Prefiguration as Strategic Practice'. *Social Movement Studies: Journal of Social, Cultural and Political Protest* 10(1): 1–20.
McDonald, Kevin. 2006. *Global Movements: Action and Culture*, Malden, MA; and Oxford, Victoria: Blackwell.
McKee, Yates. 2016. *Art Strike: Contemporary Art and the Post-Occupy Condition*. New York and London: Verso.
McRobbie, Angela. 2002. 'Clubs to Companies: Notes on the Decline of Political Culture in Speeded Up Creative Worlds'. *Cultural Studies* 16(4): 516–31.
Melucci, Alberto. 1996. *Challenging Codes: Collective Action in the Information Age*. Cambridge: Cambridge University Press.
Merleau-Ponty, Maurice. 1962. *Phenomenology of Perception*, translated by Colin Smith, London: Routledge.
Mignolo, Walter. 2011. 'Modernity and Decoloniality'. *Oxford Bibliographies*. http://www.oxfordbibliographies.com/view/document/obo-9780199766581/obo-9780199766581-0017.xml (accessed on 1 July 2015).
Moore, W. Alan. 2015. *Occupation Culture. Art & Squatting in the City from Below*. New York: Minor Compositions.
Mouffe, Chantal. 2013. *Agonistics: Thinking the World Politically*. London: Verso Books.
Nixon, Sean and Crewe, Ben. 2004. 'Pleasure at Work? Gender, Consumption and Work-based Identities in the Creative Industries'. *Consumption Markets & Culture* 7:2.
Nunes, Rodrigo. 2014. *Organization of the Organizationless: Collective Action after Networks*. London: Mute Books & Post-Media Lab.
Pruijt, Hans. 2013. 'The Logic of Urban Squatting'. *International Journal of Urban and Regional Research* 37(1): 19–45.
Rancière, Jacques. 2004. *The Politics of Aesthetics: The Distribution of the Sensible*. London and New York: Continuum International Publishing Group.
Rancière, Jacques. 2006. 'Problems and Transformations in Critical Art', in Claire Bishop (ed.) *Participation: Documents of Contemporary Art*. London: Whitechapel Ventures Limited, pp. 83–93.
Rancière, Jacques. 2010. *Dissensus: On Politics and Aesthetics*, edited and translated by Steven Corcoran. London: Continuum International Publishing Group.
Raunig, Gerald. 2007. *Art and Revolution. Transversal Activism in the Long Twentieth Century*. New York: Semiotexte.
Raunig, Gerald. 2013. 'Flatness Rules: "Constituent Practices and Institutions of the Common in a Flat World"', in Gielen, Pascal (ed.), *Institutional Attitudes: Instituting Art in a Flat World*, pp. 64–74. Valiz: Amsterdam.

Serafini, Paula. 2015. 'Prefiguring Performance: Participation and Transgression in Environmentalist Activism'. *Third Text* 29(3): 195–206.

Shiner, Larry. 2001. *The Invention of Art. A Cultural History*. Chicago: University of Chicago Press.

Sholette, Gregory. 2011. *Dark Matter: Art and Politics in the Age of Enterprise Culture*. London: Pluto Press.

Sholette, Gregory. 2016. 'Merciless Aesthetic: Activist Art as the Return of Institutional Critique. A Response to Boris Groys'. *Field 4/2016*. Available at: http://field-journal.com/issue-4/merciless-aesthetic-activist-art-as-the-return-of-institutional-critique-a-response-to-boris-groys.

Swann, Thomas and Stoborod, Konstantin (2014). 'Did You Hear about the Anarchist Manager?' *Ephemera Journal* 14(4): 591–609.

Swidler, Ann. 1986. 'Culture in Action: Symbols and Strategies'. *American Sociological Review* 51: 273–86.

Tilly, Charles and Tarrow, Sydney. 2007. *Contentious Politics*. Boulder: Paradigm.

Tucker, H. Kenneth. 2012. *Workers of the World Enjoy. Aesthetic Politics from Revolutionary Syndicalism to the Global Justice Movement*. Philadelphia, PA: Temple University Press.

Weibel, Peter (ed.). 2015. *Global Activism. Art and Conflict in the 21st Century*. Cambridge, MA: MIT Press.

Western, Simon. 2015. 'Autonomist Leadership in Leaderless Movements: Anarchists Leading the Way'. *Ephemera Journal* 14(4): 673–98.

Whybrow, Nicolas. 2011. *Art and the City*. London: I. B. Tauris.

Yates, Luke. 2015. 'Rethinking Prefiguration: Alternatives, Micropolitics and Goals in Social Movements'. *Social Movement Studies: Journal of Social, Cultural and Political Protest* 14(1): 1–21.

Chapter 1

Reimaging, Reimagining or Reimagineering
Rebranding Ulster
Sheelagh Colclough and Sarah Feinstein

Since the nineteenth century, culture has increasingly been regarded as a resource, which has accelerated in the post-industrial context as a means to revitalise economically and socially neglected urban spaces (Punter, 2010; Yudice, 2003). Concurrently, increasing civic participation through cultural engagement has become a priority in guiding policy rhetoric in Western Europe for the past thirty years (Bianchini and Parkinson, 1993; Matarasso 1997, 1998). This discursive coalescing has often manifested in a praxis of culture-led regeneration, a marriage of festivalisation and urban reanimation, underpinned by the weighty rhetoric of tourism and foreign investment whilst precariously balanced alongside audience access, inclusion, empowerment and expansion (Sassatelli, 2011; Waitt, 2008). A contingent impact of these efforts is often inscribing a reconceptualisation in the public sphere; the city and its diverse (or divergent) cultures are presented to highlight their existing assets (i.e. reimaged) or their potential utopian benefits (i.e. reimagined). Moreover, the supposed default state of a positive outcome from civic participation is entirely dependent on the culture onto which it is transposed as it must contend with broader contradictions embedded and embodied within that culture, both economic and social (Clark and Carreira da Silva, 2014). This raises the question of how agency is negotiated among the divergent social and governmental actors and particularly how various agendas are implemented and resisted by arts practitioners themselves. It also raises the issue of what aspects of participatory democracy are constructed and evoked in these manifestations of culture. Additionally, in a post-conflict urban context, there is the issue of how these dynamics affect the development and performance of reimaging, reimagining or reimagineering culture.[1]

The contemporary politics of space in Northern Ireland is in many ways defined by what has been colloquially termed the Troubles. Most often framed as a sectarian or ethno-nationalist conflict that started with the Battle of the Bogside in Derry/Londonderry in 1969 and ended with the signing of the Belfast/Good Friday Peace Agreement in 1998, the Troubles can equally be explained as a colonial conflict between British army forces, Northern Ireland state forces (predominantly Protestant), Loyalist paramilitaries (Unionist and predominantly working-class Protestant) and Republican paramilitaries (Irish Nationalist and predominantly working-class Catholic). During this time period, over 1,900 people were interned without trial, 3,600 people were killed, over 10,000 were imprisoned and 40,000 were injured (McKittrick and McVea, 2002). Aside from the militarisation of daily life in the form of checkpoints, barricades and watchtowers, public space became highly regulated and everyday movement patterns highly segregated. Needless to say, foreign investment and tourism were deeply impacted during the Troubles as well. The public culture that developed during this period was as complicated as the political culture it often reflected.

This chapter examines the cultural 'renaissance' of Belfast through the lens of creative practitioners, considering in particular the tensions between the aims and aspirations of local government, traditional indigenous groups and arts professionals. We will explore these dynamics first with a discussion of the arts policy framework developed post-Good Friday Agreement and then through an examination of the transformation of public space as interrogated through the work of artist Sheelagh Colclough. We will then turn towards public culture and the historic and symbolic role of its manifestation to unpack issues of class, collective memory and urban space as embodied by a shared or invented culture in the contemporary urban arts festival Culture Night Belfast. We situate this analysis through the myriad conundrums of the contrasting landscape of traditional community cultural forms and the emergent expressions of contemporary Ulster, asking what function does the labour of the arts serve, in both its production and its reception, to reflect the potential and limits of urban life.

REIMAGING AND REIMAGINING PUBLIC SPACE

In the rush to rebrand the historically troublesome terrain of Ulster with the economic and social benefits of a liberal peace, agencies of governance, such as the Arts Council of Northern Ireland (ACNI) and other statutory paymasters of the public purse, have attempted to depoliticise the most exigent and inevitably least affluent areas in a number of public art programmes.[2] This has primarily focused on attempts to reconfigure and recast public art forms such as 'gable end' murals away from militaristic sectarian expressions of urban life (e.g. balaclava-wearing combatants wielding machine guns) towards 'more "positive" depictions of the history and contemporary condition of Northern Ireland' (Hill and White, 2012, 72). This is part of a broader agenda to address longstanding social and cultural divisions through reconfiguring and realigning their public expressions to create a 'shared' society, as seen in policies such as the Northern Ireland Executive Office's *A Shared Future – Policy and Strategic Framework for Good Relations in Northern Ireland* (2005) and *Together: Building a United Community* Strategy (2013). The overlapping of some of the stated aims of these policies and their implementation through the work of such agencies as the Community Relations Council and ACNI, particularly those evoking the benefit of increasing the 'peace dividend' from tourism and regeneration investment for example, has led to a transformation of collective civic consciousness in terms of shared space, spectacle and sentiment post– Good Friday Agreement (McManus and Carruthers, 2014).³ However, this has arguably also served to further embed cultural and class divisions between contentious folk celebrations and contemporary cosmopolitanised ones (Carruthers et al., 2003). Moreover, in many cases this has functioned to merely decorate division, as the number of physical barriers between communities (known as peace walls) has actually increased since 1998 (Byrne et al., 2012).

Take, for example, the ACNI's 'Re-Imaging Communities Programme' (2006–2009) that funded 108 community projects under which 'symbols of sectarian aggression and racism in the form of murals, paramilitary memorials, emblems, flags and territorial colours have been removed and/or replaced with imagery that reflects the aspirations of the communities in a more positive manner' and their subsequent programme 'Building Peace Through the Arts: Re-imaging Communities' that developed and installed 32 pieces of site-specific public art (Independent Research Solutions, 2009: 115). Both programmes follow policy initiatives on reframing the contested symbolic landscape that pre-date the cease-fire of 1994 and the implementation of the 1998 Peace Agreement. From as early as 1977, there have been initiatives from various government agencies, grassroots community groups and business associations in Northern Ireland to 're-image', if not 're-imagine', public space (Hill and White, 2012). This has not gone entirely uncontested by residents or citizens with some feeling that the state-approved predetermined positivism often delivered by such projects is a type of 'peace washing', which in its haste to deliver incontestable, anodyne imagery denies communities the chance to accept, acknowledge or even examine or openly debate their recent past (Colclough, 2007, 2014; Crowley, 2011). This seems to follow that not only the reimaged projects, but the civic discourses surrounding them, illustrate what the productive labour of arts programming can expose, namely, as Debra Lisle (2006: 29) terms them, social cleavages: 'a variety of competing political struggles: community infighting . . . gender . . . race . . . age . . . and economic disparity (a disillusioned working class, increased unemployment, and capital flight)'.

To explore some of these dynamics in greater detail, we would like to focus on two bodies of work produced by Belfast-based artist Sheelagh Colclough: *Evaluate* (2007) and *Re:Evaluate* (2014), which led to the birth of The Sheelagh Foundation, a conceptual conceit providing the ongoing mechanism by which to consider the structures, language and multiplicity of meanings provoked by the work she has been involved in as an arts practitioner and administrator in Northern Ireland since 2000. Colclough has facilitated and produced arts programming for a wide variety of organisations, both those who would situate themselves at grassroots level (arts, education and social charities situated in the broad field of community development) and those seen as part of the formal elite (large art institutions, museums, statutory bodies and universities). Her own practice as a contemporary artist often explores the overlooked contradictions she has experienced both within her role as a facilitator and the larger process of community collaboration within arts programmes such as ACNI's Re-Imaging Communities Programme. To do so, she draws on the investigative tools of social research, the lexicon and management theories at the forefront of the 'creative industries' and the 'participatory arts' (and the critiques thereof) and the disciplines of drawing, painting, photography and sculpture.[4]

Evaluate! (the art of forms) an examination of community arts from the inside out (to give it its full title) was an interactive mixed media exhibition with a performative launch, masquerading as a community arts conference, debuting at the Waterfront Hall in Belfast, September 2007. It came about through the growing consciousness in Colclough's work, observing that artists, community workers, funders and the 'engaged participants' often find themselves co-opted and instrumentalised for inoffensive explorations by various agencies and ideologies.[5] In general, she sought to explore these themes through examining and encouraging multiple perspectives; using humour and a sense of the absurd to disarm, challenge and provoke thought in audiences, collaborators and participants about the social structures, postures and histories we inhabit and inherit, as well as our culture's role in shaping them. This exploration produced a counter-narrative to discourses on the affect and effect of engagement with the arts that tend to flatten nuances into a consensus of 'positive outcomes'.

The two exhibitions, *Evaluate* and *Re:Evaluate*, took as their locus community and participatory arts, delving past the 'on message' successes and redemptive failures neatly presented in the evaluation reports so often synonymous with publicly funded projects, in order to explore the largely unaired grievances of some of those involved. *Evaluate* in particular sought to examine some of the differing agendas and outlooks of individuals who had been part of ACNI's emerging Re-Imaging Communities projects. It also engaged with the wider issues of agency and collective freedom of cultural exploration and expression present in the community arts landscape at the time, including the EU Programme for Peace and Reconciliation in Northern Ireland and the Border Region of Ireland (2000–2006), known as the PEACE II Programme. Community arts, recognised as a grassroots movement emerging from civil rights struggles, has a vibrant and rich (as well as longstanding) history in Northern Ireland guided by the core principles of ownership, authorship, access and participation. However, in practice there is a vastly differing spectrum of engagement with the democratic application of those principles between participant groups in the community arts sector and funders of those projects. This is not exceptional to Northern Ireland, as many of these issues have been well documented in similar community art and participatory (or socially engaged) art projects that see both artists and the arts as agents for social, political or economic change (Bishop, 2012; Jacob et al., 1995; Hope, 2015; Mouffe, 2007).

Evaluate comprised of twenty-five confidential recorded interviews with individuals from five key stakeholder groups (funders, arts organisations, artists, community workers and participants) who were asked a range of questions, such as: What is community arts? Is there a difference between it and 'real art'? Do you think too much is asked of community arts? Do you really think it can reconcile, retrain and regenerate our society? What is an artist's role in society? Should communities/individual beneficiaries decide on their own cultural outputs and consumption or should they be guided by their benefactors? Do you think artists working in community arts have as much artistic freedom and or intellectual integrity? Have you ever felt straightjacketed by funding requirements of community arts projects? and Do you think community arts needs forms? The answers were transcribed and Colclough selected responses from which she created visual interpretations; these mixed media images were then displayed alongside experts from the interviewees' anonymised text.

Some of the questions asked, like some of the images produced, were deliberately provocative and loaded, while others were more reflective of Colclough's concerns at the time. Presenting the text alongside her visual interpretation she felt was important, as she wanted the viewer to interrogate her representation of what was being said; relating to the false construct of evaluation being touted as a neutral or factual representation of reality. For example, one of *Evaluate*'s respondents unpacked the context and a reoccurring theme that many people who had engaged with reimaging (or reimagining) projects experienced:

> I think that murals are very difficult – I think that on one level I feel really uncomfortable with this whole thing that's going on at the minute, you know to me it's like sanitising and utter revisionism and it's like war, what war? Those

murals are part of our history, of this part of the world and I feel it's really important that they are recorded in some way and then on the other hand people who do live beside them often feel very intimidated by them, it stops people going into those areas, especially Loyalist areas at the moment and that's not right, so something does have to be done . . . in the Northern Irish section of an international conference and in a panel discussion there was a woman in the audience from a Republican group who said 'but that's our history and those people and those murals are our heroes and our martyrs' kind of thing, and 'who are you to tell us . . . that's our history and we're proud of it and why should we take them down?' And yes, we will do others that aren't threatening or intimidating or whatever, but we want to keep some of those ones as well but they are our history. (Colclough, 2007)

The range of responses Colclough received confirmed her professional experiences in terms of the variety of interpretations of the increasingly monolithic and bureaucratic language of community and participatory arts and the direction public arts programmes seemed to be taking. What was also revealed was the breadth and depth of complexity that initiatives such as ACNI's Re-Imaging Communities Programme obfuscate as much as expose, one respondent commenting:

So I think it's quite fraught with difficulties . . . the Arts Council should have been going to communities in the first place rather than presenting them with a fait accompli and they would have come up with a much more imaginative programme like I think even the title – Re-imagining communities – I mean how much more powerful is that than re-imaging, re-imaging implies something that is going to be done to you. . . . What does that mean? And how much more powerful would re-imagining have been? And how much more likely to be community led? So I totally think communities should decide their own cultural outputs, yes, even if offensive to the vast majority of people. (Colclough, 2007)

This perception of the Re-Imaging Communities Programme was challenged by others who evoked the implicit and knowingly well-worn mantra of the 'shared utopia' manifesting itself with another familiar Northern Irish trope, that of the voiceless silent majority:

The programme is rooted in communities, this I think has been a bit of a misconception that it's about the government deciding that it's time for you to do something. Yes there's elements of that because we all want to subscribe to this vision, this utopia of a shared future and all that, but unless the community wants to do something I may as well run down that street with a bag full of money in the nip and give it out to whoever comes along, you know. So the groups that I'm meeting along the way, the people that I meet, the personalities are the people who are functioning within their community and who are saying, 'that wee women over there across the road has been on at me for the last 10 years to get rid of that there image', you know, we've talked about it, negotiated around it, spoke to the paramilitary communities, spoke to whoever we wanted to speak to, we now want rid of it, we could just go in with a big pot of paint and paint over it, but we've heard about this Re-Imaging Communities Programme that will connect us with an artist, that will allow us to do something in its place, that the community can then all aspire to, sign up to . . . and what have you. (Colclough, 2007)

What this begins to illustrate is a classic sociological conundrum: is this fractured understanding of such programmes a result of miscommunication by ACNI or an exigent position stated to illustrate a sentiment of disenfranchisement from an ongoing and longstanding process?

The speed of societal (albeit visual) transition from gunmen to state-approved non-contentious, aspirational visions in many communities has been undeniably rapid, but not uniform as in the case of the community worker explaining a stalemate within one Re-Imaging Communities Programme project negotiations: 'We were talking about taking one of the gunman paintings off if we were allowed to put one of the Royal family up, the funders wouldn't let us put one of the Royal family up because that would be seen as only art for one side of the community, well then we says we're leaving the gunman, so that one fell through' (Colclough, 2007).

This points to one of the central problems with reimaging, that is, the content of the image and who decides it. This problem of content in a place such as Northern Ireland is a central issue of state-administered public art programmes where the state agencies paint themselves as somehow neutral, that is, not promoting a political agenda and/or a sectarian bias.[6] Re-Imaging Communities are part of larger suite of public art interventions, along with the EU-funded Peace and Reconciliation programmes, which emphatically promote the neoliberal trickle down ideal of spending society's way to stability (known locally as the 'peace dividend'). This idea links economic stability and increased prosperity as both an outcome and a reward of peace or more specifically the cessation of violent conflict. However, when asked about this idea in relation to regeneration and reconciliation, a community worker, well versed and engaged in multiple arts programmes and projects, was uncertain: 'It can regenerate societies, or communities, as in if a place is downtrodden, doesn't look attractive, and you start putting nice stuff in, it welcomes more people in. If you get more people in, you start getting investment in, so in that side of it can. Can it reconcile? I'm not too sure' (Colclough, 2007).

These ideological contradictions of 'off message' personal misgivings, which rarely publicly surface, contained themes Colclough wanted to further frame, analyse and explore in a Northern Ireland post-global financial

Figure 1.1. *Royal Heavies*, 2007, Sheelagh Colclough (mixed media).
© Sheelagh Colclough.

crisis, where the Good Friday Agreement peace dividend carrot had failed to entirely materialise in some of the communities to which it was promised. *Re:Evaluate* was conceived therefore as a chance to critically reflect on some of the issues raised by *Evaluate*, particularly how both community and participatory arts had been increasingly subject to an accountancy culture. Interviews were conducted with academics and researchers including

Francois Matarasso, Susanne Bosch and Francis Halsall. Colclough organised a panel discussion at the Crescent Arts Centre in Belfast in January 2014 to accompany the exhibition with academics and arts professionals serving as panellists, including John Johnston from Goldsmiths, University of London and Niall O'Baoill from Fatima Groups United, Dublin. Those on the panel were asked to consider the following questions: What do we mean by socially engaged/public/community/participatory art and who is it for? Is it still a relevant or necessary practice in its present form in Northern Ireland or internationally? A brief synopsis of the panel discussion contained the following points: artists cannot control the outcomes of art and they shouldn't be expected to; there is not enough room to discuss practice; we are operating within a tick-box culture driven by accountancy and the cloak of recession; on the whole community/participatory artists engage in complex work and are undervalued; the criteria for assessment are too simplistic; and there is a collective disappointment in watching the evolution of community/participatory arts as they are slowly homogenised, utilitarianised, instrumentalised and abused.

In the wider work of *Re:Evaluate*, Bill Rolston cites what is at the crux of Re-Imaging Communities, and programmes of their ilk, is that they promote art simply as a social good without leaving room for a reflexive process or the potential to arrive at the 'wrong' answer:

> I have this notion that there's art that comes from top down, and although they may use the same words, they don't necessarily have the same meaning or same purposes. And where sometimes you see the discrepancy between means and purposes [it] is at the interface where they meet. So you may get a lot of state organisations sponsoring community arts but they may not be doing it for the reasons that a group in the community is doing it; where I see this most noticeably is when it comes to whether or not community arts has any politically articulated content or not . . . if it does the sponsors of community arts can sometimes get very fearsome – so they would prefer, let's put it this way, butterflies and fairytales because they're non-controversial no matter who you are, rather than for example trying to encourage a community to articulate its fears, its desires, even its prejudices, to put them on a wall or put them in a sculpture or whatever. So community arts, the interface, is the most interesting battle zone, as it were. (Colclough, 2014)

Francis Halsall expands on the wider notion of didactic aesthetics and problems with the limits of reflexivity offered by many public and community art programmes:[7]

> All politics is grounded in the positioning of the sensory body in space and what those spaces offer. . . . I think that sometimes with those intentions there could be a slippage into the didactic model that I'm worried about, which is, oh you

haven't experienced this oh you should try this, you haven't tasted an oyster, here's an oyster, you've never drank champagne, or you've never seen this type of art, look at this type of art. That's not enough in itself, it's when those types of experiences become enabling or enable some kind of form of self reflexivity and kind of form a transformative action, they're not good in themselves. . . . You're not a better person because you've drunk the champagne, you need to do something with that experience and think through what is at stake in having done that. (Colclough, 2014)

What both *Evaluate* and *Re:Evaluate* demonstrate is that we all need to think about what is at stake in having (been) offered and having drunk the reimaging champagne.

Figure 1.2. *Bill*, 2014, Sheelagh Colclough (mixed media).
© Sheelagh Colclough.

Figure 1.3. *Francis*, 2014, Sheelagh Colclough (mixed media).
© Sheelagh Colclough.

REIMAGINEERING PUBLIC CULTURE

These dilemmas are equally present in current responses to shifting the terrain, and territorial fixity, towards reconciliation, celebration and prospective cultural landscapes by arts and community stakeholders in Ulster engaging with public culture. This can be seen in the history of staging Belfast's largest contemporary cultural event in the urban calendar, Culture Night. In Europe, Culture Nights have been a growing phenomenon for over twenty years, mushrooming out from initiatives such as Research Center for Cultural Development's Nuit Blanche in Nantes (est. 1984), the Helsinki Festival's Night of the Arts (est. 1989), the White Nights of St Petersburg (est. 1991), and Berlin's Long Night of Museums (est. 1997). In Ireland, Culture Night

Dublin was first established in 2006, the concept spreading quickly to Cork, Limerick and Belfast. These types of festivals share strong links with tourism through their funding and official support from national, municipal and regional government, as well as private businesses and partnerships with cultural institutions and organisations.

While Culture Night Dublin may have tacitly infused itself with the common ideology of exposing its population to culture, not only as an economic resource but as an uplifting social good, Culture Night Belfast in its post-conflict context of competing class-based cultures presents a landscape of additional complexity. Since its inception in 2009, this free-to-access, multivenue arts behemoth has taken over the Cathedral Quarter (Belfast's self-styled cultural quarter) showcasing a diverse mix of performances, tours, exhibitions, gigs, talks, workshops and happenings, specifically driving audiences to decaying urban spaces and encouraging punters and performers alike to reimagine their city. As much carnival of consumption as freedom of offer *and* of expression, Culture Night Belfast sits uneasily upon the fault line of reimagining civic identity and reimagineering urban entrepreneurialism and gentrification. In its ability to mobilise tens of thousands and become, as the Chair of the Cathedral Quarter Trust puts it, 'The single biggest and most effective way of demonstrating Belfast's cultural strength' (*Belfast Newsletter*, 2015), it is difficult not to read this temporary transformation of the city into, as some have dubbed it, 'a sort of middle-class Twelfth' (Emerson, 2014), as a pointed show of hierarchical otherness. However, this is not divorced from a deeply rooted desire to transform public cultural life beyond the often-constricting identity politics of the 'two communities' narrative. Until very recently, there has been a tendency to view the 'two communities' (Unionist and Nationalist, Loyalist and Republican, Protestant and Catholic, etc.) as the only functional identities in Northern Ireland, rather than the prevailing (or perhaps even dominant) political assemblages. The question becomes: are the new traditions of public festivals hiding something or do they represent significant change in spaces for interaction? In a deeply divided society, tourism can leverage social change as much as it can entrench it. As Neil Jarman argues, the festivalisation of culture in a neoliberal peace requires the development of an infrastructure with a flexible use of public space, which in turn opens a space for a more diverse reflection of cultural practices and allows for new possibilities (or identities) to emerge.[8]

Bernadette Quinn (2010: 264) has argued that although 'festivals can deliver a series of benefits that separately meet cultural policy and urban tourism policy objectives, there is little to suggest that cities normatively engage in comprehensive, integrated policy-making for urban arts festivals'. Festivals galvanised towards the purpose of economic development 'have embraced entrepreneurial urban management policies and ideas of the "creative economy" as mechanisms to address both social alienation and the economic demise of urban centres' (Waitt, 2008: 531). However, the paradox of urban festivals, and their use as both economic engines for cities and as place-makers in the global leisure market, is that while they generate capital, it is not always the citizens of the city that benefit from it. Gordon Waitt (ibid., 515) observes, 'Allowing the masses to party in the roman mode of bread and circuses while taken for granted as fun does nothing to undermine the economic relationships that maintain social injustices'. Kevin Gotham (2007) characterises this dynamic as a complex and contradictory process that acts as an agent for change, stabilisation, exploitation and autonomy. Gotham argues that this is not a passive process of acceptance and exploitation; local actors often use these processes to leverage change that can benefit residents, as well as preserve the physical and social environment.

One example of this can be seen by the increasing recognition, support and preservation of non-elite forms of cultural expression. David Harvey (2012: 104) links the increased symbolic capital of specific locations and geographies to the now necessary 'accumulation of marks of distinction' that have become pivotal to draw the capital interest of global mobile workforces and tourist markets. The positive impact that has resulted from this, Harvey argues, has been both acknowledgement and support for 'resistance to the idea that authenticity, creativity and originality are an exclusive product of bourgeois rather than working-class, peasant or other non-capitalistic historical geographies' (ibid., 110). However, equally consistent in urban regeneration seem to be uneven geographical development and uneven financial gain (Harvey, 2000). Gotham's (2007: 5) analysis of contemporary tourism also observes similar patterns, explaining 'tourism is not exogenous to localities but is embedded within broader patterns of metropolitan development and sociospacial inequality'. This can often contribute to greater division within the cultural life of a city as David Johnston (2003: 46) points out, 'The dangerously pervasive distinctions that are drawn between the so-called high and popular arts, underpinning much of local and regional arts planning . . . also serve to justify the ghettoization of artistic activities within prescribed areas of the city'. Another consistent and crucial question in the debate of the impact of increasing a location's symbolic capital is, 'whose collective memory is to be celebrated' (Harvey, 2012: 105) and whose collective memory is to be forgotten?

A case in point, perhaps the most ubiquitous public festival in Northern Ireland, has been the Orange Order parades held on 12 July, commonly referred to as the Twelfth, to commemorate the victory of Protestant King William over Catholic King James II at the Battle of Boyne in 1690. Formed in County Armagh in 1795, the Orange Order is a Protestant fraternal organisation, self-identified as conservative British Unionist, that currently describes its function as taking 'a stand for truth in an age of secularism and in order to defend our culture and traditions' (Grand Order Lodge, 2016). Styled by some as 'Europe's largest indigenous cultural folk festival', the annual commemorations popularly referred to as the Twelfth have long been a site of symbolic discord, affirmation, conflict and celebration (A Third Way for Ulster, 2007). The parades and bonfires of the Twelfth are the climax of what is known as marching season, the period from late Easter to the end of August 'dominated by the parades of the loyal orders; but there is also a distinct nationalist parading calendar that is part of the wider culture of parading ... The Twelfth of July generates the biggest parades and crowds, the most colour and noise as well as the most disruption and protests ... THE single event that marks the Ulster identity' (Jarman, 1997). The conundrum is in how to contend with these manifestations of public life that are perceived to be part of a problematic (i.e. sectarian) identity, which is equally rooted in traditional folk culture. As one advocate of the Twelfth celebrations stated: 'We are out celebrating our culture and we have a right to do that. So those issues of how we present it, how we promote our case, and the language we use are crucially important' (Ballymacarrett Arts and Cultural Society, 1999).

The Cathedral Quarter Trust state in their Five-Year Strategic Vision and Development Plan that one of their key priorities is: 'To generate high levels of public participation to develop a greater sense of shared culture and shared space in the heart of Belfast' (Cathedral Quarter Trust, 2012). This concept of shared culture in shared space through positive shared experience is a reoccurring theme in Northern Irish public policy and a formula deeply embedded in the distribution and language of public funds and officials, drawing on the principle of parity of esteem for both sides written into the Good Friday Agreement (Hocking, 2015). While Culture Night Belfast shares the ideology of festivalisation of its European cousins, civic participation by cultural consumption is further heightened and moralised by additional layers of post-conflict complexity. As demonstrated in this quote by Culture Night Belfast former Manager: 'The macroeconomic argument for events is well understood, they encourage spend in local businesses, increase footfall to key areas and lift the image of a nation. But they are also vital for our social fabric; they improve our quality of life, connecting us with our city and provide safe shared spaces to build a community' (Turkington, 2014).

In the early years of Culture Night Belfast, a common reflection was the idea that for one night Belfast felt like somewhere 'good' or 'European' (Culture Night Belfast, 2009). As evidenced from promotional audience feedback, this characterisation seems connected to the largely unacknowledged collective consciousness of Culture Night Belfast as a type of compensation or a redressing of cultural expressions codified as sectarian (e.g. 'makes me proud to be from Northern Ireland').⁹ Within the context of showcasing 'professional culture' and the implicit exploitation involved in not paying artists or organisations for their time or efforts, Culture Night Belfast reads as a distinctly 'Middle-classified' enterprise, which is characterised by Angela McRobbie (2015, 11) as one in which 'creativity becomes something inherent in personhood . . . which has the potential to be turned into a set of capacities'. In conversations with some of its professional participants, the concern was also expressed that the event had moved away from its showcase principles and simply had become too big, an argument commonly countered with a 'bigger is better' argument by organisers. General misgivings centred around the problem of value, or indeed 'devaluation', as in lack of hard data to corroborate the idea that Culture Night audiences might come back to attend paid or even alternative free cultural offerings. The idea persists among artists and many arts professionals that those who profited most were commercial businesses in the area such as bars, restaurants, hotels or traders. For example, one participant stated, 'If you look at the PR around it, it's about a big night out in the Cultural Quarter but obviously culture has a backseat'.¹⁰

Perhaps most problematic is where the class and culture divide manifests in the cultural offer itself with an ambivalent demarcation of the 'traditional' versus the 'cosmopolitan'. This is compounded by various 'truths', that many indigenous cultural celebrations are inherently sectarian and problematic, which is something largely sidestepped by those charged with promoting them and thus further driving them into quarantine among the creative professional class. There are, of course, exceptions, not excluding Culture Night itself, which included in its 2015 programme a performance of a loyalist marching band albeit rendered palatable by accompaniment of a variety of musicians from all over the world and 'across the divide'. The *Belfast Telegraph* reported that the band members 'realised that their participation, even though they were performing along with musicians from overseas, would be viewed with suspicion by Culture Night aficionados' (Little, 2015). However, these types of hybrid manifestations are significant in resolving tension between constructs of the 'traditional' and the 'cosmopolitan', while challenging more broadly the expectations of public culture. This points to the potential for these types of festivals to, in their post-conflict context, desegregate what constitutes public life. David Thomson, Chairman of the Shankhill Road Defenders Flute Band, reflects: 'We were very nervous about going into town in full uniform with our bass drum with Shankill Road Defenders written all over it, but we reckoned our culture should be included in a Culture Night and that was the main driving force behind our taking part' (Little, 2015). The implication being that even though Culture Night Belfast's methods of creating content (i.e. through an open, generally non-curated, call for programming) claims that all creative or 'cultural' comers to the table are equally valued, it is still largely dependent on the professionalised arts organisation's gate keepers to provide the cultural context, or indeed perceived permission, to enter this sphere to those outside.

CONCLUSION

In a context such as Northern Ireland, where culture is deeply codified and thus acts as a stand-in for all manner of 'loaded guns', there is an implicit tactic to galvanise the arts towards the display and consumption of culture that can be deemed neutral and therefore accessible to all. This instrumentalises the arts as a force for civil society through participation and representation, while at the same time reflects artists' and the public's intrinsic sense of cultural manifestations as an open space for celebration and self-reflection on identity, place. and social agency. As Sophie Hope (2011) has noted, this tension can be seen in the origins of UK community arts policies through the schism between notions of the democratisation of culture and cultural democracy. A definition of cultural democracy must include, as Owen Kelly notes, 'equality of access to the means of production, rather than consumption of an already defined culture' (Kelly, Lock and Merkel, 1986). The practice of public space and public culture, and more generally culturally led regeneration, needs to be critically assessed to answer the questions of who *for*, *with* and *by* in order to move beyond the rhetoric of reimaging, reimagining and reimagineering civic and artistic practice.

This means opening up spaces, both literally and metaphorically, to host these discussions that by their very nature cannot be resolved. This is permissible in projects such as *Evaluate* and *Re:Evaluate* which take on as part of their process and their practice to critically assess but not find an answer to the questions raised. For agencies of the state, this is a more complicated proposal none the least for their mandate to deliver a concrete and finite output, be it a performance or piece of public art. More broadly, projects that take an approach similar to *Evaluate* and *Re:Evaluate* offer insight into this conundrum and also the unacknowledged power dynamic inherent in the politics of both community art and public consultation, rendering them as both process and practice.

What is at stake in presenting and representing the cultural life of a city is more than a utilitarian value codified by economic development, social inclusion or psycho-social well-being. By allowing public culture to reflect more dissonance than it is afforded when pressed into service as revitalising resource, places and spaces become a service and servants to participatory democracy. Through enabling a range of nuanced positions to be reflected and engaged with is to begin to return some of the agency and responsibility generally afforded to individual artists and cultural producers back to the public, allowing them to re-imagine their reimaging as a much more complex fairy tale. For a place such as Ulster, which must contend with the economic challenges of our neoliberal era as well as coming to terms with its particular history of civil conflict, galvanising a more self-reflective public space for its broadest cultural forms might also begin to produce through this labour a move past the sectarian or state-sanctioned binaries and confidence to engage with alternative models for being in the world.

NOTES

1. The term 'reimagineering' comes from debates raised by David Johnston in the edited volume *Reimagining Belfast: A Manifesto for the Arts*, which contains reflections on the process for Belfast's 2008 bid for European Capital of Culture. Johnston's work highlights the tensions and inequalities that are often embedded (if not produced) in municipal and state arts policy: 'The danger of an arts policy governed by the shaping and structuring of arts activity in the city – rather than enabling and fostering – is that, in the limited funding environment in which the arts exist, we are not imagining anything. We are Imagineering' (2003, 48). This applies not only to the selective nature of what cultures and geographies are invested and disinvested in, but also the social agendas of those policies to reproduce a certain type of citizenry. In this sense, the term 'reimagineering' highlights the component and conundrum of social engineering that is embedded in arts policy and programming that foregrounds the instrumental and utilitarian value of inciting social change without a component of critical engagement and/or reflection.

2. One of the conditions of liberal peace, also referred to as democratic peace theory, is the adoption of development policies in line with the prevailing economic theories of global capitalism. One major critique of liberal peace is how the markers of its 'success' often in practice involve a form of neoliberal imperialism and propagation of Northern hegemony that is characterised by an absence of critical examination and 'difficult discussions about sustainable forms of peace, legitimacy, responsibility and inequality' (Richmond and Mac Ginty, 2015, 171).

3. Reflected in public sentiment, policy rhetoric, and academic scholarship, there is a well-documented correlation between areas of highly visible expressions of sectarianism (e.g. peace walls, murals and flags) and barriers for participation in the post-conflict economy (e.g. business investment and tourism). See for example Byrne, Gormley Heenan and Gillian Robinson 2012 and Hocking 2015.

4. For discussion of the histories and evolution of cultural arts policies and projects across a range of contexts and their differing social and artistic impacts, see Belfiore and Bennett 2008, Bishop 2006, Matarasso 1997, McRobbie 2016, Kester 2004 and Sholette 2011.

5. There has been a great body of literature produced on the debate about the intrinsic versus instrumental value of the arts and culture, as well as the ways in which artists' labour comes to be used as an instrument to support and disseminate particular political and economic agendas. One aspect of this debate highlighted in the work of George Yudice (2003: 10–11) is that the producers and products of arts and culture are legitimated by their utility and expediency to serve political and economic

policies, stating that 'today it is nearly impossible to find public statements that do not recruit instrumentalised art and culture, whether to better social conditions, as in the creation of multicultural tolerance and civic participation, through UNESCO-like advocacy for cultural citizenship and cultural rights, or to spur economic growth through urban cultural development projects and concomitant proliferation of museums for cultural tourism'.

6. In framing the thorough explanation and analysis of a range of Northern Irish post–Good Friday Agreement public art programmes that Bree T. Hocking presents in her book *The Great Reimagining: Public Art, Urban Space and Symbolic Landscapes of a 'New' Northern Ireland*, the author acknowledges the added complexity of the state's role from the outset: 'In Northern Ireland, however, where the legitimacy of the state and an enduring legacy of a violent conflict bedevil inter- and intra- community relations, contestation over public space is particularly dramatic. After all, it was in public space, and in urban space specifically, where preponderance of violence in Northern Ireland occurred' (2015: 22).

7. Halsall expands on the origins of the concept of aesthetics evoking Ranciere and Foucault: 'I think there needs to be an uncoupling of what aesthetic means from the philosophy of fine art, it's only with Hegel that we get the idea that aesthetics is something that's coupled specifically to fine art. I think a more interesting definition of aesthetics is an expanded definition . . . forms of knowledge gained through the senses, I think understood in those terms, . . . aesthetic experiences . . . provide the conditions of intersubjectivity' (Colclough, 2014). Here the term 'didactic aesthetics' is used to refer to art that is created with the purpose of instruction or execution that in itself offers an answer or solution to its subject or content.

8. Neil Jarman, interview with Sarah Feinstein, 15 April 2014.

9. Culture Night Belfast. 2016. Available at http://www.culturenightbelfast.com

10. Anonymous Arts Professional, interview with Sheelagh Colclough, 30 July 2016.

REFERENCES

A Third Way for Ulster. 2007. 'Images of the Twelfth'. Accessed 1 September 2016. http://www.ulsternation.org.uk/images_of_the_twelfth.htm.

Ballymacarrett Arts and Cultural Society. 1999. 'Orangeism and the Twelfth: What it means to me'. Accessed 30 August 2016. http://cain.ulst.ac.uk/islandpublications/hall99-ip24.pdf.

Belfast Newsletter. 2015. 'Get ready for buzzing Belfast Culture Night'. 4 September. Accessed 13 February 2016. http://www.newsletter.co.uk/what-s-on/arts-entertainment/get-ready-for-buzzing-culture-night-belfast-1-6940681.

Bianchini, Franco and Michael Parkinson. 1993. *Cultural Policy and Urban Regeneration: The West European Experience*. Manchester: Manchester University Press.

Bishop, Claire. 2012. *Artificial Hells: Participatory Art and the Politics of Spectatorship*. London: Verso.

Byrne, Jonny, Cathy Gormley Heenan and Gillian Robinson. 2012. *Attitudes to Peace Walls*. Belfast: University of Ulster.

Carruthers, Mark, Stephen Douds and Tim Loane. 2003. *Re-Imaging Belfast: A Manifesto for the Arts*. Belfast: Cultural Resolution.
Cathedral Quarter Trust. 2012. *Five-Year Strategic Vision and Development Plan*. Accessed 30 August 2016. https://issuu.com/cathedralquarter/docs/developmentplan?e=2601655/2807426.
Colclough, Sheelagh. 2007. *Evaluate: The Art of Forms, an Examination of Community Arts from the Inside Out*. Didactic panel to accompany performance and exhibition presented at Waterfront Hall, Belfast, September.
Colclough, Sheelagh. 2014. Re:Evaluate. Didactic panel to accompany discussion panel and exhibition presented at Crescent Arts Centre, Belfast, January.
Clark, Terry Nichols and Filipe Carreira da Silva. 2014. 'Was Tocqueville Wrong? Buzz as Charisma, Creativity, and Glamour; New Sources of Political Legitimacy Supplementing Voting, and Civic Participation'. In *Can Tocqueville Karaoke? Global Contrasts of Citizen Participation, the Arts and Development*, edited by Terry Nichols Clark, 157–173. Bingley: Emerald Group Publishing Limited.
Crowley, Tony. 2011. 'The Art of Memory: The Murals of Northern Ireland and the Management of History'. *Field Day Review* 7: 22–49.
Culture Night Belfast. 2009. *Belfast Culture Night Survey Report 2009: Participating Organisations and Audience Surveys*. Belfast Chamber of Trade and Commerce. Accessed 30 August 2016. http://www.belfastchamber.com/uploads/document/131020101141524080404564.pdf.
Destination Cathedral Quarter. 2016. 'About'. Accessed 1 September 2016. http://www.destinationcq.com/.
Emerson, Newton. 2014. 'Class Politics Dream a Sectarian Nightmare'. *Irish Times*, 9 October. Accessed 13 February 2016. http://www.irishnews.com/opinion/2014/10/09/news/class-politics-dream-a-sectarian-nightmare-104326/.
Gotham, Kevin. 2007. *Authentic New Orleans: Tourism, Culture, Race in the Big Easy*. London: New York University Press.
Grand Order Lodge. 2016. 'What Is the Orange Order?' Accessed 15 August 2016. http://www.grandorangelodge.co.uk/what-is-the-orange-order.
Harvey, David. 2000. *Spaces of Hope*. Edinburgh: Edinburgh University Press.
2012. *Rebel Cities: From the Right to the City to the Urban Revolution*. London: Verso.
Hill, Andrew and Andrew White. 2012. 'Painting Peace? Murals and the Northern Ireland Peace Process'. *Irish Political Studies* 27: 71–88.
Hocking, Bree. 2015. *The Great Reimagining: Public Art, Urban Space, and the Symbolic Landscapes of a 'New' Northern Ireland*. Oxford: Berghahn.
Hope, Sophie. 2011. 'Participating in the "Wrong" Way? Practice Based Research into Cultural Democracy and Commissioning of Art to Effect Social Change'. Accessed 14 September 2016. http://sophiehope.org.uk/research/.
Independent Research Solutions. 2009. 'Evaluation of the Re-imaging Communities Programme: A Report to the Arts Council of Northern Ireland'. Accessed 13 February 2016. http://www.artscouncil-ni.org/images/uploads/publications-documents/Re-Imaging_Final_Evaluation.pdf.
Jacob, Mary Jane, Michael Brenson and Eva Olson. 1995. *Culture in Action: A Public Art Program of Sculpture Chicago*. Seattle, WA: Bay Press.

Jarman, Neil. 1997. *Material Conflicts: Parades and Visual Displays in Northern Ireland*. Oxford: Berg Publishers.

Johnston, David. 2003. 'Imagination and Imagineering'. In *Re-imaging Belfast: A Manifesto for the Arts*, edited by Mark Carruthers, Stephen Douds and Tim Loane, 43–50. Belfast: Cultural Resolution.

Kelly, Owen, John Lock and Karen Merkel. 1986. *Culture and Democracy: The Manifesto*. London: Comedia and the Shelton Trust.

Little, Ivan. 2015. 'The Loyalist Band That's Marching to a Different Drum'. *Belfast Telegraph*, 25 September. Accessed 30 August 2016. http://www.belfasttelegraph.co.uk/life/features/the-loyalist-band-thats-marching-to-a-different-drum-31555806.html.

Lisle, Debbie. 2006. 'Local Symbols, Global Networks: Rereading the Murals of Belfast'. *Alternatives: Global, Local, Political* 31 (1): 27–52.

Matarasso, Francois. 1997. *Use or Ornament: The Social Impact of Participation in the Arts*. London: Comedia.

Matarasso, Francois and John Chell. 1998. *Vital Signs: Mapping Community Arts in Belfast*. London: Comedia.

McKittrick, David and David McVea. 2002. *Making Sense of the Troubles: The Story of the Conflict in Northern Ireland*. Chicago: New Amsterdam Books.

McManus, Carla and Clare Caruthers. 2014. 'Cultural Quarters and Urban Regeneration – the Case of Cathedral Quarter Belfast'. *International Journal of Cultural Policy* 20: 78–98.

McRobbie, Angela. 2015. *Be Creative Making a Living in the New Cultural Industries*. Chicester: Wiley.

Mouffe, Chantal. 2007. 'Artistic Activism and Agonistic Spaces'. *Art + Research*. Accessed 15 June 2016. http://www.artandresearch.org.uk/v1n2/mouffe.html.

Punter, John (ed.). 2010. *Urban Design and the British Urban Renaissance*. London: Routledge.

Quinn, Bernadette. 2010. 'Arts festivals, urban tourism and cultural policy'. *Journal of Policy Research in Tourism, Leisure & Event* 2: 264–79.

Richmond, Oliver and Roger Mac Ginty. 2015. 'Where now for the critique of the liberal peace'? *Cooperation and Conflict* 50 (2): 171–89.

Sassatelli, Monica. 2011. 'Urban Festivals and the Cultural Public Sphere: Cosmopolitanism between Ethics and Aesthetics'. In *Festivals and the Cultural Public Sphere*, edited by Gerard Delantry, Liana Giorgi and Monica Sassatelli, 12–28. London: Routledge.

Turkington, Adam. 2014. 'Why Cut Funding for Successful Events?' *Slugger O'Toole*. Accessed 25 August 2016. http://sluggerotoole.com/2014/10/06/why-cut-funding-for-successful-events-lightsoutni/.

Waitt, Gordon. 2008. 'Urban Festivals: Geographies of Hype, Helplessness and Hope'. *Geography Compass* 2: 513–37.

Yudice, Georg. 2003. *The Expediency of Culture: Uses of Culture in the Global Era*. Durham, NC: Duke University Press.

Chapter 2

Art, Activism and Addressing Sexual Assault in the UK

A Case Study

Winnie M. Li

In April 2015, on the seventh anniversary of my own rape, a handful of other activists and I co-founded the UK's first-ever arts festival dedicated to addressing sexual assault and consent. We eventually named it the Clear Lines Festival, in a direct response to the popular song 'Blurred Lines' which had become a target for student and feminist activism on the issue of sexual consent. Fifteen weeks later, our four-day festival took place in London, drawing a crowd of up to 500, including more than sixty speakers and artists. Social media activity around the festival was rife, and mainstream media coverage included local and national television, radio, newspapers and online outlets.

In this chapter, I will examine what led to the success of the festival, as well as explore the difficulties and tensions we faced in staging an ambitious programme of engaged art on this topic. I will present Clear Lines as a case study of the recent proliferation of performance-based arts events in the London area that address the issue of sexual assault and abuse. Together, these projects provide a space for survivors' narratives to be heard through theatre, spoken word and even stand-up comedy – as well as text-based art forms like literature, film and visual art. In fact, there is a growing international network of artists, activists and audiences, eager to engage with an issue that affects the lives of many, and, yet, which they feel is often misrepresented by mainstream producers in the arts and media.[1] In enabling public audiences to bear witness to lived experiences around sexual assault – and in creating publicity and drawing mainstream media attention – these festivals are robust examples of the arts as activism.

This study will be informed largely by my own background as a rape survivor, writer and activist, and as Co-Founder of the Clear Lines Festival. The data presented in this chapter are drawn from a combination of observation and field notes during February 2015–November 2016, as well as informal interviews with practitioners and written communications (internal e-mails, websites, social media posts and media coverage). As an academic, I work from a media and communications perspective; thus, this chapter will focus on communicative strategies in the creation and delivery of a feminist arts festival addressing sexual assault and the intersection of creative, activist and emotional labour which results. One central tension to examine is the emotional involvement and very personal motivation for those performing the labour, versus the economic constraints that often challenge socially engaged art. This and other tensions underpin my ongoing work as a practitioner in arts-based activism on this issue, as well as my own academic research – both of which are my professional responses to redress an experience as personally impactful to me as sexual assault.

THEORETICAL FRAMEWORK

Writing about the impact of rape on the individual, Susan Brison (herself a rape survivor and academic) argues that narrating one's own experience is fundamental to recovery. She writes: 'In order to construct self-narratives we need not only the words with which to tell our stories, but also an audience able and willing to hear us and to understand our words as we intend them' (Brison, 2002, 51). For her, telling *and* listening to self-narratives of rape are equally important in enabling survivors to heal from the trauma caused by their assault. If we are not heard and believed – if our own narrative is not witnessed and acknowledged by another – then we cannot begin to address the truth of what has happened to us. Art created by rape survivors about their own experiences is thus a therapeutic means of self-narrative.

But who does the performing of the art, and who the listening? Nancy Fraser (1990) would call this group of narrators and listeners a subaltern counter-public, which can serve both a therapeutic, personal purpose and a political, public one. Challenging the traditional notion of the public sphere, she writes that the subaltern counter-public encompasses members from a marginalised group who band together first to redress and heal, and second, to galvanise political action against dominant forces. For our purposes, this subaltern counter-public would constitute both survivors (Ministry of Justice, 2013 statistics indicate that in England and Wales, one in five women has experienced a sexual offence), and their supporters, including feminists, frontline workers and others concerned with sexual assault. A more everyday term for subaltern counter-public might be 'community'. Several scholars have explored how this counter-public is increasingly vocal, using new, online forms of technology to publicly challenge dominant narratives of sexual assault through art, grassroots community-building and awareness-raising (Sills et al., 2016; Keller, Mendes, and Ringrose 2016; Rentschler, 2014; Salter, 2013).

But what kind of labour is required to deliver an offline arts festival where these narratives of sexual assault can be performed and witnessed? A great deal of creative labour is needed. Creative labour is defined by Banks and Hesmondhalgh as work 'geared to the production of original or distinctive commodities that are primarily aesthetic and/or symbolic-expressive, rather than utilitarian and functional' (2009: 416). Here, the 'symbolic-expressive' purpose of creative labour coincides with the need for art to express an artist's experiences around trauma, playing the therapeutic role described by Brison. Thus its value to the artist is largely an emotional one. But this definition also labels the fruits of this labour as 'commodities' – a less appropriate description, as I will argue that art addressing sexual assault is often performed and witnessed in a non-commodified sphere. Creative labour is thus seen to 'offer the possibility of personal fulfillment or self-actualization, albeit in return for considerable hard work and absence of financial security' (Conor, Gill and Taylor, 2015: 5). The emotional nature of this creative labour is not unlike that of activist work, which Hochschild (1983) defines as 'emotional labour', rooted as it is in a deep sense of injustice that needs to be righted. Yet it is precisely the depth of emotion involved which can make a social movement successful in communicating its message to the public (Gould, 2009).

These various types of labour – creative, activist and emotional – were all fundamental to Clear Lines, which sought to advance the discussion around sexual assault by creating an artistic space for performing and witnessing, and communicating this ethos to a broader public. But how did these concepts play out in practice? And how did an artistic approach compound the already strained economics of activist labour, within a feminist sphere?

CASE STUDY

This section will take the form of a narrative explaining the growing ecosystem of arts-based events addressing sexual assault in London, and the formation of Clear Lines within that sphere.

My own involvement began in late 2014, when a short play of mine was selected for the second edition of the Unheard Festival, described as 'a new writing festival featuring performance exploring the themes of sexual abuse and assault.' Tessa Hart, Artistic Director of Unheard and herself a survivor, cites reactions from theatre producers and venues, who felt no one would want to see art around sexual abuse. Frustrated, she started Unheard in 2013 specifically to address 'this huge social taboo regarding the issue of sexual violence' (Li, 2015). Hart expanded the festival for its second edition and received over 250 submissions from around the world, many with personal messages from the artists grateful that such a festival existed. My own play was one of these.

I wrote 'Everything's Normal' to encapsulate the experiences of a rape survivor going about her 'normal' life. I saw it performed alongside eleven other plays at the four-day festival in February 2015, where many performances were sold out. I was impressed by the artistic quality and the emotional intensity of the writing and acting. In addition, all the artists involved in Unheard were working for no fee, without even expenses covered. This was clear proof that there were both an audience and artists hungry to engage with the topic of sexual assault.

Unheard is not unique in depending on unpaid labour. Many fringe arts events in London and elsewhere do not financially compensate contributing talent (performers, writers, directors, producers) simply because the funds are not available. In the case of arts events addressing social issues, this is even more prevalent, as seen with the Feminist Solidarity Fest, the London Feminist Film Festival, the Festival of Choice (advocating reproductive rights), and Calm Down Dear: A Feminist Festival. It is important to note that many of these festivals are free to attend or charge very little in admission fees. This underfunded but passionate model brings with it many tensions, which I will explore later in this chapter.

In contrast, the large Women of the World Festival (WOW) at the Southbank Centre in London serves as a flagship festival for gender equality, taking place each year near International Women's Day (8 March), with a weekend always dedicated to sexual assault. Now in its sixth year, WOW benefits from corporate sponsors like Bloomberg as well as its home at one of the UK's premier performing arts centres, with public funding and a steady revenue stream. Unlike fringe festivals, WOW has paid permanent staff to organise the festival and pays a standard fee to all speakers and performers involved. Due to its high profile, WOW is also able to draw much bigger 'celebrity' names involved in gender equality who in turn drive more publicity and media coverage, as well as higher admission prices. Nevertheless, WOW often serves as a platform to showcase smaller projects and grassroots initiatives on women's issues, and many feminist activists and artists in the UK converge and network at WOW.

Inspired by this ecosystem of arts events addressing sexual assault, I decided to launch the Clear Lines Festival two months after participating in the Unheard Festival 2015. I had been invited to a casual 'coffee meet-up' for people engaged with this issue, instigated over Twitter and email by Dr Nina Burrowes, a psychologist specialising in understanding sexual abuse. Burrowes suggested the idea of 'a whole festival' on the issue of sexual assault, and I volunteered to make that festival happen. After all,

I had a background in producing film festivals, and while I had never produced a cross-arts event before, I was increasingly aware of multiple creative projects addressing sexual violence, often highlighting them in my *Huffington Post* blog on the topic. Ultimately, I wanted to create a platform for these projects to be seen, performed and discussed, connecting engaged artists with engaged audiences – again, the performing and witnessing which Brison considers essential to healing.

That sense of community – of a subaltern counter-public – was vital for Clear Lines to take shape. Over the next fifteen weeks Burrowes and I, with a small team of volunteers, worked to conceive and deliver the festival, which took place from 29 July to 2 August at the IKLECTIK Art Cafe in Lambeth, London. There were twelve panel discussions, five artistic showcases (film screenings, theatre, stand-up comedy, spoken word and visual art), creative writing workshops in poetry and memoir and a pop-up photography studio. The panel discussions addressed a variety of topics, such as media coverage of sexual abuse, male victimhood and talking to children about sexual abuse. Panellists ranged from high-ranking individuals in the Metropolitan Police and Crown Prosecution to survivors, artists, grassroots activists, social workers and an international law firm. That law firm also provided us with £1,000 in sponsorship money, joining our in-kind sponsors On Road Media, whose valuable contributions I will discuss later.

Programming was not difficult, as artists responded enthusiastically to the idea of a festival exploring sexual assault and consent. Our programme included award-winning feminist comedians like Bridget Christie, Josie Long and Sarah Kendall, and screenings of Emmy- and BAFTA-nominated documentaries on rape. After each artistic showcase, I made sure to chair a Q&A session with the practitioners, which I felt important for two purposes. First, to showcase the creative process behind the art involved, the artist's impetus and challenges. And second, as a 'debrief' session to create a dialogue for both audience and artists to release the intense emotions felt during these narratives. Often, the Q&A sessions were the most emotional moments of the festival, with tears being shed both on-stage and in the audience – to reference Brison, an important example of speaking and listening as a means to overcome trauma.

Dialogue was in fact one of our key guiding principles from the early stages of planning Clear Lines. We also emphasised diversity, inclusivity and an optimistic approach to a difficult topic. In particular, we wanted to counter the notion of sexual assault as something to only be discussed behind closed doors, distancing ourselves from the sadness associated with the lived experience, while still acknowledging it. This was reflected in our festival branding: a bold purple, modern font against a bright yellow background. Even the use of the word 'festival' was important, as we ultimately saw Clear Lines as a celebration of the human spirit and its ability to recover from sexual assault.

Much of this can be seen in the language of our programme booklets, which read: 'Help us replace the shame and silence usually associated with this issue, with insight, understanding and community'.

Social media was essential for us in reaching our subaltern counter-public. We relied heavily on Twitter, Facebook and MailChimp to spread the word about Clear Lines and post content. Leading up to the festival, we filmed and edited short videos and circulated them through YouTube and other platforms. Our most elaborate video, 'One of Us', was a two-minute, semi-scripted compilation of six survivors speaking directly to camera about their experiences. These survivors were diverse in their accents, genders, ethnicities and experiences of rape – including date rape, drug-assisted rape, stranger rape, child sexual abuse and revenge pornography. With our emphasis on diversity, we were hoping to present a more realistic portrait of the crime and challenge the stereotypical portrayal of a victim in mainstream media: the young, white, female victim of a stranger rape (Boyle, 2005). As public funds were unavailable for a brand-new organisation or within a turnaround time as short as fifteen weeks, our five-week Crowdfunder campaign was vital in raising £7,200, enough to deliver the festival on a strained budget. Thus, social media became the primary means by which we raised capital, engaged our subaltern counter-public and initiated a broader awareness of the festival and our cause. In this respect, we were in line with many other activists' usage of social media in reaching a 'networked public' (Castells, 2012; boyd, 2010; Papacharissi, 2014), particularly feminist activists (Gleeson, 2016; Khoja-Moolji, 2015; McLean and Maalsen, 2013).

Given our short lead time, festival planning was not as organised as we would have liked. Communication took place mainly by email and through semi-regular meetings, although the core work fell to a Planning Committee of eight individuals (most of us survivors), with an additional twenty to twenty-five volunteers contributing in various ways (graphic design, fly postering, data entry, offering input or advice, volunteering at the venue). Those of us on the Planning Committee felt the festival to be simultaneously energising through its teamwork and, after the event, draining. I will now examine the voluntary, emotionally intense nature of this labour and its implications for other arts-based activists working in this resource-constrained sphere to address sexual assault.

ANALYSIS

As previous scholars have examined the role of social media by feminist, activist communities, I will not be focusing on this element of Clear Lines, although our reliance on social media will naturally be included in the discussion. Instead, I will explore three aspects: the relationship between creative labour and forms of capital in producing our festival; the concept of the creative commons and a non-commodified approach to the arts; and the role of mediated visibility in activist endeavours, with a final section on longer-term sustainability. Throughout this discussion, the emphasis will be on the creative and emotional labour involved in communicating the aims of Clear Lines to both our subaltern counter-public and the broader public.

CREATIVE LABOUR AND FORMS OF CAPITAL

Clear Lines was not alone in its dependence on crowdfunding, and in 2016, subsequent artistic projects on this issue, like the theatre piece 'Foreign Body' and the photography project *The Spiral of Containment: Rape's Aftermath*, followed suit with successful crowdfunding campaigns. But it is important to realise that crowdfunding is not 'free' money. Crowdfunding backers receive rewards; for example, tickets to Clear Lines events, or signed art and books by participating artists. All this needs to be organised. In fact, a great deal of unpaid labour goes into a running a successful crowdfunding campaign, with a significant emotional cost in the form of stress and a never-ending to-do list during the campaign. Gleeson (2016) has previously explored these pressures of unpaid digital labour involved in online feminist campaigns.

Furthermore, while some of our 138 backers learnt about Clear Lines purely through social media, the majority were already friends or acquaintances of the planning committee, pledging their funds in response to repeated Facebook posts and direct email appeals. Thus, in line with previous studies on this subject (Kang, Jiang and Tan, 2016; Lehner, 2014), our experience of crowdfunding demonstrated less so 'the power of the anonymous crowd', and more so the social capital of the planning committee members – more specifically, knowing enough people with generosity and expendable funds. To invoke Bourdieu (1986), economic capital can be derived in part from social and cultural capital.

Likewise, the festival was built through the voluntary efforts of existing professionals – On Road Media, Dr Burrowes, myself, practitioners in graphic design, communications and event management – all of whom had the professional skills, the networks and the familiarity with media to deliver the festival within such a short period of time. In lieu of solid economic capital, the collective social and cultural capital of the planning committee brought Clear Lines to fruition. None of us were financially compensated for our efforts, and none of us expected to be: the festival, after all, was our 'passion project'. Panellists were not compensated – although expenses were covered, upon request. The comedians (all quite established on the stand-up circuit) and the videographers who documented the festival *did* receive a fee, but much-reduced compared to their normal earnings. Perhaps this was to acknowledge the level of professional skill these particular individuals were committing to Clear Lines. We had asked them to participate, and offering absolutely nothing felt insulting.

Similarly, I decided to pay a nominal fee to each of the artists involved in the Spoken Word and Theatre Evenings. First, I wanted to at least symbolically recognise the amount of creative labour that went into generating artistic material for the festival, whether that be a new poem written or a theatrical role that had been carefully rehearsed. As an artist myself, I knew that the relatively brief amount of time spent performing on stage was only the result of hours of artistic preparation. Second, I was aware that these artists (like myself) were freelance workers and many of them did not have regular salaries specifically so they could pursue their artistic craft. Thus, any creative labour deserved to be recognised monetarily. In contrast, many of the panellists came from organisations that paid their wages (e.g. law firms or the Metropolitan Police) or were representing an activist group of which they were a central figure. In essence, speaking at Clear Lines was an extension of their existing work. For the artists, preparing for their performance at Clear Lines was a *new* piece of creative work. These kinds of decisions coincide with scholarship on creative labour as underpaid in relation to the amount of time and effort required (Neff et al., 2005; Ross, 2009) and as precarious, taking place within a freelance 'gig' economy (McRobbie, 2002, 2015; Taylor and Littleton, 2012) where artists often are expected to work for free (Ross, 2000). For all our best intentions, the fee we were able to offer these performers was low, as concrete expenses like venue and equipment hire, printing costs and providing food for volunteers unfortunately took precedence.

Thus, there existed an uneasy tension between recognising the artistic, professional and emotional contributions of the artists and speakers involved, and being unable to adequately compensate them for their efforts. The flip side to this producer's guilt is the fact that all these individuals were willing to participate in the festival, due to their passion to addressing this issue. Scholars have commented on 'passion' as that which supposedly drives the creative professional. But, as Conor, Gill and Taylor warn, the celebratory rhetoric to 'Do What You Love (DWYL)' has profoundly 'displaced important questions about working conditions and practices within CCI [cultural and creative industries], let alone issues of equality, diversity and social justice' (2015: 2). Likewise, in scholarship on activism, the 'passion' or emotional involvement in an issue can lead to a higher risk of activist burn out (Chen and Gorski, 2015; Maslach and Gomes, 2006). Finally, scholars and frontline workers engaging regularly with the issue of sexual assault and violence run the risk of a similar emotional burnout (Campbell, 2002), especially if oneself is a survivor (Ullman, 2010).

Thus, the work involved with the creation of Clear Lines and other engaged art on the topic carries with it both financial and emotional risks. Our volunteer video editor, who worked on 'One of Us', found herself very 'drained' and 'depressed', after hours spent cutting together footage of rape survivors talking about their experiences – and this likely affected her ability to continue working on Clear Lines. As a producer, I felt guilty not knowing how to compensate her for her efforts. Thus, we tried hard not to exacerbate existing injustices regarding pay for creative labour, which often disadvantage women (Leung, Gill and Randall, 2015). But working on such a tight budget as producers, we constantly encountered that dual-sided coin of guilt and gratitude – framed on one hand by financial constraints and on the other by emotional dedication. On Clear Lines, there was a confluence of multiple stressors on those involved: non-existent to low pay and emotional involvement were concerns not just because this was creative labour, but also because it was activist labour, and specifically labour addressing sexual assault, an issue that had been personally traumatic for many of us involved. All three aspects of our work compounded to make the festival particularly challenging – but also particularly rewarding to work on.

THE CREATIVE COMMONS AND A NON-COMMODIFIED SPHERE

The concept of the creative commons advocates a culture of free sharing of intellectual material, acknowledging that cultural production thrives on access to previous creative works and encourages collaborative authorship (Lessig, 2004; Meng, 2009). In the case of Clear Lines, we can apply this concept to underline the therapeutic benefits of sharing engaged art on sexual assault. Thus, access to creative works encourages *emotional* healing, and collaborative authorship becomes the shared performance and witnessing of a narrative on this topic, enabling both the listener and the storyteller to benefit. Indeed, most of the writers contributing to our Theatre and Spoken Word Nights were drawing from their own experiences of sexual abuse. Perhaps telling their story through their artistic craft offered an inherent emotional value, such that practitioners were willing to forego financial payment for their creative labour. Hence, both the artistic content and the witnessing of it become part of a creative commons where emotional value transcends the need for economic compensation. Whether this argument is entirely ethical, given that we cannot escape the material, commodified world in which we create and consume art is another question.

Practically speaking, what this meant is that the artists were willing to create art at Clear Lines for a very nominal fee. The playwrights would likely be happy for their plays to be performed at other events, without adequate compensation – for the more philanthropic wish of positively connecting with others affected by this issue. As Brison says, we need to share our stories with each other, in order to recover. And drawing on Fraser's subaltern counter-public theory, the public needs to hear these stories, in order for societal change to occur. Thus, by subscribing to the notions of a creative commons – by making artistic material addressing sexual assault to be freely available, artists and producers are increasing the potential public impact of their work – both the therapeutic potential that other survivors might draw from witnessing this art, but also the political potential of altering public opinion. The question then becomes: where do you draw the line between making your art as available as possible for the greatest public impact, and expecting the appropriate economic compensation for the time, effort, and talent you have expended toward creating that art? The answer is not clear.

This distinctly non-commodified approach manifested not just in nominal fees paid to the Clear Lines artists, but also very nominal ticket prices charged to the audience. Most of our events were free, and except for the Comedy Night, all other tickets cost less than ten pounds. Although higher ticket prices could have raised more revenue, our emphasis was on inclusivity and accessibility – again, guiding principles for the creative commons. Ultimately, we wanted to encourage as many people as possible to be part of this new 'conversation' about sexual assault. The other fringe feminist festivals cited have a similar approach, charging no or very low ticket prices. Some, like Unheard, even donate a portion of proceeds to a local rape crisis service centre. Instead of making a profit, the ethos of these festivals is to encourage access and foster artistic practice for both artists and audiences: an ethos of performing and witnessing, which foregrounds the potential to heal.

Today digital technologies increase the possibilities of the creative commons by disseminating this art even further, for free. Prior to Clear Lines, Burrowes (2014) wrote a comic book, *The Courage to Be Me*, portraying the stories of four different sexual abuse victims in a fictional support group. She invited four different comic artists to illustrate each story, and each artist was paid from crowdsourced funds. While the hard copy of the book is available to purchase, its digital content can be accessed online for free, as Burrowes wishes that its therapeutic value be available to whoever needs it. Again, the notion of the creative commons is applicable here, along with its characteristics of inclusivity, community and collaborative authorship.

At Clear Lines, we enacted the same ethos in our use of digital technologies. With the consent of the poets, we used social media to circulate videos of their performances from the Spoken Word Night. Our Artist-in-Residence Johanna Ward ran a pop-up photography studio at the festival, inviting people to participate in a one-to-one conversation about sexual assault and photographing their eyes during this conversation. The resulting piece of art,

The Watchful Eyes, existed only in digital format, in a series of images and GIFs, interspersed with quotes from these conversations. It was made available on Johanna's website and we disseminated it through Clear Lines social media. This type of participatory art drew upon both collective and individual responses to the issue, to create a work that could only be witnessed on an online space and for free. In this sense, Clear Lines exemplified the oft-cited affordances of digital technology to expand the creative commons, freely circulating art to a broad audience to enhance the artistic, emotional and societal value of the works created (Lessig, 2001).

MEDIATED VISIBILITY

If social media became a fundamental tool for disseminating content to a subaltern counter-public, mainstream media also played an important role in 'validating' the Clear Lines Festival and publicising it to a larger audience. In the weeks leading up to the festival, we found ourselves drawing attention from media producers via two different routes. First, an 'organic' route, whereby media producers noticed our social media activity and approached us. This happened when we reached our initial crowdfunding target of £3,500 and were subsequently covered by *The Huffington Post* and London Live television station, as well as local and feminist online publications. Second, there was a more professional public relations route, whereby our sponsors On Road Media issued a press release before the festival and solicited their existing media contacts. Eventually we were covered by Channel 4 News, *The Daily Mail*, *The Telegraph* and BBC Radio, resulting in a catalogue of articles and video clips which, in terms of Clear Lines as activism, serves to validate and legitimise the impact of our organisation (Gamson and Wolfsfeld, 1993). Interestingly, many of the mainstream outlets specifically asked to interview a festival organiser who was a rape survivor – which ended up being me.

A few learnings can be derived from this experience. First, mainstream media remains fascinated by the topic of sexual assault, but tends to report it according to established tropes (Boyle, 2005). In this case, that trope is of the 'rape victim's life made good' (Orgad, 2009). In their Femail section, *The Daily Mail* ran a long, photo-heavy article on me: this turned out to be primarily the story of my own rape and recovery, with only a very small mention of Clear Lines towards the end.[2] Here, the clichéd narrative of an individual survivor's journey from stranger rape (Boyle, 2005) eclipsed the collective story of a group instigating social change through art. This has subsequently been the case for media coverage of other activist projects addressing the issue, such as the My Body Back Project in London (covered by many major media outlets in the UK). Second, mainstream media producers are largely reliant on social media content – websites, crowdfunding campaigns, Twitter trends – to fuel their enquiries into grassroots activist projects. Third, despite the role of social media in suggesting content, it is still very much social and cultural capital or centrality in a communication network (Pilny, Atouba and Riles, 2014), which determines the stories that are covered in mainstream media. In this case, without On Road's network of contacts, we would have never secured the Channel 4 interview, our most visible media coverage. Related to this is my fourth point: a significant amount of labour went into soliciting and handling the media coverage of our event and this should not be overlooked. In addition to organising the festival itself, I underwent multiple media interviews – all of which require communication skills, time, energy and – especially when addressing one's own experiences of sexual assault – emotional labour.

An interesting conundrum arises: while mainstream media coverage is seen as a bonus, as 'best evidence' of an event's success (Pilny, Atouba and Riles, 2014), we should not underestimate the kind of labour involved in generating it. Established organisations have their own communications and PR teams, skilled to generate media coverage so others can move forward with the regular operations. But grassroots activists and artists do not. In an already underfunded, voluntary field, how does one balance the actual activist work with the labour of handling the media? But more importantly, why is mainstream media coverage even seen as a marker of status and achievement, particularly when we realise how much social capital is required to penetrate the closed world of mainstream media producers? Surely there is an inherent worth in the activist work itself – in the live performance and witnessing – that we do not need the press files as validation of the event's success. And when considering the value of an event addressing sexual assault, why should an article by a professional journalist carry more weight than a blogged testimonial by an individual survivor who has lived the impact of rape?

Added to this are the dangers of mainstream media coverage, where messages can be misrepresented to conform to dominant narratives. Unlike social media, where activists can control the content of their own posts, mainstream media coverage often results in a loss of control and a distortion of the initial message. In addition, for activists opening up to the media in interviews, talking candidly about their experience of sexual assault involves a great deal of emotional labour. Emily Jacob, Founder of The ReConnected Life, a social enterprise for rape survivors, admits the hardest part of her work involves 'the telling, and re-telling of my story', which is nevertheless necessary for raising the profile of her venture: 'There's a real vulnerability in seeing "rape survivor says" in the Metro article headline'.[3] Though perhaps unique to sexual abuse survivors, the emotional exposure of media visibility is a more acute version of the emotional labour required for professionals to maintain a personal brand in the creative industries (Adkins and Jokinen, 2008).

But for an activist organisation like Clear Lines, what Thompson (2005) terms 'mediated visibility' is a form of recognition which will help in our next round of fundraising. Pilney, Atouba and Riles (2014) consider this 'media visibility' in an ecosystem alongside legitimacy, solidarity, networking, perceived influence and support, which surrounds a social movement organisation. And yet, that ecosystem is a world away from the private, intimate world of each survivor's journey towards recovery, which relies upon storytelling, listening and community. Arts-related activism around sexual assault attempts to traverse both these public and private worlds, with resulting tensions. On the one hand, an event like Clear Lines is largely organised, performed and witnessed by a subaltern counter-public of rape survivors, supporters and activists often connected through social media. On the other hand, activism aims to bring about societal change – and media visibility is still seen as the most effective tool for public impact (Gamson and Wolfsfeld, 1993). Events like these show how producers in mainstream media and social media interact, feeding off each other for content and validation – alternately implicating the power of the crowd and the perceived status of mainstream media attention – to demonstrate the public importance of an issue.

Activists must ask: for whom are we organising this event? For individual survivors, to help them recover and find a community, or for the public sphere, so a broader audience can witness and understand these narratives of sexual assault? For Clear Lines the answer was both – and subsequently our labour was doubled by the need to both organise the event and cater to mainstream media. Other activists and artists may well desire mediated visibility, but this is not without its additional cost of unpaid emotional labour.

COMPETITION WITHIN A CROWDED ECOSYSTEM

Paradoxically, within this ecosystem, organisations addressing sexual assault find themselves in competition with each other – at the same time that they support each other ideologically and substantively. On social media, many of these groups and activists form a networked community, re-tweeting and re-posting each other's event announcements, and starting conversations around relevant articles. Offline, too, many of these organisers network informally over coffee and at events, sharing curatorial advice, ideas and expertise.

For Clear Lines, we curated much of our Theatre and Spoken Word night from the previous Unheard Festival. Some of this was performed subsequently at the One Billion Rising Festival and Keble Arts Festival, and individuals attending Clear Lines were inspired to start their own activist ventures like the Survivors Collective in London and the first Reclaim the Night in Norwich. Seen in one light, this supportive ecosystem of dedicated activists and artists seem to collaborate on various public events in order to address sexual assault, drawing upon a sense of solidarity in a networked public (boyd, 2010) and the creative commons (Lessig, 2001). But in another light, because this ecosystem is so underfunded and non-commodified, these events and organisations perhaps compete with each other for resources like mediated visibility, creative labour, leadership and funding. If activists and artists cannot hope to earn a living from addressing the issue of sexual assault, there is a limited amount of time, energy and emotional involvement they can dedicate to it. And yet, the finite nature of these resources is in stark contrast to the endless amount of work that can be done on this topic.

Elisa Iannacone mentions 'compassion fatigue or empathy fatigue' in her ongoing photography that engages survivors. Jacob and Burrowes both emphasise the need for self-care to mitigate against burn out, which is reiterated in the literature on activism (Gorski, 2015). It is often difficult to draw a line around the amount of effort one expends, knowing there is so much ignorance and suffering out there related to sexual assault. How long can an individual activist continue working unpaid on this issue before their own mental health and well-being are affected?

Furthermore, if activists are not going to be paid anyway, many choose to start their own endeavour on their own terms, because an emotional sense of gratification (running your own event, being in charge) can at least replace the lack of financial gratification. What this unfortunately leads to is an overcrowded ecosystem full of grassroots activists and artists, all wanting to make their own mark, often supporting each other ideologically, but rarely pooling together their resources and skills in an organised, financially compensated way.

Other resources are scarce, such as mediated visibility. Media producers can only report on so many festivals addressing sexual assault before it is no longer news. Likewise, public funding for such events is severely limited and often tied to proof of public impact (i.e. mediated visibility, which is in turn tied to social and cultural capital). And yet, without sufficient funding, activist organisations can rarely move beyond the grassroots level or transcend the subaltern counter-public to address the larger public sphere. In this precarious world, the personal and psychological cost of undertaking activist and creative labour to address sexual assault must not be underestimated. But while this ecosystem proves there is a fertile ground full of ideas, energy and talent wanting to challenge this issue, not all of those efforts can take root and grow.

CONCLUSION

Clear Lines is a clear example of the many challenges and triumphs encountered by contemporary activists addressing sexual assault. One participant wrote: 'What you've done is pretty miraculous and you could see how the festival lit up those people. I haven't experienced such positivity and hope like that, possibly, ever, especially in the face of such a tough subject'.[4] But my own contribution to Clear Lines equated to three months of full-time work, unpaid. It is not a labour model I wish to replicate again, for the sheer fact that I need to earn a living. Indeed, in 2016, while the desire was certainly there on our part, we were not able to stage a second edition of Clear Lines, primarily because paid work took precedence for the individual organisers. Nevertheless, we hope to organise Clear Lines in 2017, especially as the issue of sexual assault has continued to gain mainstream visibility and galvanise more activists and survivors.

But we are wary of the challenges involved, in relation to labour and capital in this underfunded activist sphere. In particular, the combination of an individual's deep emotional involvement and personal motivation to address the issue of sexual assault, compounded with the existing financial precarity of creative labour, can lead to multiple stressors on those performing the work to make the festival and its art possible. While these factors help create a non-commodified sphere within which Clear Lines and other socially engaged feminist art are performed, ultimately, this is not sustainable in the long term, neither for the events nor for the practitioners. 'Passion' cannot be the only fuel driving an activist or artistic enterprise, because inevitably this can lead to burn out. And yet, how do we solve the problem of raising enough capital to economically compensate our artists and producers?

With such an overcrowded field, we would suggest that the many artistic and activist ventures addressing sexual assault start to join forces in a more official capacity, so we can collaborate rather than compete with each other for limited resources. I am in talks with other London organisers about merging festivals and events. This may require a sacrifice of ego and personal vision in order for progress to take place, but ultimately this seems like the best route for building a more sustainable, better resourced activist effort. The cultural commons remains a relevant concept when we understand the therapeutic capacity of performing and witnessing, enabling artists and audiences alike to heal. But if we wish to adhere to this concept – divorcing the emotional, artistic value of a work from its economic value and making the work as accessible as possible – then we must find other ways to adequately compensate our artists for their creative labour. With a less crowded field, organisations may be in a stronger position to unlock funding from either traditional cultural institutions, public funds, corporate sponsors or other forms of revenue. And a stronger infrastructure will also enable better resources to provide emotional support, mitigate against burn out and communicate with mainstream media producers for more effective media visibility. In this way, we can best serve the subaltern counter-public of those affected by the crime and reach the broader public in challenging the public conversation around sexual assault.

Until this happens, continued engagement with the issue of sexual assault appears to be an unsustainable and precarious practice for individual activists and artists. And yet, many remain passionate.

NOTES

1. See Unheard Festival, Women of the World Festival, Calm Down Dear: A Feminist Festival, Tell It Festival: Acting Out, Creative/Disruption.
2. Emily Wadsworth: 'Woman Who Was Raped by 15-Year-Old in Broad Daylight While She Was Hiking Reveals She Did Not Feel Threatened at First . . . Because He Was So Young'. *Mail Online*. 30 July 2015. http://www.dailymail.co.uk/femail/article-3179721/A-woman-raped-15-year-old-boy-decided-write-book-traumatic-experience.html.
3. Emily Jacob, email message to author, 30 November 2016.
4. Name withheld, email message to author, 3 August 2015.

REFERENCES

Adkins, Lisa, and Eeva Jokinen. 2008. 'Introduction: Gender, Living, and Labour in the Fourth Shift'. *NORA – Nordic Journal of Feminist and Gender Research* 16: 138–49.

Ainger, Katharine. 2016. 'The Social Fabric of Resilience: How Movements Survive, Thrive or Fade Away'. In *Sites of Protest*, edited by Stuart Price and Ruth Sanz Sabido, 37–53. London: Rowman & Littlefield.

Banks, Mark, and David Hesmondhalgh. 2009. 'Looking for Work in Creative Industries Policy'. *International Journal of Creative Policy* 15: 415–30.

Bourdieu, Pierre. 1986. 'The Forms of Capital'. In *Handbook of Theory and Research for the Sociology of Education*, edited by John Richardson, 241–58. New York: Greenwood.

boyd, danah. 2010. 'Social Network Sites as Networked Publics: Affordances, Dynamics, and Implications'. In *A Networked Self: Identity, Community, and Culture on Social Network Sites*, edited by Zizi Papacharissi, 39–58. New York: Routledge.

Boyle, Karen. 2005. *Media and Violence: Gendering the Debates*. London: SAGE.

Brison, Susan. 2002. *Aftermath: Violence and the Remaking of a Self*. Oxford: Princeton University Press.

Burrowes, Dr. Nina. 2014. *The Courage to Be Me: A Story of Courage, Self-Compassion and Hope after Sexual Abuse*. London: NB Research.

Burrowes, Dr. Nina. 2015. YouTube channel. Clear Lines 2015 videos. 'One of Us'. Published 6 July. https://youtu.be/O-l9QwPrH2E.

Callaghan, Sharon. 2011. 'The Weeks of Work That Make the Day: Looking at All the Activities in Activism'. *Social Alternatives* 30: 5–9.

Campbell, Rebecca. 2002. *Emotionally Involved: The Impact of Researching Rape*. London: Routledge.
Castells, Manuel. 2012. *Networks of Outrage and Hope: Social Movements in the Internet Age*. Cambridge: Polity.
Chasteen, A. L. 2001. 'Constructing Rape: Feminism, Change, and Women's Everyday Understandings of Sexual Assault'. *Sociological Spectrum* 21: 101–39.
Chen, Cher Weixia and Paul C. Gorski. 2015. 'Burnout in Social Justice and Human Rights Activists: Symptoms, Causes and Implications'. *Journal of Human Rights Practice* 7: 366–90.
Clear Lines Festival. 2015. 'Thanks for Making Clear Lines a Success!' Last modified 6 August. http://clearlines.org.uk/2015/08/thanks-for-making-clear-lines-a-success/.
Clear Lines Festival. 2015. Programme booklet. 30 July–2 August 2015. Published 28 July.
Conor, Bridget, Rosalind Gill and Stephanie Taylor. 2015. 'Gender and Creative Labour'. In *Gender and Creative Labour*, edited by Bridget Conor, Rosalind Gill, and Stephanie Taylor, 1–22. London: Wiley Blackwell/ *The Sociological Review*.
Crowdfunder. 2015. 'Clear Lines'. Accessed 30 August 2016. http://www.crowdfunder.co.uk/clear-lines/.
Fraser, Nancy. 1990. 'Rethinking the Public Sphere: A Contribution to the Critique of Actually Existing Democracy'. *Social Text* 25–26: 56–80.
Gamson, William A., and Gadi Wolfsfeld. 1993. 'Movements and Media as Interacting Systems'. *The Annals of the American Academy of Political and Social Science* 258: 114–25.
Gleeson, Jessamy. 2016. ' "(Not) Working 9–5": The Consequences of Contemporary Australian-Based Online Feminist Campaigns as Digital Labour'. *Media International Australia* 161: 77–85.
Gleeson, Jessamy. 2016. 'Online Change in an Offline World: Perceptions of Social Transformation among Feminist Campaigners'. In *Sites of Protest*, edited by Stuart Price and Ruth Sanz Sabido, 163–78. London: Rowman & Littlefield.
Goblin Baby Theatre Company. 2014. 'UNHEARD Focus Festival 2015'. http://www.goblinbaby.com/festival-overview.html.
Gorski, Paul C. 2015. 'Relieving Burnout and the "Martyr Syndrome" Among Social Justice Education Activists: The Implications and Effects of Mindfulness'. *The Urban Review* 47: 696–716.
Gould, Deborah B. 2009. *Moving Politics: Emotion and ACT UP's Fight against AIDS*. London: University of Chicago Press.
Hochschild, Arlie. 1983. 'Comment on Kemper's "Social constructionist and Positivist Approaches to the Sociology of Emotions" '. *American Journal of Sociology* 89: 432–34.
IndieGoGo. 2016. 'Foreign Body, a New Play'. Accessed 28 November. https://www.indiegogo.com/projects/foreign-body-a-new-play#/
Kang, Lele, Qiqi Jiang and Chuan-Hoo Tan. 2016. 'Remarkable Advocates: An Investigation of Geographic Distance and Social Capital for Crowdfunding'. *Information & Management*. 4 September.
Keller, Jessalyn, Caitlyn Mendes and Jessica Ringrose. 2016. 'Speaking 'Unspeakable Things': Documenting Digital Feminist Responses to Rape Culture'. *Journal of Gender Studies* 25: 1–15.

Khoja-Moolji, Shenila. 2015. 'Becoming an "Intimate Publics": Exploring the Affective Intensities of Hashtag Feminism'. *Feminist Media Studies* 15: 347–50.

Khroudina, Victoria. 2015. 'The "Clear Lines" of Sexual Consent'. *SheRa Mag*. 28 July. http://www.sheramag.com/clear-lines-festival/.

Kickstarter. 2016. 'The Spiral of Containment: Rape's Aftermath'. Accessed 28 November. https://www.kickstarter.com/projects/961196631/the-spiral-of-containment-rapes-aftermath.

Lehner, Othmar M. 2014. 'The Formation and Interplay of Social Capital in Crowd-Funded Social Ventures'. *Entrepreneurship & Regional Development* 26: 478–99.

Lessig, Lawrence. 2001. *The Future of Ideas: The Fate of the Commons in a Connected World*. New York: Random House.

Leung, Wing-Fai, Rosalind Gill and Keith Randall. 2015. 'Getting In, Getting On, Getting Out? Women as Career Scramblers in the UK Film and Television Industries'. In *Gender and Creative Labour*, edited by Bridget Conor, Rosalind Gill and Stephanie Taylor, 50–65. London: Wiley Blackwell/*The Sociological Review*.

Li, Winnie M. 2015. 'UNHEARD Stories: An Upcoming Theatre Festival about Sexual Violence'. *The Huffington Post*. 17 February. http://www.huffingtonpost.com/winnie-m-li/unheard-stories-an-upcomi_b_6691792.html.

Maslach, Christina, and Mary E. Gomes. 2006. 'Overcoming Burnout'. In *Working for Peace: A handbook of Practical Psychology and Other Tools*, edited by Rachel MacNair and Psychologists for Social Responsibility, 42–59. Atascadero, CA: Impact.

McCosker, Anthony. 2015. 'Social Media Activism at the Margins: Managing Visibility, Voice and Vitality Affects'. *Social Media + Society* 1: 1–11.

McLean, Jessica and Sophia Maalsen. 2013. 'Destroying the Joint and Dying of Shame? A Geography of Revitalised Feminism in Social Media and Beyond'. *Geographical Research* 51: 243–56.

McRobbie, Angela. 2002. 'From Holloway to Hollywood: Happiness at Work in the New Cultural Economy'. In *Cultural Economy: Cultural Analysis and Commercial Life*, edited by Paul du Gay and Michael Pryke, 97–114. London: Sage.

McRobbie, Angela. 2015. *Be Creative: Making a Living in the New Culture Industries*. Cambridge: Polity.

Meng, Bingchun. 2009. 'Articulating a Chinese Commons: An Explorative Study of Creative Commons China'. *International Journal of Communication* 3: 192–207.

Ministry of Justice, Home Office and Office for National Statistics. 2013. *An Overview of Sexual Offending in England and Wales*. Statistics Bulletin. 10 January.

Neff, Gina, Elizabeth Wissinger and Sharon Zukin. 2005. 'Entrepreneurial Labour Among Cultural Producers: "Cool" Jobs in "Hot" Industries'. *Social Semiotics* 15: 307–334.

Orgad, Shani. 2009. 'The Survivor in Contemporary Culture and Public Discourse: A Genealogy'. *The Communication Review* 12: 132–61.

Papacharissi, Zizi. 2014. *Affective Publics: Sentiment, Technology, and Politics*. Oxford: Oxford University Press.

Pilney, Andrew N., Yannick C. Atouba and Julius M. Riles. 2014. 'How Do SMOs Create Moral Resources? The Roles of Media Visibility, Networks, Activism, and Political Capacity'. *Western Journal of Communication* 78: 358–77.

Rentschler, Carrie Anne. 2014. 'Rape Culture and Feminist Politics of Social Media'. *Girlhood Studies* 7: 65–82.
Ross, Andrew. 2000. 'The Mental Labor Problem'. *Social Text* 18: 1–31.
Ross, Andrew. 2009. *Nice Work if You Can Get It: Life and Labor in Precarious Times*. New York: New York University Press.
Salter, Michael. 2013. 'Justice and Revenge in Online Counter-Publics: Emerging Responses to Sexual Violence in the Age of Social Media'. *Crime, Media, Culture* 9: 225–42.
Scharff, Christina. 2015. 'Blowing Your Own Trumpet: Exploring the Gendered Dynamics of Self-Promotion in the Classical Music Profession'. In *Gender and Creative Labour*, edited by Bridget Conor, Rosalind Gill and Stephanie Taylor, 97–112. London: Wiley Blackwell/*The Sociological Review*.
Sills, Sophie, Chelsea Pickens, Karishma Beach, Lloyd Jones, Octavia Calder-Dawe, Paulette Benton-Greig and Nicola Gavey. 2016. 'Rape Culture and Social Media: Young Critics and a Feminist Counterpublic'. *Feminist Media Studies* 16: 1–17.
Silverstone, Roger. 2007. *Media and Morality: On the Rise of the Mediapolis*. Cambridge: Polity Press.
Taylor, Stephanie, and Karen Littleton. 2012. *Contemporary Identities of Creativity and Creative Work*. Abingdon: Ashgate.
Thicke, Robin, featuring T. I. and Pharrell Williams. 2013. 'Blurred Lines'. Star Trak Recordings.
Thompson, John B. 2005. 'The New Visibility'. *Theory, Culture & Society* 22: 31–51.
Ullmann, Sarah E. 2010. *Talking about Sexual Assault: Society's Response to Survivors*. Washington: American Psychological Association.
Wadsworth, Emily. 2015. 'Woman Who Was Raped by 15-Year-Old in Broad Daylight While She Was Hiking Reveals She Did Not Feel Threatened at First . . . Because he Was So Young'. *Mail Online*. 30 July 2015. http://www.dailymail.co.uk/femail/article-3179721/A-woman-raped-15-year-old-boy-decided-write-book-traumatic-experience.html.
Ward, Johanna. 2015. 'The Watchful Eyes'. http://www.johannaward.co.uk/the-watchful-eyes-1/ (site taken down as of January 2017).
Warner, Michael. 2002. *Publics and Counterpublics*. New York: Zone Books.

Chapter 3

Macao before and beyond Social Media

The Creation of the Unexpected as a Mobilisation Logic

Alberto Cossu and Maria Francesca Murru

Macao was officially born in Milan on 5 May 2012 with the occupation of Galfa Tower by a group of art workers. It defines itself as the 'new centre for arts, culture and research of Milan' and its activities, still in progress, are based on two main strands. First, Macao has been fighting for the liberation of abandoned urban spaces, both public and private, so that citizens can participate in the cocreation of the city. The main tools used by Macao are both discursive and performative in their nature and they are meant to counter urban policy, first of all on the imaginary plane. Following this logic one can understand the choice of Macao to enter the public arena occupying the Galfa Tower – a thirty-storey skyscraper located in the business centre of Milan and unused for fifteen years – and thereby obtain wide media coverage. Faithful to the idea of art as more and more social, radical and urban, Macao has been working to connect its socio-cultural critique to 'performances' that can detonate the contradictions of the surrounding reality, recreate a new possible city and engage an audience of participating citizens and not of mere spectators (Whybrow, 2011). The occupation, as well as giving Macao a physical space, introduces both the issue of urban public spaces and the critique of the forms of life and production that are being currently promoted in the so-called creative cities into public debate.[1] It is precisely the latter issue that forms the second line of intervention, whereby Macao fits into the larger 'National Network of Occupied Theatres'. Driven by the occupation of Teatro Valle in Rome, the day after the referendum victory of 12 and 13 June 2011, new occupations of theatres have spread throughout the national territory and have formed a network, with regular national meetings, activities and shared projects.[2] In a context of linear cuts in funding to culture and performing arts, the theoretical perspective of 'commons', already present in the referendum campaign against the privatisation of water services, has thus expanded to encompass culture, its spaces and its processes.[3] Macao's participation in the Network went beyond effective partnerships; its links with this wave of mobilisation were consolidated in the sharing of a symbolic struggle that has targeted the perceptions of the artist's role in society. The decision to call themselves 'art workers' indicates the attempt to overcome the cliché that associates the artist to a politically pacified subjectivity and abstracted from social and economic contradictions. Finally, Macao's actions critique the so-called event economy (Bologna and Banfi, 2011) upon which a substantial part of the cultural and artistic production in Milan is based. The economy of the event designates a particular production method, based on short-term events open to the public (festivals, universal exhibitions, fairs, etc.) and characterised by structural instability. In this sense, the mobilisation of Macao is part of a wider cycle of protest on precarity (Mattoni, 2012) through links with its main actors, such as San Precario,[4] and by sharing a post-workerist[5] theoretical framework. An innovative aspect is given by the articulation of artistic subjectivity within which the fight against precarity – and the distinctive issue of national mobilisation that started with the occupation of Teatro Valle in Rome in June 2011 – is performed in substantial terms but not in terms of framing. It should be stressed how Macao addresses the working conditions within the creative industries more than the other actors in the Network because of the specific urban context in which it acts. In fact, Milan shows the highest concentration of people employed or in education in the creative sector (Bonomi, 2008), a fact that is reflected in the peculiar constituency of Macao, and which differentiates it from the other theatres that are part of the Network. In the first place, Macao's choice not to occupy a theatre entails that in its constituency the craftsman and other technicians usually employed in the performing arts are not predominant. Moreover, starting from a relative homogeneity in terms of class composition within Macao's founding group, there has been a progressive diversification due to the substantial expansion of participation triggered by the occupation of the Galfa Tower. New profiles have joined the initial artistic component, including workers employed in the city's creative industries (both freelancers and employees of large global corporations) and in higher education. Based on the results of an investigation conducted by Macao on their constituency,[6] we can trace the average activist profile: a thirty-four-year-old person with a university degree, who has more than one job – no full-time contracts or permanent positions – dissatisfied with both the earnings and the nature of their jobs, and who dedicates to Macao an average of thirty hours a week.

Along the different phases of its development, the mobilisation of Macao has been characterised by its effective and strong visibility throughout the most popular social networking platforms. From the beginning media coverage has alternated between favourable attention and hostile indifference, which has resulted in a systematic and articulated presence in digital media. As will be seen here, Macao is one of the most advanced nodes in terms of media platforms used and visible online activity within the 'Theatre Network'. This element allows us to draw a parallel with some of the important empirical cases that inspired much of the recent literature on the use of new technologies by social movements. Within the field of political sociology and contentious politics (Tilly and Tarrow, 2007), many contributions have tried to understand how information and communication technologies have been transforming the political mobilisation practices. This chapter fits within this line of research with the aim to account for the role that digital media practices have had in the Macao mobilisation. To this end, we develop an analytical path divided into two phases. The first constitutes an exploration of the applicability of three analytical models offered by more recent literature to our case study: the connective logic proposed by Lance Bennett and Alexandra Segerberg (2013), the concept of communicative cultures developed by Anastasia Kavada (2013) and the aggregative logic developed by Jeffrey Juris (2012). Once we have established the eccentricity of Macao with respect to these interpretative frameworks, the study moves on to a second phase that consists in the creation and the testing of a hybrid analytical approach and mixed methods. More specifically, the study of media practices (Couldry, 2012), realised by means of digital ethnography sessions and semi-structured interviews, is combined with a critical discourse analysis (Fairclough, 1992) applied to the symbolic production that Macao has conveyed through its website and various social profiles and by which it presents itself to the public as a collective entity capable of action. Thanks to the use of different disciplinary perspectives, it is possible to understand the role of digital communication practices in the light of the activation of a peculiar logic of action and storytelling that, in the case of Macao, is due to a 'semantic of the event'. As will be more fully discussed in the chapter, this logic has emerged as a red wire between the technological affordances, concretely enhanced by digital communication practices, and the symbolic structuring of Macao's agency, observable in the discursive traces of its digital presence.

MEDIA IN MOBILISATION: AGENTS, MIRRORS AND LOGICS

The first step of the analytical path proposed here is to investigate the phenomenon of Macao in the light of three specific analytical perspectives, present in the most recent literature and selected because of the affinity between Macao and the case studies that inspired it. This is the logic of connective action identified by Bennett and Segerberg (2013), the connection between communicative cultures and organisational/decision making/strategic cultures identified by Kavada (2013) and the aggregative logic outlined and explained by Juris (2012) in relation to Occupy.

Three analytical perspectives have been chosen as emblematic of three different approaches to the role that media technologies play in mobilisation. If, in the first case, they are considered agents of collective action, in the second, they reflect collective action with its underpinning strategic, organisational and communication cultures. In the third case, finally, they are seamlessly embedded in the interpretive logic that guides and motivates mobilisation. In the next section, the three approaches will be applied to Macao in the attempt to assess the extent to which their heuristic potential fits into the complexity of our case study. The discussion aims to contextualise and justify the conceptual and methodological choices that have led to the development and testing of the hybrid and mixed-methods analytical model that is the subject of the next sections. What happened during and after the occupation of Galfa Tower in May 2012 relates to what Bennett and Segerberg (2013) define as 'connective action', indicating a protest dynamic animated by self-organised networks and personalised action frames. The ideal-type developed by the two scholars includes a number of parameters that could be applied in Macao. As shown by the data gathered during the research (see the Media Practices section), we are faced with an undoubted success in managing the visibility of the movement in the most well-known social networking platforms. We can also see in Macao a discrete organisational autonomy that distinguishes it from the subjectivity of more established forms of protest. In this regard, it is significant that whilst Macao chose to join the 'national network', they avoid identifying their struggle with a specific space, such as a theatre, on both a symbolic and a professional level. Equally important is the emphasis on horizontal and a-hierarchical participatory practices. Thanks to their organisational capacity and a sound constituency of militants, their strategic aim is to continue to facilitate the social aggregation that has emerged around Macao in order to avoid pre-existing associations that could colonise the innovative drive. Several factors therefore seem to contribute to making Macao one of the possible manifestations of connective action ideal-type described by Bennett and Segerberg (ibid.).

Yet, on closer inspection other elements emerge that differentiate the case investigated by the connective logic model. The first one is related to the level of personalisation of the action frames. Despite the structural independence from previous memberships or rigid ideological identifications, despite the constitutive openness to the invention of the unexpected and innovation of social practices, Macao marks the attempt of a reaffirmation of a subject more collective than individual. Not only was Macao's birth linked to a subjectivity that is already the 'us' of the proponents, but is also constantly projected towards a project of action and thinking that aspires to be rooted in the experience of the subjects transcending singularity and idiosyncrasies.[7] Rather than an affinity with the various forms of political individualism that distinguish the mature democracies (Beck and Beck-Gernsheim, 2002) and that according to Bennett and Segerberg (2013) would be at the origin of the personal action frames mobilised by the action connective, we have observed an original attempt to create the conditions for a new collective dimension, innovative in its form and premises.

Similarly, if we carefully observe the data reflecting the activity of their social media profiles in the preparatory phase and in the first days of mobilisation, we see how their digital channels are much less active (see the Media Practices section). The role that digital media has played in the mobilisation of Macao cannot be explained in the light of the connective logic model. Social networking platforms have not supported the organisation of the protest, at least in the initial phase of mobilisation that also coincided with the visible *exploits*[8] of the movement. The increase in online presence came later, especially during the first eviction, suggesting that if there was an agency that explains the mobilisation, it certainly cannot be their actions through digital networks. Similarly, the relevance of digital media cannot be found even on a symbolic level. Where Bennett and Segerberg (ibid.) observe the capitalisation of 'private' politics that finds in social media its most obvious incarnation (Papacharissi, 2010), we record the spread of collective, non-exclusive action frames in which Macao experiments with new forms of protest subjectivation.

In the interpretative model of Kavada (2013), the communication practices of the movements are reduced to their 'communicative cultures', or to those patterns that drive the concrete processes of human interaction. These communicative cultures refer, first of all, to specific beliefs according to which one decides what to write, whom to talk to and how to do it (Carey, 1989). According to Kavada it would be possible to detect correspondence between communicative cultures and decision-making cultures (inspired by the principle of representation or that of participatory democracy), organisational (defined according to the formalities in the definition of roles and objectives, the degree of hierarchical structuration and the levels of professionalisation of skills and resources) and strategic (related to insights that guide the efforts of social movements for the transformation of society) cultures of social movements that exert them. From empirical research on the European Social Forum in London in 2004, Kavada (ibid.) develops a typology of network cultures between the two extremes of the broadcasting and the interactive, respectively corresponding to the two polarities of the vertical and horizontal, which are related to decision-making, organisational and strategic cultures of social movements. This elegant correspondence between communicative culture and its organisational background, however, does not adapt to the case of Macao. Long participant observation sessions allowed us to observe participatory and inclusive decision-making processes, during which the expressive richness and complex layers of participation were never sacrificed to the efficiency of the action. Activists have always paid attention to the sharing and making use of the personal experiences of everyone involved, as well as the emotional aspects of their professional lives and their experiences of protest. We therefore found ourselves facing a strategic decision-making culture very similar to those that Kavada (ibid., 79) defines as 'horizontal', a culture in which one is not limited to claims for change in the external environment but in which conditions are created for the alternative to be actualised and experienced by the militants themselves. In contrast to what is suggested by Kavada's model, Macao's communicative culture appeared much closer to the broadcasting mode. Starting from ethnographic research we have been able to verify the high level of professionalism of the website management activities, social profiles and event communications. In addition, there is a boundary that separates the public and media presence in Macao from the decision-making processes that take place in the assembly and on the internal discussion platform. The Macao website, in its public part, tends to play the role of a showcase for the events organised and the dissemination of topics close to their political sensibility.

With respect to the analytical model taken into consideration in this case, our empirical case is eccentric. The nature and function of the communicative practices of Macao cannot be explained in the light of the values brought into play by the culture that inspires its strategies and the decisions.

The third analytical reference, the aggregative logic outlined by Juris (2012) and inspired by the transnational mobilisation of Occupy, presents interesting affinities relating to Macao. It allows us to temporarily bracket the strictly communicative dimension that directs our attention to the symbolic value of spatiality. This dimension draws Macao closer to that wave of international protests that made an emblem and vehicle out of the occupation of urban spaces and which clearly identifies their political approach. The 'aggregative logic' is understood as 'a cultural framework that is shaped by the interactions of people with social media and generate particular patterns of social and political interpretation' (ibid., 266). Unlike the networking logic (Juris, 2012), the aggregative logic does not use mailing lists or websites to start complex and dialogic communication exchanges but relies solely on social networking platforms to disseminate large amounts of information and links, scaling large ego-centric networks and taking advantage of the potential of viral circulation of the contents. For a social movement structured on weak ties and thus with no stable interaction, the occupation of physical space becomes both a goal and premise for the existence of a mobilised crowd and the performative evolution through which to flesh out and provide cohesion for crowds mobilised online.

The culture of Macao, so distant from its organisational culture, could be plausibly attributed to 'aggregative logic': social media and the website are not used as discursive contexts in which to put at stake identity and relations, but only as channels through which to mobilise people within specific physical and highly symbolic spaces. The empirical verification of this first inference required more operational conceptual tools than the concept of 'logic', abstractly defined by Juris as a 'semiotic framework . . . through which people interpret their world and their interactions with others' (2012: 266). Taking for granted that the significance of digital media in mobilisation cannot be understood unless it is based on a culture or logic that they emerge from, we decided to choose two privileged observation points for our empirical investigation. The first is represented by media practices (Couldry, 2012), intended as actions marked by a certain regularity and oriented to the media or which media have made possible. The media practices approach has been developed in literature on social movements from Alice Mattoni (2012) and, in the original formulation of Nick Couldry (2012), it responds to the need to map the varied ways in which the media has become relevant for social action and its objectives. To the extent that it understands media as dependent on the socio-cultural dynamics that make them significant and, at the same time, not losing sight of the regularity and structuring effect implied in media use, this perspective has the merit of avoiding the temptation of both technological and social determinism. Instead of abstractly assuming that a specific mobilisation logic is materialised in a given technological platform, our analysis has explored which affordances (Hutchby, 2001) are actually grasped and actualised by their users.

The second viewpoint is represented by the analysis of the discursive production that Macao has conveyed through their website and social media profiles. The aim of this second part coincided with a focus on the symbolic elaboration through which Macao has presented itself to the public and was formed as a collective entity capable of action. As pointed out by Alberto Melucci (1996), the literature on social movements has investigated this dimension mainly through the concept of framing (ibid., 348 ff.), neglecting the ideological aspect. As a process constitutively relational, by which collective actors present their actions to themselves and to others, the framing activity is always conditioned by the particular position of the actor who develops it. It follows that the symbolic production of a movement is always necessarily determined by pre-existing social relations and at the same time is able to condition them actively and strategically. This dialectic can be successfully grasped through critical discourse analysis (Fairclough, 1992), an approach that we have chosen to apply to a selected sample of all the public speeches published from April 2012 to May 2013 on the 'diary' section of Macao's website. According to critical discourse analysis, discourses are conceived as influenced by the surrounding social context and, at the same time able to regenerate it and shape it. Its aim is therefore the analysis of communicative events – which can be texts, discursive practice and social practice – and the way in which they are constructed and simultaneously contribute to the construction of social identities, relationships and systems of meaning. The analysis has favoured those texts in which the agency of Macao – its objectives, its instruments and its relationship with the environment – was more explicitly discursive.

These two dimensions were analysed through a mixed-method approach that contemplated, in addition to the critical discourse analysis, participant observation in the period between April and July 2013, semi-structured interviews with twelve activists and digital ethnography sessions on social platforms on Macao's website.[9]

MEDIA PRACTICES

This section explores the digital presence of Macao, first presenting and interpreting the quantitative data gathered during the research and then tracing a typology of practices that Macao has implemented in its social media activity.

Macao's presence on social media is highly diversified and includes Facebook, Twitter and YouTube. Fifty-three thousand people follow its Facebook fan page. To provide a wider frame, the Occupied Valle Theatre of Rome has 84,000, while the Nuovo Cinema Palazzo has 13,000 followers. Smaller nodes in the network include the Teatro Pinelli Occupato – Messina and the Ex-Asilo of Naples, with 9,400 and 1,700 followers, respectively. Macao's fan page was created on Facebook on 8 May 2012, three days after the Galfa Tower occupation. Since then it has capitalised on the urban and media effervescence that had previously coalesced around Macao. The total number of users who view at least one of the contents published by Macao on Facebook grew from 102,840 on 8 May to 490,000 viewers on 15 May. This constituted the peak of visibility and coincided with Macao's eviction from the tower. From that moment onwards it decreased to 89,000 during the post-eviction of Palazzo Citterio and finally it stabilised at a daily average of 30,000 in the following months.[10]

A Twitter profile was created on 1 April 2012, and this has around 12,000 followers and 8,000 tweets, with an average of seven tweets per day. Even if internal data concerning the Twitter audience are not available, thanks to external databases[11] it is possible to state that the buzz around Macao during its first phase of intense mobilisation followed the same dynamics that characterised the Facebook page. Be that as it may, as the Twitter profile was active from early April, the time of Macao's launch campaign, it is fair to interrogate if, and to what extent, tweets actually supported the digital aggregation of Macao's constituency. As is visible in the graphic (cf. Graphic 1), during April daily tweets – from and about Macao – range between two and fifteen: a number that is insufficient to explain the following explosion. Deepening the analysis of these tweets, during April the profile activity was limited to an interaction with the other nodes of the network of theatres and Macao was not capable of attracting, at least digitally, a wider audience. Furthermore, even if we consider the relative peak, around eighty tweets, the day before the Galfa Tower was occupied – when the idea that Milan would soon have an 'artistic' occupation was quickly spreading in the offline world – it appears substantially less intense compared to the 3,000 tweets (produced by or directed to Macao) that constitutes the absolute peak during the day of eviction from the Tower.[12]

Concerning the YouTube channel, this comprises of 113 videos that have gathered 180,000 views and 671 subscribers. As we have mentioned already, it is this platform that hosted Macao's launch campaign. Starting on 1 April and concluding on 4 May Macao produced twenty-seven videos. Each of them has a number of views that ranges from 241 to a maximum of 6673,[13] an average of 1,868 views per video. Finally, if we consider the 50,000 views gathered across the whole campaign, it seems plausible that a viral propagation of Macao's message took place on YouTube. What must be taken into account in this case is that only 10 per cent of views[14] are accountable for in the pre-occupation phase, proving that the Galfa event induced sympathisers, media professionals or fellow citizens to inform themselves retrospectively about what Macao was about and how it became possible.

Leaving for now the quantitative data, we can present the practices identified in Macao's social media strategy. One point of reference, in this endeavour, is the concept of media practices elaborated by Nick Couldry (2012), which makes it possible to identify 'what people do with media in the context

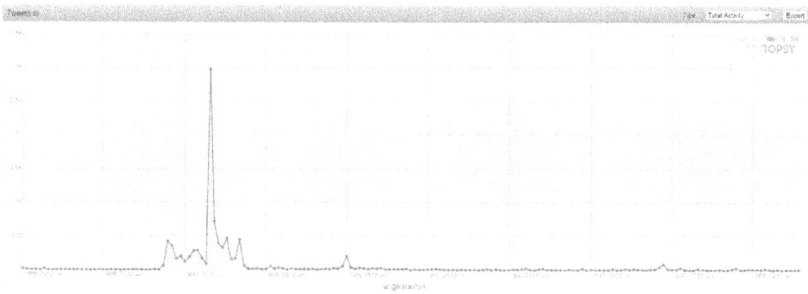

Figure 3.1. Total of tweets created by Macao or directed to Macao (from 1 April 2012 to 30 June 2012).
© Alberto Cossu.

in which they act' (Couldry, 2012: 35). Following this conceptualisation, media practices are those practices addressed specifically to, and involving, media but in which media is not the primary object and practices that rely on a pre-existing media system (or on a specific way of functioning of such a system) in order to fully develop. Practices are always about regularities: that is, regularities of action; they are a social product and, as such, they embody shared knowledge, power relations and constraints on action. Based on semi-structured interviews and digital ethnography (Rogers, 2013), Macao's social media activity can be pinned down to four distinct media practices:

a) Information
b) Announcement
c) Dissemination of imagery
d) Strategic incursions into the media

Information practices refer to the regular and daily diffusion on social media, and particularly on Twitter, of a certain amount of news reports from independent media outlets on themes selected as having an affinity to Macao's identity (e.g. the extensive coverage granted to Gezi Park events in May 2013). The second category includes communications that concern the diffusion of news regarding events organised by Macao or 'service announcements' during mobilisation phases. This kind of activity is performed especially through Facebook. The dissemination of imagery aims to evoke rather than inform, creating expectations and transmitting an aesthetic mood. One example is provided by the campaign that preceded the blitz-occupation of the 'Maestoso' Cinema, set up in order to celebrate Macao's first birthday on 5 May 2013. This was a visual campaign that attempted to arouse interest by foreshadowing the imminent event providing no explanation at all on its concretisation in the urban space. In this manner, media practices were deployed online, with the aim of producing effects offline. Lastly, strategic incursions that focused directly on the media with the goal of disrupting the symbolic order in the media ecosystem showed a strong affinity with the situationist détournement. A concrete example of this kind of practice was the complex 'subvertising' campaign elaborated to critique the 'big event' of Milano's design week held annually in April, complemented by its 'off' side, the 'Fuorisalone', which nowadays has become more influential than the former.

To conclude, Macao's social media use appears to have been inspired by a vertical approach (Kavada, 2013) and represents a strategic tool in which both the Macao activists' decision-making processes and their organisation culture are not openly involved. For Macao, social media platforms are not spaces in which things 'really' happen – they are, rather, vehicles for making things happen in the real urban space.

DISCURSIVE PRODUCTION

When analysed from the perspective of critical discourse analysis (Fairclough, 1992), each communicative event opens an opportunity of contingency and innovation into the pre-existent social structure. This intrinsic productivity of discourse can be grasped by focusing on three main dimensions:

1. The practices of production, grasped through the identification of mobilised genres and discursive orders
2. The texts, with a specific attention to thematic structures, keywords, metaphors and transitivity (which subjectivities receive attention, have voices, and are attributed roles and responsibility)
3. The social practices surrounding the discourses, which have been explored through interviews with activists aimed at identifying their professional identities and the background of the concepts, values and beliefs which have inspired their actions.

The findings have pointed at two distinct phases within the symbolic production of Macao: the *exploit* phase and the 'stabilisation' phase.

The *exploit* Phase: from April to May 2012

Macao appears for the first time in YouTube on 1 April 2012 and then, on following days, in the main streets of Milan through a videobox where bystanders were asked to play with the word 'Macao' considering it as acronym of what they would have expected and desired by a centre for art and culture based in Milan. The textual debut of Macao is characterised by the co-presence of two main discursive genres, that of cultural jamming (Cammaerts, 2007) and that of political manifesto.

The first one is emblematically represented by a YouTube video showing a sketch of an Italian television programme that was very popular during the 1980s, *Indietro Tutta*. It had an imaginary commercial sponsor that was called 'cacao meravigliao', a wonderful and exceptional type of cocoa available in various versions whose names were parodies of Brazilian words (delicacao, spregiudicao and depressao). In this first video, Macao changes the initial letter from 'c' to 'm' and recalls the fictional advertising of this imaginary product. Macao makes its first appearance with the parody of a parody or better, the détournement of a détournement. It introduces itself as something that doesn't exist: (1) it is suggested by the discourse uttered by the presenter that Macao coincides with the commercial product that doesn't exist, which is presented as essential to the world but that is in the end imaginary and fictional (2) at the end of the video, the sentence 'coming soon' creates the expectation of something that is not yet available but it is going to arrive. Macao is something that is going to happen or to appear. There is not at this stage any exhaustive, narrative and accomplished self-presentation. Macao finds its only defining features in the playful and surreal dimension subverting the advertising and commercial language.

The genre of political manifesto is found in three videos showing three leading personalities in art and culture describing the current crisis of economic and cultural systems and calling for a revolutionary intervention into it. They are Antonio Caronia and Franco Berardi, two prominent theorists and activists in the Autonomist tradition and cyber-punk social movements, the Nobel Laureate Dario Fo and the filmmaker Alina Marazzi. Their videos are 'political discourses' in the full sense of definition insofar as they contain both the diagnosis of a conflict between a system that hinders humanity, freedom and solidarity and excludes people, who are constantly damaged by it and constrained to live in metropolitan areas that don't answer to the logic of human association and a way out of this conflict through the constitution of new subjectivities.

However, Macao emerges indirectly – it is implied most of the time and is only once named as a 'centre for art and culture' – as an actor that doesn't still speak for itself; it is rather 'spoken out', anticipated but not directly introduced by speakers. Their discourses outline the kind of subjectivity that Macao should take on, the kind of context that it should address and cope with, the various social and cultural needs that make its intervention essential and required, the aims and the ways for enacting them. At this stage Macao is a plan of action – a need, an aim, a set of means – but not an actor that carries out a specific will and presents itself.

The two discursive genres share two relevant elements: the way in which the agency of Macao is discursively built and the kind of engagement that both genres require of the reader. The first element points out the discursive emergence of Macao as an actor that is embedded in a dialectic of absence/presence. Macao is evoked rather than displayed in the discursive genre of cultural jamming of popular and media culture. It is implied, but not directly quoted, in the political discourses of intellectuals that call to action and point to the need for some kind of collective revolution. This dialectic of presence/absence of Macao is something that is very peculiar to the event as described by Derrida – a kind of 'waiting without a specific horizon of expectation' (Di Martino, 2009). In the event there is an intrinsic dialectic of offering and withdrawing. The event is something that, on the one hand, opens itself to be experienced, understood, perceived; on the other hand it is something that escapes and opposes a sort of resistance towards any attempt of comprehension. This is the reason why the event requires a predisposition to experiencing and receiving it, an original openness to something that cannot be predetermined in advance, but at the same time the event is primarily something that we cannot understand, it is the happening that we cannot understand, the unexpected, the absolute surprise, the newness that cannot be discovered in advance.

The second element deals with the interactive engagement that both genres require of the reader. From the cultural jamming discourse, a web meme (Shifman, 2012) is launched from the wordplay made by the presenter Macao Meravigliao: the web meme is represented by the wordplay of surreal aphorisms made by the presenter which can be endlessly reproduced with slight and creative variation on the main logical structure: same syntactic structure ('like . . . without') and a link between the two variable words that consists in sharing one or more syllables and that could, possibly but not necessarily, result in unexpected and always open semantic outcomes.

At the same time, a group of posts with the same title and the same graphic format of these meme wordplays (a coloured poster named 'aphorism', identified by a number and containing only words) starts to clarify the ideological frame of Macao. They show sentences extracted from longer discourses published and discussed during assemblies organised in the previous month by 'Lavoratori dell'Arte', a group of artists/immaterial workers from which Macao was born.

In these discursive fragments, we can find some of the main pillars of what will become the political discourse of Macao: (1) **political action** as action with the aim of liberating the transformative capacity of society (2) **common good,** as opposed to public good, constituted through the political action of violation, divestiture, appropriation and restitution (3) **emancipation**, not as appropriation of common good but as collectivisation of 'capacities invested on the scene of dissent' (4) **public spaces** whose property and management should be given to those that actively and culturally inhabit them.

The sentences are completely decontextualised and they produce an effect of disorientation insofar as they appear to be a prosecution or synthesis of some premises that are not made explicit. Immediately, we can see the appearance of the 'narrative logic' of this fragmented manifesto: not a circular and self-accomplished discourse but fragments of a wider discourse in which producers and their conditions are not manifest or exhibited. These fragments are rich with demonstrative pronouns without clarification of the referred subject (e.g. 'we insist on that because . . .') and full of implicit information: the need of a struggle against the system is implied but not further articulated or legitimised; in two of the posters an 'us' is implied by the speaking subject but we don't know who he/she is and if he/she is speaking in the name of a groups of artists, of a political organisation or a simple group of citizens; the implied subjectivity emerges as a dialectic agent that argues in favour of one specific path of action among possible others: representation

Figure 3.2. Macao aphorism from the launching campaign.
© Macao.

versus struggle – 'to represent the world that we want instead of struggling against the political/economic/cultural system' and a positive versus negative logic of action – 'time is over for a specific negative logic that has marked language and aesthetic of recent years'. Macao is deliberately presented as a 'budding' discourse that has been already initiated by someone and probably has already had an audience but we cannot find any explicit reference to this antecedent; its buds are redistributed as autonomous unities aggregated through a cumulative logic instead of a narrative one. This cumulative logic requires a great effort by the reader who is asked, before adhering to the text and its call to action, to actively engage with it by filling in the empty space of missing logic connections.

The Stabilisation Phase: from October 2012 to October 2014

In the following months, the 'diary' section of Macao's blog and the posts on social media deeply changed, becoming something similar to a noticeboard announcing activities organised by Macao, from press releases to concerts or workshops leaflets. In a sense, the shift from the old to the new diary could be interpreted as change in the focal point: from the need to communicate who they are, and how they managed to become Macao, to what they do (which also defines what they are). Macao's identity now emerges as constantly reshaped by its ongoing projects, the activities it hosts and the people that always contaminate it.

Thanks to discourse analysis, it has been possible to point out that Macao has used and valued social media platforms as linguistic devices, where specific linguistic conventions, habits and games were already stratified. In deploying the discursive genre of cultural jamming, Macao has appropriated not the device of social media platforms in themselves, rather a peculiar cultural and linguistic model incorporated in them: the mimicking practice of mashups, remixes and other derivative formats that is typical of the so-called participatory culture (Jenkins et al., 2006). Coherently with the main aim of its contentious action, Macao has woven a narrative fabric where the digitally enabled social networks are not considered as places where things happen, rather as fragments of meanings that allow facts to concretely take place in physical spaces.

CONCLUSION: THE EVENTFUL LOGIC

On the basis of the analysis of the long cycle of protest for global justice, della Porta (2008) proposes that we consider mobilisation and demonstration not just as an effect of a given political opportunity, structure and organisational resources but rather as an event capable of triggering a transformation of the affective, relational and cognitive dynamics of a movement. Inspired by the concept of eventful temporality elaborated by Sewell (1996), according to which events are defined as occurrences capable of transforming the social structure, della Porta proposes that we think in terms of eventful protest in order to focus on those events which, within certain cycles of protest, affect structures by creating new organisational networks, connecting pre-existing frames of action and establishing new bonds.

Going back to the results of the analysis conducted on Macao, it is possible to understand how linking communication practices and artistic production is a shared eventful logic. The study of media practices reveals how online activity mainly consisted in the dissemination of an imaginary functional to the deployment of the event in the urban space. The occupation of the Galfa Tower can be considered as a 'big event' in its own right, as a surprising occurrence that actualised the unexpected and disclosed unforeseen possibilities.[15]

In line with the founders' desire to oppose the neoliberal logic of cultural events, Macao's first major public act deployed a new meaning of an 'event', as an opportunity for change, insurgence of the unpredictable and irruption of new generative forces in society. 'The event is not the solution to predetermined problems, it is rather the opening of new possibilities that pose new questions and solicit the imagination of new replies' (Lazzarato, 2005: 13). Bringing back to life the inanimate space of the Galfa Tower created the conditions in which it was possible to start and develop a political discourse on the social role of art and on cultural expression, on the value and the practice of the commons. At this point we can recuperate the notion of logic elaborated by Juris and apply it to the case of Macao, specifying an eventful logic based on the strategic and cultural appropriation of that generative dynamic highlighted by the notion of eventful protest proposed by della Porta. The strategic character of the appropriation is due to the symbolic rupture triggered by the occupation of the Galfa Tower, which provided the context for the legitimation of a new political discourse. The consolidation was based on a deep cultural rootedness capable of interacting with both the professional competencies of the activists and the recreational and convivial habits of the metropolitan public intercepted by Macao.

In contrast to the paradigmatic definitions that we have found in recent literature (i.e. the connective logic by Bennett and Segerberg, 2013), we propose a pragmatic concept, in which the relevance of digital media for mobilisation has to be empirically detailed in the light of cultural logics that appropriate them and make them significant. It is likely that the empirical eccentricity of Macao, compared to the analytical models discussed, not only indicates its contingent specificity but also calls into question the applicability of conceptual categories derived solely from the technological characteristics of the media investigated. The analysis of communication practices combined with the analysis of Macao's process of coming into existence has enabled us to empirically establish the notion of eventful logic as the fil rouge between the technological affordances concretely valorised and the structuring of the agency of Macao. To conclude, what we would like to suggest for future investigation and verification is not so much a new label: it is, rather, an analytical method in which the role of mediated communication practices is investigated as a dynamic interdependence between the digital tools used, the cultural contexts and the subjects who inhabit them and their specific skills and strategies.

However, even in the stabilisation phase, the event has continued to play a crucial role in the symbolic mediation of Macao. The diary of the last year looks like a patchwork of concerts, workshops, theatre performances, meetings and festivals hosted in the new occupied space. It is no longer possible to find on Macao's website a coherent discourse about what Macao is and what its objectives and its purposes are. The progressive chain of events is the only framework of discursive production by Macao in recent months, when resources for self-narration began to dry up. This development naturally responds to the needs of economic sustainability, but it is also consistent with the professional skills of the people involved, being knowledge workers who are able to set up events and communication campaigns in a very short time. Paradoxically, the activists themselves have exported their own eventful language to Macao, intended as a symbolic framework of the signs and meanings they have learnt in the creative industries in which they work and against which they are mobilised.

NOTES

1. Following the decline in industrial production as the main vehicle of urban development, the creative city model identifies elements in culture and creativity on which to find a new path to economic growth. A key subject to this process is the 'creative class' (Florida, 2002), composed of knowledge workers capable of producing a high added value that will accrue not only to the productive sector of belonging (creative industries, art, hi-tech) but to place themselves at the heart of urban regeneration projects and competition among cities to attract the best creative workers. Criticisms have emerged against the concept of 'creative class' – to the extent that it represents rather a taxonomy of the 'creative' jobs whose borders appear rather uncertain (Pratt, 2008) – and the creative city model, marked on a neoliberal governance that leverages culture and creativity to revitalise and make the city more competitive in the global arena (Peck, 2005). To date, the promises of the creative city model to guarantee growth, social inclusion and well-being remain largely betrayed, while leaving room for the casualisation of large sections of the 'creative workers' (McRobbie, 2011). In this context, cities have developed mobilisations in an attempt to build an alternative to the creative city discourse, claiming a 'right to the city' (Harvey, 2012).

2. For cartography of the network, see the digital publication edited by Silvia Jop (2012) which collects self-narratives of the spaces involved. See also the book by

Lidia Cirillo (2014) for a more recent collection of interviews with the main actors of the network.

3. On this, see the *Rapporto sul futuro del Teatro Valle* (report on the future of the Teatro Valle) by Faccioli et al. (2014).

4. San Precario has been a key player in the promotion of a critical discourse on precarity in Italy. Active in Milan since the early 2000s, it is an economic and political laboratory and organiser of the annual Mayday Parade, the 'First of May of the precarious workers'. To retrace the historical and intellectual profile of San Precario see Cristina Morini and Paolo Vignola (2015).

5. Beyond the endorsement of its fundamental theses, Macao has also engaged in a shared research program with the leading members of Italian post-workerism, as evidenced by numerous seminars and research (see on this the Macao magazine, available at: http://www.macaomilano.org/rivista [accessed on 11 October 2015]). It is impossible to account for the complexity of the workerist debate in the space of this article. We refer to this excellent essay by Cristina Corradi (2013). See also the contributions by Maurizio Lazzarato (1996), Sergio Bologna and Andrea Fumagalli (1997) and Antonio Negri (2009). Moreover, see the contribution of Roberto Ciccarelli and Giuseppe Allegri (2013) for an analysis of the Italian context and to Rosalind Gill and Andy Pratt (2008) for an international review.

6. On this, see the enquiry conducted by Macao in autumn 2012, entitled *69,300 hours*, available at: http://issuu.com/macaomilano/docs/69300_ore (accessed 12 June 2015).

7. It is perhaps no coincidence that the 'about us' section of the site is entitled 'Who is Macao', indicating the impartiality of a person who is born from the desire of specific people but who is ready to live its own life and take shape through action practices and from all those who decide to live his 'common constituent territory' (on this see: http://www.macaomilano.org/chi-e-macao/ (last accessed 12 June 2015).

8. We refer here to 'exploit' as a noun referring to a 'notable or remarkable deed', a meaning attested both in French and English. For reference: https://www.merriam-webster.com/dictionary/exploit.

9. The authors jointly conducted critical discourse analysis (Fairclough, 1992), semi-structured interviews, digital ethnography and some sessions of participant observation during the months of April, May and June 2013. The reflections on the strategic and decision-making cultures of Macao, which have been formulated in relation to the analytical model proposed by Kavada (2013) and presented in section 3, have benefited from a wider ethnography independently conducted by Alberto Cossu as part of his doctoral research. In particular, the research methodology can be traced within the posture of militant research (Mirzoeff, 2013) to the extent that the research was conducted working 'in and with' the movements who are objects of study. Beyond this political choice, the idea of producing research that is relevant to the movements themselves is not only the heritage of a cultural approach to social movements but demonstrates the will to overcome the 'scholastic debates on the character and dynamics of collective action' (Barker et al., 2013: 2).

10. Source: Official insights from Macao's Fan Page on Facebook, access to which was generously granted.

11. Source: data gathered from Topsy (www.topsy.com).
12. If we consider all the hashtags related to Macao on those days (#macao, #tuttisumacao, #iostoconmacao, #torregalfa), we can count a grand total of almost 20,000 tweets published during 15 May.
13. Views updated till 20 August 2013.
14. Source: elaboration of public data available on Macao's YouTube channel.
15. The concept of event is deeply rooted in Western philosophy; however, it was especially since the 1968 that post-metaphysical philosophy deeply reinvented the understanding of event. Badiou, Derrida, Deleuze and Heidegger before them are the fundamental thinkers who have considered events. Although they have significant differences – at the ontological level, regarding the singularity or plurality of the event, on its immanence or transcendence or its susceptibility to a hermeneutic or dialectic comprehension – all these authors attribute in a relatively consistent manner the following features to the event: it is contingent, unpredictable, radically transformative. Nestled in the epistemological struggles of the time, the notion of an event constitutes a hinge between structuralism and subjectivist approaches. As this research has empirically observed concerning the various possible interpretations of event, the notion of an event also appears 'amphibious' in philosophical terms, to the extent that the boundary that separates the event-break from the event that reproduces the status quo is treacherous.

REFERENCES

Barker, Colin, Cox, Laurence, Krinsky, John and Gunvald, Alf N. (eds.). 2013. *Marxism and Social Movements*. Leiden: Brill.
Beck, Ulrich and Beck-Gernsheim, Elisabeth. 2002. *Individualization: Institutionalized Individualism and Its Social and Political Consequences*. London: Sage.
Bennett, Lance and Segerberg, Alexandra. 2013. *The Logic of Connective Action. Digital Media and the Personalization of Contentious Politics*. New York: Cambridge University Press.
Bologna, Sergio and Banfi, Dario. 2011. *Vita da freelance. I lavoratori della conoscenza e il loro futuro*, Milano: Feltrinelli.
Bologna, Sergio and Fumagalli, Andrea. 1997. *Il lavoro autonomo di seconda generazione: scenari del postfordismo in Italia*. Milano: Feltrinelli.
Bonomi, Aldo. 2008. *Milano ai tempi delle moltitudini. Vivere, lavorare, produrre nella città infinita*. Milano: Mondadori.
Cammaerts, Bart. 2007. 'Jamming the Political: Beyond Counter-Hegemonic Practices'. *Continuum: Journal of Media and Cultural Studies* 21(1): 71–90.
Carey, W. James. 1989. *Communication as Culture*. Boston: Unwin Hyman.
Ciccarelli, Roberto and Allegri, Giuseppe. 2013. *Il quinto stato*. Milano: Salani.
Cirillo, Lidia. 2014. *Lotta di classe sul palcoscenico. I teatri occupati si raccontano*. Roma: Alegre.
Corradi, Cristina. 2013. 'Panzieri, Tronti, Negri: le diverse eredità dell'operaismo italiano'. *Consecutio Temporum* 3 (5).

Couldry, Nick. (2012). *Media, Society, World.* Cambridge: Polity Press.
della Porta, Donatella. 2008. 'Eventful Protest, Global Conflicts'. *Distinktion: Scandinavian Journal of Social Theory* 17(2): 27–56.
della Porta, Donatella and Diani, Mario. 2006. *Social Movements. An Introduction.* Malden: Blackwell.
della Porta, Donatella and Mattoni, Alice. 2012. *Cultures of Participation and Social Movements*, in Aaron Delwiche and Jennifer J. Henderson (eds.), *The Participatory Cultures Handbook.* New York: Routledge.
Di Martino, Carmine. 2009. *Figure dell'evento. A partire da Jacques Derrida.* Milano: Guerini Scientifica.
Faccioli, Franca, Gallina, Mimma, Iaione, Christian, Leon, Alessandro and Melotti, Marxiano. 2014. *Rapporto sul futuro del Teatro Valle*, available at: http//www.academia.edu/7825873/Rapporto_sul_Futuro_del_Teatro_Valle (last accessed 1 March 2017).
Fairclough, Norman. 1992. *Discourse and Social Change.* Cambridge: Polity Press.
Florida, L. Richard. 2002. *The Rise of the Creative Class: And How It's Transforming Work, Leisure, Community and Everyday Life.* New York: Basic Books.
Gill, Rosalind and Pratt, Andy. 2008. 'In the Social Factory? Immaterial Labour, Precariousness and Cultural Work'. *Theory, Culture and Society* 25 (7–8): 1–30.
Harvey, David. 2012. *Rebel Cities: From the Right to the City to the Urban Revolution.* London: Verso.
Hutchby, Ian (2001) 'Technologies, Texts and Affordances'. *Sociology* 35 (2): 441–6.
Jenkins, Henry. 2006. *Fans, bloggers, and gamers: exploring participatory culture.* New York: New York University Press.
Jop, Silvia (ed.). 2012. Com'è bella l'imprudenza. Arti e teatri in rete: una cartografia dell'Italia che torna in scena, available at: http://www.lavoroculturale.org/imprudenza/ (last accessed 1 March 2017).
Juris, S. Jeffrey. 2012. 'Reflections on #Occupy Everywhere: Social Media, Public Space, and Emerging Logics of Aggregation'. *American Ethnologist* 39 (2): 259–79.
Kavada, Anastasia. 2013. 'Internet Cultures and Protest Movements: The Cultural Links between Strategy, Organizing and Online Communication', in Bart Cammerts, Alice Mattoni, and Patrick McCurdy (eds.), *Mediation and Protest Movements.* Chicago: The University of Chicago Press.
Lazzarato, Maurizio. 1996. *Lavoro immateriale: forme di vita e produzione di soggettività.* Verona: Ombre corte.
Lazzarato, Maurizio. 2005. *La politica dell'evento.* Soveria Mannelli: Rubbettino.
Mattoni, Alice. 2012. *Media Practices and Protest Politics. How Precarious Workers Mobilise.* Farnham: Ashgate.
McRobbie, Angela. 2011. 'Re-Thinking Creative Economy as Radical Social Enterprise'. *Variant* 41, available at: http://www.variant.org.uk/41texts/amcrobbie41.html (last accessed 1 March 2017).
Melucci, Alberto. 1996. *Challenging Codes.* Cambridge: Cambridge University Press.
Mirzoeff, Nicholas (ed.). 2013. *Militant Research Handbook.* New York: New York University Press, available at: http://steinhardt.nyu.edu/scmsAdmin/media/

users/dhp238/Faculty_Projects/MRH_Web_SinglePage.pdf (last accessed 1 March 2017).
Morini, Cristina and Vignola Paolo. 2015. 'Introduzione' in Cristina Morini and Paolo Vignola (eds.), *Piccola enciclopedia precaria*. Milano: AgenziaX.
Negri, Antonio. 2009. 'Arte e lavoro immateriale', in Marco Baravalle (ed.), *L'arte della sovversione. Multiversity: pratiche artistiche contemporanee e attivismo politico*. Roma: Manifestolibri.
Papacharissi, Zizi. 2010. *A Private Sphere. Democracy in a Digital Age*. Cambridge: Polity Press.
Peck, Jaimie. 2005. 'Struggling with the Creative Class'. *International Journal of Urban and Regional Research* 29(4): 740–70.
Pratt, Andy. 2008. 'Creative Cities: The Cultural Industries and the Creative Class'. *Geografiska Annaler: Series B, Human Geography* 90 (2): 107–17.
Rogers, Richard. 2013. *Digital Methods*. Cambridge: MIT Press.
Sewell, H. William. 1996. 'Three Temporalities: Toward an Eventful Sociology', in Terrence J. McDonald (ed.), *The Historic Turn in the Human Sciences*. Ann Arbor: University of Michigan Press.
Shifman, Limor. 2012. 'An Anatomy of a YouTube Meme'. *New Media and Society* 14(2): 187–203.
Tilly, Charles and Sidney Tarrow. 2007. *Contentious Politics*. Boulder: Paradigm.
Whybrow, Nicolas. 2011. *Art and the City*. London, I. B. Tauris.

Chapter 4

The Political Value of Techno-Future
Emanuele Braga

Let's play a kind of game, and gamble on two different hypotheses. The most probable and strategic scenario in order to invent new modes of production is deeply rooted in the integration of two different components: democratic participation and technological innovation.

If this is the case, I would like to immediately put forward a fundamental question: can the capital produced by social cooperation be economically sustainable by means of new forms of self-organisation? What form will such a self-organised production take?

What if, on the contrary, we are facing an even more fundamental risk in our discourse? What if creativity, innovation, participation, cooperation, what we call the 'new technologies' embedded in the sharing economy, were nothing but empty watchwords, new simulacra of old ways of doing business plans and creating monopolies? What if they serve to foster new neoliberal governances and gentrification processes?

This is a central question: in a future in which machines, that is, the digital and physical automation of production, will substitute most part of the work once carried out by humans, how will it be possible to maintain a purchasing power? In the past, wealth was redistributed through salaries and wages. Significantly, the salary was also pivotal for workers' struggles and unions' demands. But what will happen if the wage relation becomes less and less central? What kind of models of struggle and organisation can we imagine?

Around 2008 – knowing how financial markets, the system of production and control exercised over every single life, are evermore defined by the synergies of algorithmic machines – a group of hackers and activists, inspired by open source culture, mostly anarchists and anti-systemic (some of them sympathetic to a certain anarcho-capitalism rooted in Austrian economic thought and developed in the San Francisco area), developed a protocol under the name of Bitcoin.[1] Their line of thought appeared to be rather linear: since capital accumulates value through the control of the information regarding our behaviour, we should construct a technological infrastructure in which there is no central accumulation (property), no traceability of profits (anonymity) and where everything is guaranteed by computers working in synergy.

The crisis of the past ten years has been a crisis of trust: debts, loans, derivatives – all means by which capital produces political control in neoliberalism. It is a crisis of relationships, of reliability. What we have to aim for is a new economic environment, a new ecology in which the unit of value is based on a fairer infrastructure. That is the starting point of another good example worth mentioning: FairCoop[2] and Fair mutual credit systems; ambitious projects that attempt to provide an alternative economic environment for cooperatives and grassroots independent productions on a worldwide scale.

Currently this field is extremely lively, many participants are start-ups – also business-oriented – and research programs that are investing in Blockchain technologies. In this trend we can also find initiatives based on very skilled and independent teams such as Freecoin[3] and D-cent.[4] Rather than creating another alternative currency in order to pressure the market, their goal is to create tools to foster participatory processes, decision-making systems and crypto-currencies based on the needs of specific communities. Each specific community may adopt these tools in order to shape them to their specific goals and needs.

Macao[5] is a centre for art and research, presently based in an occupied building in Milan, Italy. It was born out of a mobilisation in 2012, within the cultural sector of creative industries and art workers. Macao started to collaborate with Freecoin and D-cent in order to design a platform conceived to share means of production and co-production in the art/creative/cultural field. This collaboration is rooted in the network of occupied art spaces that emerged during the political mobilisation of the past five years.

Macao is currently proposing to design a crypto-currency (Commoncoin) with very specific features.[6] The primary and radical question in this process was: can we use an algorithmic, decentralised and peer-to-peer technology rooted on a process of political decision making? Can we base an algorithmic machine on a shared and community-based political value?

The future we imagine is made of decentralised technological infrastructures, distributed and based on algorithms; these are governed by democratic discussions and decisional processes, put into place by communities that share values and ideas. In other words: in a plausible future in which algorithms control our economical, relational and spatial behaviours, the real challenge is to find a way to question them without creating democratic deficit as a collateral effect.

The fundamental challenge around the Sharing Economy and technological innovation lies in the attempt to avoid these extreme outcomes:

- On the one extreme, allowing algorithms to be privatised, as in the case of Uber, Amazon, Apple, Airbnb and so on.
- Or, on the other extreme, to conceive of completely autonomous algorithms in which political decision dissolves into computing power and anarcho-capitalism. Therefore, the political challenge we are facing implies binding algorithms to democratic decisional processes, in ways that are dynamic and at the same time based on solidarity.

Ultimately, issues concerning the relationship between human and machine may look very current today, but in fact run through all of the past century. The intention of this chapter is to understand current experimentations in the field of activism and techno-politics coming from the experience through a historical analysis of Macao. In particular, it connects the Italian worker-ist's reading of the 1960s – which started reflecting on concepts such as the machine and technological innovation – with current reflections on how decades of post-Fordism and neo liberal policies have given their first notice-able results.

In the first section I look at the relationship between the concept of a machine and that of social cooperation, investigating how social movements can break some machinic ties and invent new forms of organisation. In the second section, inspired by the case of Macao, I focus on the relationship between machine and desire: if bio-political control, value extraction mechanisms and concentration of capital are realised through the use of new technologies, what are the possible tactics of emancipation from this form of slavery? In the last section I focus more clearly on what I think is the challenge that links new technology and politics: the question of the body and the collective desire: not being subject to an alienating mechanism but earning a cooperative dimension that is creative power.

THE FORM OF THE ORGANISATION

In 2007 financial capitalism declared its crisis. Over time, many people realised that this 'crisis' was nothing more than a sadistic strategy to strengthen and increase the value-extraction mechanism, concentrating even more wealth, making governments weaker, capturing more 'slaves', and disciplining the 'many'. In reaction to this, a global movement emerged taking different names, especially in the West, such as Occupy Wall Street in the United States, the 15M in Spain, Intermittent du Spectacle in France and the anti-austerity movements in other parts of Europe. In Italy this was most clearly expressed through the mobilisation of knowledge and art workers – several cities saw new institutions of the commons, brought about by organisations such as Macao in Milan.

All these struggles occupied public spaces both physically and in the media and they became both instituting and constituent laboratories. They were not just instances of protest or examples of agencies working on a certain political agenda, but they became experimental laboratories for other forms of socialisation. Using creative strategies, they aimed to liberate social relations from capital. It was social cooperation that wanted to be emancipated from capital in the form of a struggle conceived as the creative act.

Nowadays, the aesthetics of this are well established: people sitting in a circle, discussing, inventing new gestures and rituals, avoiding the reproduction of the same forms of capital (hierarchy, delegation, fascism, sexism, slavery at work, etc.). It is very interesting how social cooperation began to tentatively and awkwardly design new algorithms of public space, a new kind of unstable, monstrous bureaucracy, for example to demonstrate ways in which to signal that I want to intervene, how to know how much time I have before I bore others and how to communicate disagreement. During the first Macao assemblies in May 2012, everyone seemed somewhat embarrassed to see people pushing their hands upwards in unison to communicate appreciation and so on; the social machine was hacking itself. Almost immediately new rituals and behaviours appeared, and although embarrassing for many, they revealed a strong collective consciousness: we must find a meaning that we lost, and to do this we have to invent other forms of sociality.

After a few years, the most common criticisms of this wave of struggles was related to questions of the primacy of horizontality, that is, direct democracy, claiming it was incompatible with processes of political organisation. In short, within mobilisations in a few years there was a great outcry against the horizontality of the streets in comparison to the verticality and the effectiveness of the political organisation.[7] Although the tactical-political level of these positions is understandable, if the issue is framed in these terms one risks failing to grasp a very important conceptual node from which to imagine the future.

The real question, which also constitutes the backbone of the relationship between technology and politics, is the following: what form of social organisation represents the expression of our needs?

Our collective and social being always expresses itself in an antagonistic movement, placing rights before the law, needs before the code, the movement of legitimisation before the reason of the state, in the processes of appropriation of space (urban space, but also migration and post-colonial dynamics), and through a conception of the frontier as a constantly moving border, a nomadic and constituent organisation. We express ourselves necessarily in collective and organised forms that change in time by successive approximations to perfection. History is the form of this instituting resistance, the production of limits and constructivist borders. The horizon, the boundary of our landscape, is always articulated, organised, defined and at the same time never definitive.

Here, to put it more concretely, there is no opposition between the organisation's form and its movement, because to subvert the actual situation we always act through forms of organisation. And to explain better the subject of this intervention, every form of subversion is expressed through the creation of machines.

When Macao was born, a goal was stated: to gradually invent new forms of production and social relations that respond to current production processes (debt, insecurity, gentrification, destruction of the welfare, etc.), which make us sick. I still remember with amazement that one of the terms used to define Macao was 'an experiment in social engineering'. This monster-institution that we were creating was using terms borrowed from social science and indeed from an idea of society as a machine. To use the term 'social engineering' indicated that in the end, we might actually think about social relations as modules that can be removed and installed and in which parts can be removed and replaced with other parts – and that these processes can be innovative. At that time (around 2011), the old Italian cultural institutions (museums, huge theatres, the concert hall) were clearly in decline, big dinosaurs kept alive thanks to heaps of public money and negligible audiences. Those were the years in which politicians declared that culture was an unnecessary expense, since it was unable to create profit. They were wrong. The phenomenon of creative cities,[8] already tested in other states of the West, was coming even to 'old Italy'. Creativity as an industry would become, within a few months, the backbone of the metropolitan ransom. Creative industries became widespread, featuring start-ups, business models, urban regeneration and new apps able to digitise everyday life. The city was about to become smart.

Even in Macao we could have tried to join forces and create a great start-up. But we did not. We could have organised Macao, optimising time, trying to work to our best, with primary emphasis on efficiency, using only the evaluation criteria that we know so well: assessment, audience engagement and return on investment with repayment schedules.

During the first year of activity in Macao, we did the exact opposite: a self-enquiry,[9] which we then titled *69,300 hours*. We handed a survey to all participants and activists involved in Macao, and during the compilation we conducted in-depth interviews with them. We wanted to know who we were, where we came from, what we had studied, where we lived, how we were indebted and, especially, what we wanted to achieve through forming and participating in Macao; all of this because we were spending so much time on this experiment. In short, we wanted to build a common sense of Macao.

Rather than myopically jumping into the machinic, engineering, organisational and technological aspects, we asked very simply: who are we?

In order to highlight the history of this concept, I would like to go back to the 1960s in Italy, within the movement called Operaismo (Workerism), by remembering a magazine called *Quaderni Rossi*, where the translation of *Fragment on machines* by Karl Marx appeared in the fourth issue. This well-known text is often discussed for its contemporary relevance. Although this chapter will not refer to it in depth, I would like to pick out some elements as reference points to our discussion. Marx says that the machine is not an instrument for production, but it is the automation of production itself. It is not the worker who uses the machine to produce, but it is the machine that incorporates the worker in an automated process. Workers are no longer needed because of the living labour they embody, and they are instead bound to be the guardians and custodians of the machine. The second point I want to emphasise is that, according to Marx, on the one hand the machine increases productivity, but on the other it does not diminish the workload. The machine is not a substitute to living labour; it is rather conceived for being massively used by humans only when labour is already massive. This step is particularly interesting because it ignores some of the stereotypes regarding the relationship between automation and work. Automation increases productivity but does not diminish human labour. In fact, it needs the work of the masses. What does this mean? Marx notes that the machine automates and objectifies collective knowledge as social labour in the form of both science and knowledge. Through the machine, capital puts the general intellect to work. What does it mean that the machine objectifies the general intellect? It means that the machine is the result of the production of knowledge dispersed in society. The third point I want to mention: money, in the form of salary, is paid to the worker who must immediately spend it to keep the machinery in motion. Through the automation of production, money becomes transformed into debt, internal to a machinic circuit. Only within a machine is capital able to transform social cooperation into value. Fourth, Marx also speaks about the concept of innovation: the machine objectifies collective knowledge and needs to innovate constantly, not so much to improve production, but rather to continue capturing social production. Since social production is mainly the production of knowledge, capital must continually innovate itself to continue capturing the value produced by the multitude.

Pursuing this issue, I would also like to recall a passage in the first issue of *Quaderni Rossi* by Raniero Panzieri[10] entitled *Sull'uso capitalistico delle macchine nel neocapitalismo* (On the capitalistic use of the machines in neocapitalism).

Social cooperation is a result of the production of capital ratios. In the assembly line, social cooperation is subject to both technological innovation and the machine. The technological innovation rhetoric is the propaganda of capital, guaranteed by the successful processes of subjectivity. The struggle for wages is only a struggle for a wealthy slavery: Panzieri calls them slaves in 'golden chains'. In some way Panzieri stresses that sociability, including what was considered leisure time, time to not work, the set of social relations, including resistance and workers' struggle against capital, is considered by capital internal to the relations of production. It is rather a question of capturing the true value, much more central than profit rates and marketing of goods. This step raises the stakes on the classical question of the ownership of the means of production. Through machines, capital controls the social in all its forms or conversely by controlling the shape of machines, sociality can overturn this power-struggle with capital. But does this mean that social production is subject to technological innovation? It means that the relationship between social cooperation and machines within capital is one of slavery. But a new form of slavery. What then are these gold chains?

The most obvious and concrete answer is that the gold chains are the latest smartphone with its infinite applications, the electric car, Uber, the beautiful apartment booked on Airbnb, geolocation that finds an unknown address – the gold chains are capital's ability to deploy a certain well-being through the machinic control. This is a point I want to investigate further, because I argue that the gold chains have less to do with technology and more to do with the theme of the body, of desire and of happiness. We express ourselves by creating machines, but we can also be passively captured within highly machinic processes, even though they may seem infinitely ethereal and abstract.

This is the point. There are machines without subjectivity, but the processes of subjectivity can be very parched, exploited by machinic processes.

The problem is the social control exercised by machines. But what do we want from the automation? What do we desire through the machine? If social relations are internal to the machine, we must reestablish a government of machines, machines should go back to being prepared for a production of humans for humans. Cooperation and multitude (not the individual) are the precondition of the machine. The machine and its technological innovation are relational to the multitude's exploitation. And not just by a principle of misery and scarcity. Even where wages redistribute health, the machine strengthens a relationship of slavery: the gold chains. The gold chains are well-being without happiness, a healthy lack of meaning. We have to steer the machine as a collective movement, as social production, but what does this mean?

THE NIGHTS OF TAGGING

In 2013 Macao decided to study how a creative city might be governed through machinic processes. A tempting opportunity arose during Milan

Design Week. This is a very important event for a large city and generates investment opportunities for the urban territory of Milan. It is a highly emblematic form of production of Milan as a Creative and post-Fordist City, because it brings together the interest of many international corporations in the event-economy form, controlled by profiling mechanisms and digitally automated financing. To return to our theme, through a co-research method and direct action we observed how algorithmic automation was organising behaviours in the urban social fabric and the development processes: a great performance by social networks, finance, mapping, urban planning and culture, in which machinic processes worked synergistically.

Macao first conducted a series of interviews with workers and executives of the Design Week and understood the following: the programme is aggregated through an open call for showrooms scattered on the map of the city who participate in exchange for visibility. International sponsors give money to those who manage the programme, proportionally to the visibility of the event, and this visibility is measured based on how much the public speaks of the event on social networks and how often the program's website is visited, according to a 'page rank'. With this type of arrangement the central event agency collects 300 million euros for a week of events. This wealth is not redistributed to the workforce (mostly temporary workers or people working for free) or to the programme participants.

The algorithms not only profile our behaviour in order to create profit, but also work as a kind of prosthesis of the bottom-up self-organisation. This is the great insight of the latest generation of capitalism, which is allied with the libertarian ideology that feeds the Silicon Valley. The digital automation, including algorithmic deep learning, does not impose a paternalistic rule in order to control the behaviour of masses, but learns from these, from their actions, and extends as a social prosthesis, incorporating the repetitions and the anomalies that it detects. The algorithms elongate entropy production or organisation and differentiation. The questions being: who benefits from this? What do we want? What role does the human have? What about the collectivisation of needs? What is the relationship between workforce and algorithms? Are these relations of production? What is the relationship between social production and digital organisation? Who is writing and articulating these algorithms?

This is why, during one edition of the Design Week, Macao's collective planned to carry out an action that was both a hacking and an investigation. We created a fake website for Design Week and asked all workers exploited by the event to generate its contents. At the same time, during the event we placed critical questions to the public on social networks. We asked audiences to evaluate the contents of the programme, and specifically we asked if they were conscious of being the true wealth producers of the event. The Twitter storm was so successful that our cluster surpassed those of the official agencies and the mainstream media, so that Twitter, after three days of action, suspended our account for unknown reasons.

We also downloaded 10,000 photos from Instagram, taken by members of the public during design week. If the production of social cooperation (the audience of the event), that is, free labour, was the real living labour that gave value to the event, those photos were the advertising and informational content that hundreds of thousands of people had made without knowing that they were working for the event. We wanted to know what the content of those photos was, which processes of subjectivity were involved. That is why we invented 'the nights of tagging'.

We gathered in a room to display on various computers all the downloaded photos in order to tag them. We did what machines usually do, dividing the photos by categories, marking differences and redundancies, and tried to produce meaning. Collectively, we profiled and shared what an algorithm usually does. We discussed and tried to make sense of the images. I mention this now because for me it was very significant. In a political community, for once we managed to do what an exploitative algorithm usually does, but we tried to resignify the result through a discussion that could make sense. We gave body to what usually works in an abstract way and yet strongly influences our lives, how we pass through the city and how we use our time.

Perhaps the dominant grammar of the contemporary is the algorithm. Throughout history, writing has undergone many changes and assumed different grammars and syntaxes. We can say that a form of contemporary writing is algorithmic. We prepare a message, a sense of that kind of articulation. Structuralism and post-structuralist theories have strongly developed this relationship in the history of languages and literature. Derrida[11] puts great emphasis on the impossibility of ensuring the message. In any text the writer has to accept a form of death that at the same time is the only way to create the chance for someone else to understand and articulate a common environment. But the text cannot be insured; it can only be 'caught' by someone else. Consequently, as we have seen, there are many pitfalls in the present day, for example when we write a post on Facebook. Who can guarantee how it will be used? What can preface a post? Sometimes on your Facebook wall prefaces appear or notes, like, 'I prevent Facebook from using my information'. But we know that this kind of prevention is totally short-sighted and futile in the face of a machine that as Panzieri said is also fed by this type of resistance. What assures me that the post is used in the right way? What predisposes an algorithm?

It is this emphasis on individual security that prevents us from grasping the point. The individual profit, the value of use, safety and anonymity do not grasp the power of a physical process and joyous emancipation.

What is the difference between human materialism, ontologically rooted, and a technocratic post-humanism? It is the collective desire, rooted in a relationship – a desiring intelligence, which produces and organises the being of which the technological prosthesis, the means of production, is not the expression. In this ontological horizon, where automation takes a normative and coercive position over the collective movement, technocratic domination is only an absence, a 'not yet'. The Artificial Intelligence speeds up, but who does it speed for? It is an expression, but whose?

POST-HUMAN OR POST-MACHINE?

Capitalistic society is a sadistic machine, a machine that renders relational processes meaningless. It is a sadistic machine in the sense of the progressive cancellation of sensations, of the flattening of perceptions of ever fewer images. It decreases visible space. This aspect is very important. We see it for example developed by Henri Lefebvre when he speaks of urban space. Space is an ideological construct of capital that uses the rituals of the body as a machine. Is how a woman sits on the subway, or around a table, different from how a man sits? Urban space is the scene of great social choreography and behavioural codes, in which we train every day. And these sets of codes and patterns often limit our actual possibilities, domesticating our needs and desires. So the theme of the body intensifies this question: either the instrument works as a human implant, or it is absorbed so that the social machine defines the human. The problem is not just anthropo-technical. There is something beyond efficiency and optimisation, beyond rational functions. The problem is that efficiency can lead to boredom. The machine is an information transmission system. Developing the idea of 'feeling', we might ask whether machines can cut off the organs that allow us to feel, or whether they multiply the organs of sense. While a society flattens machinic dimensions, it diminishes the subject to an interconnected element within a pre-established pattern. By addressing this node, Tiziana Villani in *Ecologia Politica*[12] recalls the myth of Narcissus who dies by drowning in his own image. The man in front of a static visual field, trapped in the automation of fragmentation, with no possibility to escape, falls and dies almost not realising that there is no air. This appeal to the myth of Narcissus, to explain the human–machine relationship, is very pleasant. Living labour drowning in fixed capital. A fixed capital reduced to a surface among others, which are almost incorporeal. The 'nights of tagging' reveal a sense of how an apparently bored public moves frantically from one location to another during Design Week, snapping pictures to post on social networks, much like a contemporary Narcissus dying in a continuous recurrence of selfies: a possible exegesis of the gold chains, the lack of *ex-stasis*, that is, the exit from stasis. The movement of this machine does not coincide with itself. Also interesting is the concept of the unexpected: the unexpected creates a qualitative difference. The unexpected is not the abnormal, the not-yet-rule, the non-catalogued, the not yet taggable, but soon taggable. In deep learning the rule rewrites itself, incorporating difference. On closer inspection deep learning produces no difference, but searches it in order to cancel it.

Villani, in more than one text, emphasises this apparent play on words: to institute is to become what one is. This immanence of life is our power to produce difference. We are genetic codes. Our very existence depends on writing. DNA is like an algorithm. We have the power to activate the code, and the power to differentiate. The sensors and actuators (the Internet of things), however, do not represent feeling. For the human there is a difference between acting and suffering. For a shield or a card connected to the sensors and programmed by a code, there is no difference between acting and suffering if not in terms of communication. For a machine, communication is just a matter of information transfer. From this point of view, to suffer and to act are the same thing. The subject has a power of life that is not commensurate to cybernetics. The subject takes possession not only of what the machine does not see, what is abandoned, but it appropriates what does not exist yet, what is not yet differentiated. This is creating: the power of life. And we can only do it in an ecology, in a relational system of more subjects, it can only happen as *moltitudo*. This is the difference between artificial intelligence and general intellect; the general intellect desires to have a body.

In *Grammatica della moltitudine* Paolo Virno makes a small note: fixed capital has been completely impaired: after 1977 the machine lost its body.

The machine is no longer the factory with its heavy assembly lines, but it is algorithmic, made of bits. It has ever less body. The more it enhances the general intellect, the more the machine loses its body. From which we can derive the concept of the abstract machine.

In 2015 Macao and Sale Docks[13] addressed this concept of abstract machine through a series of meetings and actions, titled Abstract Strike (ABStrike). The question was very simple: If we are governed by algorithms, what kind of strike can we conceive of? What kind of strike is a strike to an abstract machine? Among others, Toni Negri participated in this discussion, writing for the occasion a text entitled *Notes on the abstract strike*.[14] In this text Negri first comments that never before has social cooperation been so close to having regained possession of the means of production. The problem is that the capital mining machine has taken a step back; it has become more and more abstract. Algorithms are machines, and there is no machine without subjectivity. Thus, even if abstract, every machine requires a minimum of physicality. Without subjects, machines do not exist. But the governmentality of capital on living labour is extremely impalpable, it has lost the body, it is not as accessible as the factory environment. Even those who tried to operate on a more abstract level to regain possession of the machine were duped and replaced in a controlled space. As Negri rightly emphasises, it is not so much a sort of competition for who has the most powerful machine, but a more ontological one and on more substantive grounds. For Negri, the act of regaining possession of the machines must have two main reasons: the first being the production by human for the human, the second should be an opportunity to multiply networks, to federate the struggles. The reappropriation of the means of production is not a technological problem and is rather a problem of resignification.

Finally, I want to recall one last concept well explained by Virno in *Grammatica della moltitudine*:[15] Communism of Capital. The outcome of the struggles of the 1970s – the refusal of work, the sharing, the transforming of factories into social factories – was the precondition of a counter-revolution by capital that gave birth to post-Fordism. It placed value on the general intellect and the coexistence of work and life. But this calls for a question, obvious in its triviality. Is it a victory or a defeat? Are these really gold chains?

That is to say (and we can say it perhaps only nowadays): new technologies allow for social cooperation to hack the abstract machine, to make a real 'assault to the sky'. Negri says that now, more than ever, the multitude is close to having regained possession of the means of production. But how should we do this?

Hackers are of course the heroes of this era. They showed up in Macao in 2013 asking to work with us for a month. They came from all over the world and locked themselves in a room with dozens of laptops and projectors on the walls, to discuss and write code. They were the developers of Bitcoin and at that time they were simply running away. They were discussing a certain Dark Wallet – a new tool to get away from the financial market and the U.S. government that was trying to take possession and control of Bitcoin through assets and administrative law. We are now at the heart of the topic discussed here.

During a period of six months in Macao we discussed these issues with a network of Italian subjects: the value of inventing new economic and financial infrastructure, discussing the concept of money and the relations of production. Together with the collective *Effimera*[16] and the *dyne.org* group we disassembled and reassembled the concept of money through a historical perspective involving several economists, and parallel to a practical point of view we gathered around us many projects that were reprogramming financial spaces. They were inventing digital coins, banking, finance and small and large experiments to try and have a different relationship with forms of organisation, new technologies and essentially with machines.

On this path we met Enric Duran and the Faircoop project. Enric Duran is a Spanish activist who years ago, with an insolvent bank loan, had stolen half a million euros from banks, donating money to the many realities of the Spanish movement. As an internationally wanted criminal, he started working with other Catalan, Spanish and European activists, creating a digital platform called Faircoop that would provide alternative financial services. This platform aims at globally pooling various independent producers and using a crypto currency to regulate the exchanges. The protocol of this coin was slightly different from Bitcoin, both from the point of view of the plan (less subject to financial speculation) and from the point of view of governance (controlled by members of an open cooperative). From that moment we started working with Faircoop, adhering to the foundation of a new project: an open cooperative called Freedomcoop. We did this by pooling legally different production nodes scattered across Europe on a transnational level with ethical and political protocols.

What I most want to emphasise of Enric's work was his method: in a calm manner he travelled extensively going from community to community, through different territories, observing different contexts and technically explaining what he was working on. And so the project has grown. The Bitcoin users live in anonymity, they do not know each other and do not even have the desire to do so. In the FairCoop circuit one perceives the need and the desire to enter into a relationship. Since the beginning, a collaborative environment was created, given that a number of groups are on Telegram and meet through Skype: there are those who translate, those who seek to understand aspects of various national laws, those who start projects. Sometimes all this is debated and sometimes it goes unnoticed. The project is neither icy nor machinic; it is instead intended as a means to create a relational fabric.

In recent years Macao has also collaborated with another important project: Robin Hood Minor Asset Management. They invited me to a meeting in Dublin, where their work method was in the nomadic form of temporary offices in different cities of the world. They are also a cooperative, made of economists, artists, hackers and academic researchers. They created a cooperative fund that speculates on the financial market using a parasite algorithm that ensures high performance. Essentially mimicking larger speculative investment funds, they bring in a cooperative fund and the shareholders are united in wanting to invest the profit in political activism projects with high social impact. Through an algorithm written by them, they subtract value to the financial markets to redistribute it in processes of resistance to the capital.

In the summer of 2014 we organised a conference with the collectives of Macao and Effimera, entitled *La moneta del comune*.[17] The challenge was to figure out a set of assumptions for a financial system, with a base of production by humans for humans, designed to build the commons. On that occasion, some of the participants suggested that we write a manifesto. At this solicitation, Jaromil, a hacker from the dyne.org project, replied that this was not the time to write manifestos, but rather to write manuals.

So it was that we began to work on the architecture and design of a coin. We set off from the need of a region, a network of relationships and a sequence of nodes and subjects. And we began to design a form of currency that we called Commoncoin. The idea was to understand how different productive organisations could decode certain social needs and activate new political prospects. We tried to design a financial system and to decide collectively what to assign value to. The themes that emerged were how to put into question the wage form, introducing a self-managed basic income, how to stimulate collaboration between multiple projects, such as inscribed mutual aid and a fairer redistribution of wealth in the form of a financial circuit. Beyond the form that can never be definitive, this path was capable of drawing attention away from the charm of new technologies as a panacea for all ills and placing instead more attention on the values we want to automate. Automation is not the goal, but only a means to the construction of the commons. The size and space in which we are repositioning the machinic function is this debate, the sharing of vision and needs, this relational space that creates the social space.

This is the problem of 'the becoming other' of the machines. The 'instituting' always provides a machinic element, incorporates it, or is embodied through it, as well as the organisation codes and rites. The point is that the constitutional process is inscribed in that code.

This is evident in the case of crypto-currencies. That is, creating an alternative infrastructure that regulates social relations through money. Very often, the focus is on machinic design elements. If the design contains certain elements like anonymity, decentralisation, proof of work, as in the case of Bitcoin, the virality and dissemination of the coin is machinic. One does not need to activate relational or emotional chaining. Many individuals will begin to be slaves of yet another machine without establishing anything. In place of the extraction mechanism governed by the relation between debt and finance, which is the euro or the dollar, we will have another currency governed by another protocol that will only transform many opportunities into a loss of sense. But we do want forms of organisation and differentiation to become the expression of a process of emancipation, of a creative gesture, that institutes and allows for the needs of being to emerge through an act of liberation.

A machine that is not too complicated, which is capable of being an expression of real needs, is better than a highly sophisticated and complex machine that automates people's time in an exploitative relationship. How do we become aware of the difference between the gold chains and the machines with which we are liberated? Do we prefer the iPhone, or an old phone which we never got rid of, or a phone produced independently but that cannot do all the things that the iPhone does? In this way the question is misplaced. The essence of the problem lies not in the shape of the machine. On the contrary, the relationship is the fundamental issue.

In the continuous questioning of the system – of the machine that puts us in a position to organise our space and our time – the act of appropriating the conflict, refusing to answer to it nor dialectically or ideologically, enables us to live it as an expressive process, not fearing collective and relational dimensions, not being afraid of becoming something else. To do this enables us to continuously exit the stasis, to not coincide with the still image, to feed the appetite of our needs and continually redraw the environment, keeping it in a continuous check and buzz. We cannot talk about the machine unless we want to be happy.

The Luddites ideological perspective is the result of an artificial opposition between machine and human. We should rather conceive machines in a new way, more like a game where the rules are an excuse for fun, for discovery, for the expansion of the visual space. We must love the machines in a post-machine perspective, so as to be able to drag them into a line of flight together with our needs and our daily struggles. The real question is how to consider machines as important organs that allow us to institute this movement, which will allow us to intensify the affective, sexual, environmental and visual dimension. At stake is the ongoing maintenance of our social body as a desiring machine.

CONCLUSION

Contemporary capitalism has reorganised through new technologies, structurally changing the relationship between society and production. In other words, this is in line with one of the main post-workerist statements: the site of production is not the factory anymore, as it nowadays coincides with the whole society. In this context, waged labour, as well as the distinction between work and non-work time, is a term that cannot describe the reality of contemporary work. A new production model is emerging, in which all the aspects of life, including the emotional, the relational, care, are put to work and enter the financialisation of capital circuits.[18] New technologies, the core of new capitalistic platforms, the big corporations such as Facebook, Netflix, Apple, Amazon and Alibaba are developing services, relational environments and hardware implants, specifically in relation to this type of social control and concentration of capital. Through technological innovation, today more than ever, the capital is mimetically extracting value from life, from the organised society in its most varied forms.

In the coming years, the paradigm shift will be evident and shocking. The knot that binds capital and technological innovation will cross, like a razor, the theme of post-democracy, nationalism, the role of the state, the concept of work and the concept of money, health and education – this is the battlefield of the future.

For this reason, as collective intelligence, cooperating societies, relational fabric, we have to figure out how to trigger processes of appropriation, of counter-expropriation, within and against capitalistic platforms. The challenge today is to regain possession of the means of production, reappropriate technologies, desiring through collective processes. The issue of private property, of the monopolies of data and hardware infrastructure are the points of attack. This is why the fields of struggle are: infrastructures for economic redistribution, mutualistic circuits, cooperative platforms, co-management of common services and enabling a bottom-managed welfare system.

POST-SCRIPTUM: NARCISSUS AND THE TORTOISE

Two symmetrical but opposite movements are encountered on the surface. First: the human who dies in his own image; moving from land into water to coincide with his own image and then die. Second: the turtle that comes out of the water, becomes human, and as a human it cries. An animal becomes human because it has feelings, compared to a human who dies because he becomes a machine.

The tortoise, like the crocodile, breathes air and not water, but it eats in seawater. In doing so it swallows great quantities of salt. For this reason, when they end the apnoea, and resurface to breathe air, their eyes cry, to eject the excess of salt they ingested. The turtle comes out of the water to cry.

Presumably the human's DNA descends from a mammal that lived in the sea and began to colonise the land. But this organ that actually expels brine from our eyes became a gesture strongly linked to feeling, affection and relationship. We do not cry harder to digest, but we weep to feel affected. Perhaps our species inherits this useless function: the non-coincidence between the value in use, the function and affection. In eugenics, the human comes out of the water and transforms a mechanical element, functional and animal, in an organ of feeling, in affection. While on the other side Narcissus enters the water and dies, believing he coincides with his own image.

NOTES

1. Bitcoin is a digital and global money system (currency). It allows people to send or receive money across the Internet, even to someone they do not know or trust. Money can be exchanged without being linked to a real identity. The mathematical field of cryptography is the basis for Bitcoin's security.

2. For FairCoop see: www.fair.coop.
3. For Freecoin see: www.freecoin.ch.
4. For D-Cent see: www.dcentproject.eu.
5. For Macao see: www.macao.mi.it.
6. For CommonCoin see: http://www.macaomilano.org/rivista/IMG/pdf/commoncoin-2.pdf.
7. 'We believe that the most important division in today's left is between those who hold to a folk politics of localism, direct action and relentless horizontalism, and those who outline what must become called an accelerationist politics at ease with a modernity of abstraction, complexity, globality and technology. The former remains content with establishing small and temporary spaces of non-capitalist social relations, eschewing the real problems entailed in facing foes that are intrinsically non-local, abstract, and rooted deep in our everyday infrastructure. The failure of such politics has been built-in from the very beginning. By contrast, an accelerationist politics seeks to preserve the gains of late capitalism while going further than its value system, governance structures, and mass pathologies will allow' (Williams and Srnicek, 2013). The Accelerationist Manifesto had quite a big impact in political and theoretical discussion concerning the relationship between horizontalism and accelerationist politics. On the issue of horizontalism and verticality see also Negri (2014) and Cossu (forthcoming).
8. See Richard Florida (2008).
9. The research was inspired by the workerist practice of 'con-ricerca'. Cf. Alquati (1993).
10. Panzieri (1961).
11. Derrida (1967).
12. Villani (2013).
13. S.a.L.E. Docks is an independent space for visual arts and experimental theatre born in Venice in 2007 thanks to a group of activists coming from the experience of the 'Centri Sociali' and the autonomous social movements.
14. Negri (2015).
15. Virno (2001).
16. Effimera is a 'virtual' collective and consists of more than 200 persons, interconnected with each other, living in various parts of the world. It is a network of researchers and activists who share a practice of militant research that originates from the Italian workerism, starting from Quaderni Rossi in the 1960s, to the most recent theories on capitalism and biopower. http://www.effimera.org.
17. See http://www.macaomilano.org/rivista/spip.php?rubrique8.
18. Fumagalli (2007).

REFERENCES

AA.VV., *Quaderni Rossi* (1961–1966). Milano: Sapere Edizioni.
Alquati, Romano. 1993. *Per fare conricerca*. Padova: Calusca Edizioni.
Braga, Emanuele and Fumagalli, Andrea (eds.). 2015. *La Moneta del Comune*. Milano: Alfabeta Edizioni.

Cossu, Alberto. 'Beyond Social Media Determinism? How Artists Reshape the Organisation of Social Movements'. *Social Media + Society*. (forthcoming)
Derrida, Jacques. 1967. *De la grammatologie*. Paris: Editions de Minuit.
Kleiner, Dmytri. 2010. *The Telekommunist Manifesto*. INC Publications, Amsterdam.
Lefebvre, Henri. 1974. *The Production of Space*. Oxford: Blackwell Publishing.
Florida, Richard. 2008. *Who's Your City? How the Creative Economy Is Making Where to Live the Most Important Decision of Your Life*. New York: Basic Books.
Fumagalli, Andrea. 2007. *Bioeconomia e capitalismo cognitivo*. Roma: Carocci.
Fumagalli, Andrea and Lucarelli, Stefano. 2015. 'Finance, Austerity and Commonfare'. *Theory, Culture & Society* 32(7–8): 51–65.
Marazzi, Christian. 2010. *Il comunismo del capitale*. Napoli: Ombre Corte.
Negri, Antonio. 2015. 'Notes on the Abstract Strike'. *E-flux journal 56th Venice Biennale*. Available at: http://supercommunity.e-flux.com/texts/notes-on-the-abstract-strike/.
Negri, Antonio. 2014. 'Reflections on the Manifesto for an Accelerationist Politics'. *E-flux journal* #53. Available at: http://www.e-flux.com/journal/53/59877/reflections-on-the-manifesto-for-an-accelerationist-politics/.
Panzieri, Raniero. 1961. 'Sull'uso capitalistico delle macchine neocapitalismo'. *Quaderni Rossi 1*.
Piironen, Pekka. 2015. 'Democratizing the Power of Finance' in Lovink, Geert (ed.), *Money Lab Reader*. Amsterdam: Inc. Publications.
Villani, Tiziana. 2013. *Ecologia Politica*. Roma: Manifestolibri.
Virno, Paolo. 2001. *Grammatica della Moltitudine*, Rubettino: Catanzaro.
Williams, Alex and Srnicek, Nick. 2013. '#ACCELERATE MANIFESTO for an Accelerationist Politics'. *Critical and Legal Thinking*. Available at: http://criticallegalthinking.com/2013/05/14/accelerate-manifesto-for-an-accelerationist-politics/.

Chapter 5

Changing the Narrative
Highlighting Workers' Rights in Environmental Art Activism

Paula Serafini

Historically, the relationship between the labour movement and the environmental movement has been marked by tensions in the Global South as well as in the North. In the Global North, this is due in part to the fact that environmental issues do not have a set place on the political spectrum (Godfrey 2012: 1). In other cases, mostly within the Global South, there have been tensions between labour and environmental causes often intertwined with indigenous land rights and with policies and discourses of development (Gudynas, 2009: 200–01). Furthermore, environmental issues are intrinsically connected to race and class (Cutter, 1995), and this is evident in the disproportionate way in which people of colour and working-class people are affected by both pollution and climate change across the globe. This connection, however, is not made visible by the composition of environmental movements in the North, where people of colour and their perspectives are underrepresented (Dhaliwal, 2015).

At the same time, there are increasingly more campaigns and movements that are making the connections between environmental issues, human rights and labour struggles more visible, highlighting the need for 'just transition' of workers in the energy sector towards secure, green jobs (Kohler, 2010), equating climate and/or environmental justice to social justice (Schlosberg, 2007) and exposing the human rights violations of multinational fossil fuel companies driving climate change.[1] Considering the current landscape of social, political and environmental crisis, it seems more crucial than ever to develop strategies for effective political action that can simultaneously address issues of human rights, labour and climate change in an effective manner. With that in mind, this chapter seeks to explore the ways in which activists are currently constructing narratives that bring together the aforementioned issues.

I will approach this subject by analysing the performances of BP or not BP?, an environmental activist theatre troupe that stands against oil sponsorship of the arts in the UK, and for a culture beyond oil.[2] I will look at how their creative actions generate narratives and how they have incorporated issues of human rights and workers' struggles in an attempt to construct a more holistic approach to an environmental anti-fossil fuel stance. I will specifically look at how the group generates these narratives through the medium of art activism,[3] looking at performance actions (Serafini, 2014) and 'guerrilla exhibitions' as two forms of aesthetic-political practice that enable the construction and sharing of these narratives. By presenting the case of BP or not BP?, this explorative, empirical chapter hopes to provide a partial yet timely account of how environmental groups in the UK are incorporating issues of labour in their narratives and provide an analysis of how this is done through the medium of art activism as a vehicle for narration and political action.

NARRATIVE AND POLITICS

In politics, the 'struggle for the narrative' has become a frequent theme. In a conflict, the use of the term narrative to refer to the way in which opposite sides frame an issue 'suggests the existence of competing truths' and 'implies that each version is not a neutral account of events, but an attempt to naturalise what is, at bottom, an ideological stance' (Rimmon-Kenan, 2006: 11). Narratives intrigue audiences because they call for our interpretive participation, for us to struggle in filling the gaps. 'We struggle because the story's end is consequential; it is not only outcome but moral of the events which precede it' (Polletta, 1998: 423).

There are certain features of narrative that make it a useful tool and form of communication in and about social movements, such as 'its reliance on emplotment, point of view, narrativity, and a canon of familiar plots' (Polletta, 1998: 420). In the words of Terry Eagleton, 'Think of narrative as a kind of strategy. Like any strategy, it mobilises certain resources and deploys certain techniques to achieve specific goals' (Eagleton, 2013: 105). It therefore makes sense that activists construct narratives in order to communicate their ideas to the organisations they are protesting against, to the general public, and to themselves. But in addition, the narratives explored in this chapter emerge out of a context of performance-based activism, and as a result, my approach to these narratives will abide by a perspective that challenges the Platonic/Socratic distinction between narrative (diegesis) and drama (mimesis) (Rimmon-Kenan, 2006: 10), considering also how narratives emerge out of other discursive and performative media, such as exhibitions.

Narratives can be powerful vehicles for giving voice and presence to a group or an idea (Rimmon-Kenan, 2006: 15), and, indeed, 'stories are possible because some initial order is disrupted' (Eagleton, 2013: 104). It is this power that warrants a focus on narratives in the study of social movements, and in the intersection between environmental and workers' movements in particular. However, rather than providing an analysis of the narrative elements of these performances from a narratology perspective, in this chapter I will instead look at what the narratives are and how issues of labour are incorporated into actions coming from an environmental campaign, exploring the processes behind this as well as the challenges faced by art activists and the possibilities that art activism opens up for holistic climate and social justice campaigns. I situate this chapter in between an analysis of narratives and a study of how these narratives are shaped and conditioned by their setting (Polletta, 1998: 425), considering as well their role and potential as tools for evolving campaigns.

ENVIRONMENTALISM IN THE UK: THE CAMPAIGN AGAINST OIL SPONSORSHIP OF THE ARTS

Fossil fuel companies have for long been patrons of the arts in the UK, with companies like BP and Shell sponsoring some of the most prominent cultural institutions in Britain, including the Royal Opera House, the National Portrait Gallery and the British Museum. But while the relationship between oil and culture goes back decades, it has for long been challenged by environmental groups who claim that fossil fuel companies are drivers of climate change, and as such their sponsorship of cultural institutions is unethical (Evans, 2015). Beginning with Rising Tide's *Art Not Oil* campaign, which later grew into a coalition of artists and activist against oil sponsorship of the arts, groups like Platform, Liberate Tate and BP or not BP? have brought their combination of art and activism to the halls and exhibition rooms of these institutions. These protests have gained significant media attention and succeeded in generating a public debate on the ethics of sponsorship,[4] which was followed by the end of some high-profile BP sponsorship deals in 2016, including that with Tate.

Activist theatre troupe BP or not BP? started out as a Shakespearean ensemble targeting the Royal Shakespeare Company's BP-sponsored plays. Inspired by traditions of agitprop theatre, participatory arts and the Bard himself, BP or not BP? engage in what we can refer to as 'performance actions', a type of political action that borrows from the processes and forms of performance art and theatre, and that 'is defined by the double role of participants as political activists and performers' (Serafini, 2014: 324). Once the sponsorship deal between BP and the Royal Shakespeare Company came to an end, the group moved on to performing at the British Museum, swapping stage invasions for larger and more durational performances, participatory actions and flashmobs that question BP's place in said institution. Their change of venue not only resulted in a move from the stage to museum halls, but also the group's performances gradually became more inspired by the themes of the BP-sponsored exhibitions, as was the case of the BP Vikings flashmob, a large-scale performance that featured a human-made Viking longship (Serafini, 2015). Furthermore, staging protests at the British Museum introduced a series of new factors into the mix. First, it spotlighted the undeniable imperial past of this cultural venue. In the words of Jess, one of BP or not BP?'s *actorvists* (a term often used by BP or not BP? to describe their position as actor-activists), the museum 'is a powerful icon of British colonial power, as is BP'.[5] Second, it was revealed that BP was specifically sponsoring exhibitions and events about Global South countries where they are operating or in the process of brokering new deals with (Art Not Oil Coalition, 2016). And finally, BP or not BP? had to consider the fact that the British Museum was the site of other controversies, including the museum's links to former blacklisting company Carillion (Smith and Chamberlain, 2015).

BP or not BP?'s response was to begin creating performances that make explicit the connections between corporate power, climate change, human rights and (neo)colonialism, in relation to both the British Museum and BP. These connections were manifested in different ways in the scripts of performances and were prompted by solidarity work and collaborations with frontline communities, which took a variety of forms. In Jess's words, 'I think the thing that we didn't really foresee was how well [the British Museum] would lend itself to solidarity campaigning, and how it would broaden out our messaging and our mission in ways that has felt really good and important'. She then adds 'our messaging has broadened out from "BP is bad, you should drop them" to "and these groups are advocating for these changes and we're gonna advocate for them as well"'.

This shift in perspective and objectives makes BP or not BP? a unique case for analysing the production of narratives, and for tracing how these new narratives incorporated issues of human and workers' rights into their environmental campaign. The remainder of this chapter will look at two of BP or not BP?'s actions against oil sponsorship of the arts that attempted to build, in different ways, connections to human rights and workers' struggles in the UK and abroad. I will focus on the construction of narratives and the internal and contextual factors that allowed these narratives to come to life, looking at how art activism can facilitate the construction, communication and performance of those narratives.

COMEDIC PERFORMANCE AND PERFORMATIVE STORYTELLING: THE CASE OF GILBERTO TORRES

Gilberto Torres Martínez is a Colombian activist who was kidnapped by paramilitaries in Colombia in 2002, following his leading role in a campaign protesting the disappearance of fellow trade union leader Aury Sará Marrugo. Gilberto, who was at the time a union activist for the oil workers' union USO, was held captive for forty-two days before being released due to national and international pressure. He was one of the only two trade union activists in Colombia to ever survive their kidnapping.[6] The investigation and trial conducted in Colombia after Gilberto's release revealed that his abductors had been hired by the company Ocensa, which produced oil pipelines, of which BP was a shareholder. In 2015, Gilberto travelled to London to raise awareness of his story and to announce that he was working on a legal case against BP for its alleged role in his abduction. BP or not BP? and Gilberto first got in touch through War on Want, a UK-based organisation that was coordinating Gilberto's tour of public appearances in the UK. The result of this new connection was the plan for a performance action at the British Museum that would involve Gilberto – and originally also his colleague Francisco, who unfortunately could not make it to London – and would shed light on BP's record of human rights violations and Gilberto's case specifically, in addition to the environmental issues usually highlighted by the group's actions.

But turning the story of Gilberto's kidnapping into a performance action about BP and its sponsorship of the British Museum was a challenging task, which brought about four major concerns. The first was getting the facts right, and constant consultation, which was ensured through a collaborative script-writing process with Gilberto and Francisco, was crucial towards this. The second was ensuring Gilberto and Francisco had agency in the performance, considering it would revolve around Gilberto's personal story. The third was successfully broadening the scope of BP or not BP?'s narrative and making the links between sponsorship, climate change, and human and workers' rights clear. In reference to this, it is important to acknowledge the different perspectives involved in this joint fight against BP, as Gilberto is an engineer and trade union leader who used to work for the oil industry in Colombia, not an environmental activist based in the UK. The group therefore needed to construct a frame for the action as well as a narrative for the performance that brought together all these different issues and perspectives in a coherent manner. And the forth and probably most crucial concern of all in terms of the performance, was tone. Jess from BP or not BP? shared: 'My gut feeling was "how could we possibly do any kind of a performance when he has been tortured, you know?"' In line with many of BP or not BP'sf? previous performances, which rely on the element of humour, it was agreed by the group that this performance would also have a comedic element, something that both Gilberto and Francisco agreed with. However, as Jess expressed, there were concerns about the comedic aspect of the performance and the potential dangers of getting the tone wrong: 'I was feeling really like, this could be horrible if we get the tone wrong, if we judge this wrong. This could be really disrespectful'.

The Performance

The performance takes place on 11 October 2015 and begins with two comedic characters or jesters drawing in an audience in the British Museum's great hall in a vaudeville style. The two performers wear colourful waistcoats and shirts and introduce themselves as the Truth Translators (TT1 and TT2 in the script). They show off a big horn bearing the words 'truth translator' and announce they will test this apparatus out on 'one of the most practiced liars in the world: BP'. At this point, a woman dressed in sleek black clothes with a BP badge and her hair pulled back enters the scene. She begins to make statements about BP's corporate responsibility policy, including some with particular reference to BP's operations in Colombia.[7] After each of the statements the BP representative makes, one of the Truth Translators yells out 'translation!' and the other uses their translating horn to decipher the truth behind BP's statements:[8]

> BP: We truly believe in the importance of art & culture, and want to support great British cultural institutions.
>
> TT1: Translation!
>
> TT2: 'We believe in the importance of moving attention away from the terrible destruction we cause elsewhere. Our sponsorship here is just Greenwash'.
>
> BP: We strive to contribute to *development* in the places where we operate.
>
> TT1: Translation!
>
> TT2: 'We always contribute to . . . *destruction* in the places we operate'.
>
> BP: Such as Colombia, where our carefully managed operations have been welcomed by farmers and stimulated the local economy.
>
> TT2: 'Such as Colombia, where BP has been sued by farmers for polluting their land and destroying their livelihoods'.
>
> BP (*looking concerned but ploughing on*): Our operations are built on respect. We value diversity of thought, and aim to build strong relationships with our workers and local communities.

At this point the performance is stopped by another performer/translator who announces that 'there is someone here who knows the truth'. Gilberto enters the scene as the Truth Translators step back and proceeds to share his story and that of fellow trade union leader Aury Sará Marrugo, using maps of Colombia and photographs as visual aids.[9] Once Gilberto concludes, the Truth Translators ask BP what she has to say about that. BP gets worked up and loses her composure. She spits out corporate statements, which are countered by the Truth Translators with great speed:

BP: Er, Personal . . . personal relationships!

TT 1: Persecution of locals and trade unionists.

BP: Er. Er. Development!

TT 2: Destruction.

BP: Corporate responsibility!

TT 1: Climate change.

BP then breaks down. Begins to yell 'Money! Money! Money!' and oil comes out of her mouth. BP falls to the floor, and the performance concludes with the Truth Translators stating:

TT 1: BP. A well-oiled PR machine.

TT 2: But the truth always comes out in the end. . . .

Figure 5.1. Gilberto Torres holds a picture of kidnapped trade union activist Aury Sará Marrugo while standing outside the British Museum with two BP or not BP? performers, 11 October 2015.
© Paula Serafini.

Narrative, Plot, Performativity

When I asked Gilberto about his views on the connection between environmental issues and workers' rights in Colombia, he offered the following thoughts:

> It is social processes that the capitalist system attacks today in terms of human rights, peoples' rights, environmental rights, indigenous communities, afro communities and LGBTI communities, and its principal actors are transnational and multinational companies – without forgetting the role of local capital and businesses – all with the aim of protecting their economic interests.[10]

Gilberto places capitalism as the force tempering with both human rights and the environment for the sake of profit and identifies multinational companies as main actors, aided by local governments and joined by the power of local capital. In his words once more, he sees 'the State and the multinationals merged under a voracious capitalism that does not measure consequences'.

The concept for this performance action emerged out of the conversations with Gilberto and Francisco, in which they emphasised how companies like BP say they bring progress and development to countries in the Global South, but this is not the reality they see in Colombia and in other countries in the region, both in terms of economic development and human rights, and in terms of the consequences that the operations of BP and other oil companies have had in the environment. The idea of fake promises of progress versus the reality of environmental damage and human rights violations became the main message of the performance and gave place to the plot presented earlier.

Despite the obvious differences between traditional theatre and social movement performance, the latter 'employs many of the same considerations as 'proper' theatre in its highly 'improper' work, including compelling and/or outrageous characters, [and] crafted plotlines with clear and exciting dramatic conflict' (Shepard et al., 2008: 14). When looking at this performance action, a crucial element is the character of BP. BP, a clear villain, sounds like a machine. This represents the lack of humanity of corporations and anticipates the blind profit-driven agenda that is manifested towards the end of the performance, when BP breaks down and shouts 'Money!' repeatedly. BP's corporate machine-sounding character also makes evident the distinction between the top tiers of the company – including its PR machine – and other oil industry workers, such as Gilberto himself. It is worth considering, however, the limitations of the agitprop-inspired approach of BP or not BP?, and the way their narratives present villains and heroes. In today's post-modern Britain, the 'enemy' is not as easily identifiable as in the age of grand narratives – one could focus on policy makers who enable fossil fuel companies instead, for instance – and also, 'the chief oppositional formations – the counter-cultures – are not all programmatic in their ideologies, making any kind of didacticism difficult' (Kershaw, 1992: 80). In a climate of austerity, the targeting of cultural sponsors is controversial, and the environmental and human rights narrative that drives it is often countered with neoliberal economic arguments.

In her study of narratives in social movements, Polletta argues that 'as a logic linking events, plot is both heuristic and normative, since the end of the story is also its 'end' in the sense of purpose or telos' (Polletta, 1998: 421). The end of the performance, in which BP breaks down, pours oil from her mouth and lets her true colours show, embodies the aim of BP or not BP?'s campaign: to establish BP as an unethical sponsor and severe its links to cultural institutions in the UK. It also manifests the objective of Gilberto's cause: to expose BP's lies and its role in his abduction, as well as other human rights violations in Colombia. This brings us to considering issues of performativity, as another characteristic of performance-based forms of political action (Pal, 2010: 52) that was integral to this performance. In this performance, Gilberto shares his story as a way of denouncing BP, exposing its lies, and eventually causing BP to crash. Gilberto's performance is therefore a performative act – understanding here that 'the meaning of a performative act is to be found in this apparent coincidence of signifying and enacting' (Butler, 1995: 198). His storytelling not only symbolically destroys BP, but it is also part of a performance that raises the profile of his lawsuit against the same company, and thus directly addresses BP beyond the stage and in the context of a current conflict.

Another issue to consider in reference to this performance and the narrative it creates, however, is the central role that Gilberto's story has in challenging BP's rhetoric. Using Gilberto's story as 'proof' of BP's lying means adopting his perspective, and there might be difficulties then shifting back into a wider Colombian, Latin American, or global perspective on issues of environment and human and workers' rights, considering that 'if you tell your story from the standpoint of a specific character, it may not be easy to step outside this perspective' (Eagleton, 2013: 85). On the same issue, Polletta warns us that 'the protagonists of stories stand in for larger groups or identities . . . yet stories often do not specify criteria for their representativeness. The danger is that the story presents a unitary picture and obscures difference within a group or experience' (Polletta, 1998: 440). In the case of the narratives presented here, it is worth asking which of the workers' perspectives are presented. Is the trade union perspective representative of the whole labour movement? And in the case of Gilberto's story and his statements about corporations in Latin America, can his particular case articulate the struggle of a whole continent and the complex position that multinational corporations have in different countries in the region? The challenges faced in the production of this narrative are therefore not restricted to properly honouring Gilberto's story as testimony, but also related to how this story stands in for wider struggles.

Play and Humour in Activist Theatre

Jess shared that after BP or not BP?'s first few performances, the group realised that 'using performance, using creativity, and something really important: using humour to engage audiences on this issue, had really resonated with a lot of activists, and it was what they were looking for, what they felt was missing from the climate movement'. In the context of social movements the importance of play lies not only in the fact that it provides a mode of expression and action for activists, but also in the fact that it serves to blur the distinction between activists and the public by drawing in audiences, and providing affective modes of relating to others. Play can also provide the emotional support to build and maintain communities, even among heterogeneous groups (Shepard et al., 2008; Shepard, 2011). Furthermore, carnivalesque and playful interventions also act as disturbances in the system, which engage with and respond to the systems and power structures they oppose (Lane, 2007: 358). Seattle 1999 and other protests against the World Trade Organisation, during which people were dancing in the streets, carrying giant puppets, and wearing costumes, are examples of how play and the carnivalesque play a part in 'making the revolution irresistible'. In the fight against big oil, 'play and political performance create spaces where activists feel compelled to challenge seemingly insurmountable targets' (Shepard et al., 2008: 3).

In this performance, the Truth Translators were playful vaudeville figures. They used play and humour to draw an audience in, and also to ridicule the figure of BP, thus undermining its authority. This approach can be compared in spirit to the rebel clowning of the Clandestine Insurgent Rebel Clown Army (CIRCA) (Bogad, 2016), 'a form of radical political activism that brings together the ancient art of clowning and the more recent practice of non-violent direct action' (Fremeaux and Ramsden), using play as a 'political performance' of freedom from repressive forces (Shepard et al., 2008: 2). The Truth Translators used comedy and play as a way of enabling the temporary reappropriation of that space, presenting as non-threatening performance what is in fact a transgression of the rules and boundaries of the institution, and generating as well a kind of unexpected complicity with museum visitors (turned audience).[11]

Play and humour were used as vehicles for platforming Gilberto's voice, but the tone of the performance changed once Gilberto came on stage, and his storytelling shifted the performance towards a more earnest one. Gilberto's performative storytelling acted as testimony against BP's activities, in a direct – albeit mediated by translation – communication of Gilberto's life narrative to a UK audience. Play and humour regained their place, once again, after Gilberto's story, with BP's grotesque crash. In reference to this, Jess says that the performance felt 'disjointed' and that it was 'a performance of two halves'. This raises a question regarding the limits of play, as a strategic performance approach might, on occasion, conflict with the tone of the narrative constructed.

A HISTORY OF BP

In April 2016, BP or not BP? set out to accomplish one of their most ambitious projects so far: a guerrilla exhibition at the British Museum. The exhibition was titled *A History of BP in 10 objects*, and the title, as well as the concept, was a mischievous wink at the museum's landmark exhibition *A History of the World in 100 objects*. This new exhibition brought together slightly over ten artefacts that spoke, in different ways, of BP's history, their practice and what BP or not BP? refer to as a record of environmental and human rights violations. For this action, BP or not BP? worked with frontline communities in places like Canada, West Papua and Colombia who contributed objects representing BP's mark on their land, people and history, which became part of a narrative against BP's sponsorship of the British Museum. The exhibition included objects such as a tear gas cartridge from Egypt, a photo album of a refinery in Indiana, United States, an oil lamp recovered after the floods in Calder Valley, UK, and crude oil from the Gulf of Mexico spill.[12]

The official exhibition text read as follows:

> For the last twenty years, BP has sponsored the British Museum. Over the same period, they've been linked to countless human and environmental abuses, while working to a business plan which makes climate breakdown inevitable. This exhibition brings together objects sent from communities around the world and asks: why does the British Museum continue to work with this corporate criminal?

The objects in display were loosely arranged around four main themes: environment, workers' rights, repression and positive futures. While the set-up of the exhibition morphed during the several hours it ran for, and the location of artefacts changed, these four themes still came through, either through objects that clearly addressed one of the issues specifically, or through objects that addressed several of these issues at once. The crude oil from the Gulf of Mexico, for instance, was an object that brought all of these different struggles and places together, and it also held a specific symbolic power – and a sense of irony – found in the act of bringing real oil as a form of testimony into a space that is sponsored by BP, and which activists are fighting to make 'oil-free'.

Arpillera

Another artefact that was at the centre of the display, and that embodied several of the main themes of the exhibition, was the *Arpillera* (Figure 5.2). The *Arpillera*, a large embroidered piece, was one of the largest and most eye-catching items in the exhibition. Following the tradition of Chilean arpilleras which were used during the military dictatorship as a form of storytelling and spreading news of the atrocities happening in Chile, the embroidered piece was collectively made by a number of London-based groups that are involved in solidarity work with frontline communities in the Global South, and/or working towards the decolonisation of the environmental and social justice movements in the UK. The groups that contributed to the *Arpillera* were London Mexico Solidarity (who acted as coordinators), Expresión Inka, Movimiento Jaguar Despierto, Wretched of the Earth, and BP or not BP?

Figure 5.2. Image of the *Arpillera* being displayed by members of London Mexico Solidarity and The Wretched of the Earth at the *History of BP* exhibition.
© Paula Serafini.

María from London Mexico Solidarity (LMS) shares that for her group, taking part in the exhibition was 'a way of placing Mexican struggles on a global scale, in dialogue with other countries, or with struggles elsewhere'.[13] She adds that it was important to make the object with other groups as well, so it would not just be LMS's vision, but rather 'a more general one of solidarity with struggles of Latin America'.

As María explains, the *Arpillera* features a wealth of images and symbols that represent different aspects of Mexican and broader Latin American struggles and imaginaries:

> The red stars ... are the Zapatista symbol. We put Zapatista women because for London Mexico Solidarity the issue of gender is very important. Corn, flowers, things that represent Mexico. Colours, the mountains, and [on the mountains] we included the issue of BP and the oil spill in the Gulf of Mexico, in order to link what happened in Mexico and the issue of human rights – which is also represented with the silhouettes – with the theme of the exhibition, which was BP and its impact in the Global South and the world more generally. . . . There are some silhouettes that say '43', which stands for the 43 disappeared students of Ayotzinapa. And it says 26,000, which stands for the 26,000 disappeared, and another says 150,000, which stands for the 150,000 people murdered in the last ten years in Mexico in the war against drugs. . . . And one important thing was the issue of natural resources, and how in Mexico the expropriation of natural resources and the privatization of natural resources have led to this war against drugs.

Other elements found on the *Arpillera* include the phrases 'BP is colonialism' and 'They wanted to bury us but they didn't know that we are seeds', the latter embroidered in both English and Spanish.

London Mexico Solidarity strives to combat the narratives that dominate the environmental movement – and its public reception – in the UK and it points out two things. First, the need to talk about colonialism in present tense, in terms of the extraction of resources and violations of human rights that are happening in this day and age by the hand of Global North cconomies. And second, the need to challenge misconceptions of climate change as a non-pressing issue that only middle-class activists have time to worry about. As María explains, 'In these countries of the Global North the environmental issue is seen as something abstract, something concerning polar bears and seagulls, while in our countries people fighting for the preservation of the environment are persecuted and repressed'. Their *Arpillera* challenges these attitudes by creating a visual narrative that shows the links between neo-colonialism in the form of corporate power, human rights, gender and environment.

The *Arpillera* can be seen as a performative object that brings together not only a number of stories into a collective narrative about human and environmental rights in Latin America, but also as a tool and a platform for political action in itself. In the first place, the arpillera, as a medium, is an object of denunciation, with a charged, gendered, political history in Chile. In fact, María shared that after the exhibition LMS and other groups expect to use the *Arpillera* again, seeing it as an object that allows them to speak of what they do and of their solidarity with struggles in Mexico. She says the *Arpillera* can 'enhance the power of the discourse that we have, and occupy other spaces'. Furthermore, the arpillera was performative in its process. Each little house was individually cut out and stitched and carried the name of one of the groups that contributed to the making of the *Arpillera*. The embroidered houses came together on the fabric in order to form a community, while the performative act of collaborative craft making enacted that community (Ravetz et al., 2013).

Presenting and Representing Workers' Struggles

Another object in the exhibition was a hard hat provided by the Blacklist Support Group, which had been creatively intervened with by means of carved words and designs calling for justice for all blacklisted workers. Their participation in the exhibition was prompted by the fact that Carillion, a multinational company that was involved in the blacklisting of workers who were fighting for higher safety standards in the construction industry (Smith and Chamberlain, 2015), is a facilities manager for the British Museum. This hard hat is part of a collection of 'Art Hats'. In the words of the Blacklist Support Group: '"Art Hats" are a visual statement connecting collectivism and environmentalism to express our goal of justice. They render the hard hat neither safe nor functional, drawing on parallels with the multinational construction corporations who Blacklist their workers and people fighting for a sustainable environment before profit'.[14] In a video produced for the exhibition website (see previous endnote), Dave Smith, Secretary for Blacklist Support Group, draws attention to the eleven workers who lost their lives during the Deepwater Horizon spill, and the sixteen workers who died and several who were injured during the Texas City Refinery explosion in 2005, both at the hands of BP. He points to the unaddressed safety issues in both cases and relates them to the struggle of the Blacklist Support Group, referring as well to the environmental consequences of BP's spills. With these statements, the Blacklist Support Group bridge environmental and social justice issues, focusing on the one hand on the case of workers' safety in relation to two companies present at the British Museum – Carillion and BP – and on the other situating their struggle in a wider movement for social and environmental justice, against the power of multinational corporations.

The hard hat was joined in the exhibition by a sunflower (a crafted protest object) from the PCS union; another object that represents the struggles of

UK workers, and in particular the long struggle against the privatisation of National Gallery staff. It is worth noting that the PCS union, which represents a large number of cultural sector workers (including many at the British Museum), officially joined the Art Not Oil coalition in 2015. This is evidence of workers' commitment to environmental issues, but it also reinforces the position that, as Clara Paillard from PCS has argued, 'Privatisation and sponsorship by oil companies are two sides of the same coin'.[15]

When speaking with Jess of the role of workers' struggles in this exhibition, she explained that:

> [O]ur top level ask is 'drop BP', but we are not a single-issue campaign that sees that ask in total isolation from everything else. We want to transform the museum, we want to free the museum from private interests, and when you look at other things that are going on within the museum you realise that there are real challenges for staff, threats of privatisation – privatisation has already happened, it's created multiple tiers of members of staff that have different rights and different pay grades, and different levels of security. . . . So I think [the sunflower] represented the fact that we are trying to work in solidarity with all the groups that are affected by BP, climate change, [and] privatisation of arts and culture.

A 'Disobedient' Exhibition

This action differed from previous BP or not BP? actions in that it did not follow a play script. While there was a performance element to it, found in activists' roles as 'curators' and 'gallery assistants', the 'History of BP' was told through the objects and the accompanying texts and not performed for an audience by a set of characters delivering lines. The exhibition could indeed be read as an installation as well as a performance.

Despite being an activist action and not achieving the display standards of the venue where it was taking place, the exhibition was well received by museum visitors and staff, many of whom dedicatedly went through each exhibit. The collaborative creative labour that went into the exhibition was in fact a reflection of BP or not BP?'s own stance on cultural labour, enacting a DiY, grassroots, collaborative approach that borrows from institutionalised forms – in this case, the exhibition – and subverts this for political use; rather than an exhibition of 'disobedient objects',[16] this was a disobedient exhibition.

In addition to the evident interventionist nature of this particular unsanctioned exhibition, curating can become an activist act in terms of developing the content or theme of an exhibition, the attitudes about the content presented, and the way this is made accessible to an audience, for instance through discursive programming (Cachia, 2014: 259). In this case, the exhibition was not only political in terms of its interventionist approach and its narrative about BP. While acting as testimony of BP's activities, the presence of frontline perspectives from across the globe and from local workers' struggles also contributed to a widening and a decolonisation of the narrow environmental narrative of the Global North.

The form of the exhibition also brings us to consider issues of space, both physical and symbolic. Maria asks, rhetorically: 'The British Museum is "the" representation of Empire. They have stolen everything from all over the world. So, how can you decolonise or re-appropriate a space that is constructed, even physically, as empire? How can we go and appropriate those spaces and make a formal exhibition?' McNamara and McNeill argue that the discourse of politicians usually references 'a particular reading of the spatial history, imagination, and personalities that have a significant claim to' spaces of power (2012: 273). BP or not BP? activists adopted this approach, albeit coming from a grassroots context instead of an institutional politics one. By turning the British Museum's most famous exhibition against them, and doing this within the British Museum walls, BP or not BP? referenced the spatial history of the museum and adopted its language, in order to present evidence of BP's wrongdoings with the aim of pressuring the museum into breaking its sponsorship deal.[17]

CONSTRUCTING NARRATIVES

Polletta (1998) explains that people often resort to narrativity as a way of giving sense to unfamiliar events or changes in the social configuration. The actions presented here created narratives in order to present a conflict, establish the sides in that conflict and make the links between issues such as human rights, workers' struggles, climate change, corporate power and colonialism explicit and visible at a time of environmental, economic and social crisis.

When looking at these narratives, it is important to differentiate between the narratives generated for each performance, and the overarching narratives that lead BP or not BP?, its allies and collaborators (these narratives are at the same time embedded in, and sometimes challenging, the wider narrative of the environmental movement). Looking at the work of BP or not BP? and the statements provided by Jess, Gilberto and María earlier, we can see that environmental issues and workers' rights issues are brought together under a narrative of corporate power, in turn related to a logic of accumulation and forms of neocolonialism that allow the savage extraction of fossil fuels and other resources, particularly in the Global South, tampering both environmental and human rights.

Most of BP or not BP?'s performance actions communicate this overarching narrative in different ways, often through the construction of other sub-narratives. Gilberto's performance told the story of BP's lies being uncovered by the Truth Translators and by his own testimony, which caused BP's true intentions to be exposed and eventually caused BP to crash. In this narrative we can identify a moral, made evident by the Truth Translators' final lines: 'But the truth always comes out in the end'. The narrative took the form of a comedic dramaturgical performance and of performative storytelling, two media (one embedded in the other) that allowed different parts of the narrative and different tones to be communicated.

A History of BP in 10 objects, on the other hand, communicated the overarching narrative against BP through a different subnarrative, and through the practice of curating, itself a discursive medium (Smith, 2015) and a narrative space (Groys, 2013: 44). In the exhibition, the themes of environment, workers' rights, repression and positive futures came together to tell a (hi)story of BP through objects and their accompanying texts. The exhibition format allowed for a different type of narrative, which can be pieced together by visitors as they wander through the displays. The four themes mentioned previously do not tell a progressive story with a beginning and an end, but rather, together they provide a picture of the different facets of BP's practice as perceived by people in places where they operate, and they also hint at the possibility of a future where these instances of repression, environmental damage and suppression of workers' rights are non-existent. The exhibition engages in a dynamic of play, but contrary to Gilberto's performance, this is manifested in the playful subversion or 'culture jamming' (Farrar and Warner, 2008) of the exhibition format and the appropriation of both space and medium as political tools. In this sense, the exhibition is also delving into the field of the curatorial as opposed to curating (Martinon, 2013), as it is a commentary on the role of the exhibition as a medium, and a performative subversion of the format into a political act that challenges the museum, as well as its sponsor.

Another issue to consider in relation to these different narrative levels is that the relationship between subnarratives and the overarching narrative of the group is reciprocal, as they feed into each other and result in an evolving group narrative that changes with every action, determining in turn the subnarratives of subsequent actions. These are also influenced by the narratives put forward by collaborators and allies, and external factors regarding the (spatial) history of the British Museum, such as its imperial past, the themes of its exhibitions and the struggles of its workers.

One final consideration, as pointed out by Jess, is two major challenges of creating performances that bring together a number of different issues, namely tokenism and media coverage:

> How do you create a performance that brings these things, that you can connect but are essentially two different campaigns, calling for two different outcomes, together? How can you do that in a way that isn't just kind of tokenistic? And

then I think as soon as you do try to do that, and you have a more complex or nuanced message or series of messages, it's very difficult to get media coverage for that or to get decent media coverage that gets the connections.

However, she adds, 'one of the things about having multiple messages, is that different bits of media will pick up on different messages and actually you can be getting several different messages out at once, and that can still be a really useful thing to do'. This was the case for Gilberto's performance, Jess shares, and it was the case for other previous actions. The different responses that the media can have to complex narratives and Jess's emphasis on this issue lead us to consider how media coverage and the hope for proper representation of these issues by the media are factors that can condition how actions are planned and hence which narratives are built, when widespread coverage is a key objective in mind.

CONCLUSION

The narratives generated by BP or not BP? in the two actions presented in this chapter show that the group and its collaborators put forward an understanding of social justice and environmentalism as intrinsically connected, and tied to an anti-corporation stance. The narrative that frames the group's work has evolved from an environmental focus and a clear demand: 'drop BP!' to a wider campaign that not only advocates for a fossil-free culture, but also wishes to decolonise the museum and free it from all forms of corporate power and exploitation. The two actions presented here also suggest that human rights and workers' struggles are making visible the connections with environmental issues, from the Blacklist Support Group's statement for a 'sustainable environment before profit' to London Mexico Solidarity's denunciation of corporate and state power's crimes against human rights for the sake of extraction of resources, and consequent environmental damage.

Creating narratives is necessary in order for these movements to generate and sustain cohesion between different elements or facets of the struggle, namely human and workers' rights, the environment, corporate power and neocolonialism. These activists bring into play a series of creative tools that allow them to both generate and share these narratives. These include the theatrical performance, the act of performative storytelling and the guerrilla exhibition. Within these forms, art activists use tools such as humour, performativity and visual symbols for generating these stories, and making the complex links between issues legible to different kinds of audiences.

While there are challenges when bringing together issues of workers' rights and environment into one performance and one clear, coherent narrative – despite the intrinsic connections between these struggles – BP or not BP? moved away from being a single-issue campaign, prompted by collaborations with local groups and frontline communities across the globe, and by a current social climate of austerity that is having its effects felt across issues and sectors of society. This signals a new way for the environmental movement towards a more decolonial approach that is committed to social justice and moves away from single-issue approaches.

NOTES

1. See in relation to this numerous reports published by Platform, including *Dirty Work: Shell's Security Spending in Nigeria and Beyond* by Ben Amunwa (2012).

2. This chapter brings together my first-hand observations from two actions by the group in 2015 and 2016, and interviews with three activists involved in those actions. It is also based on years of involvement with BP or not BP? as a researcher and participant. My analysis of these actions adopts a critical reflection perspective that addresses the internal processes and challenges faced by the group when planning public actions and situates them within wider theoretical debates on art, narrative and activism.

3. I am employing here the term 'art activism' to refer to forms of political action that employ art as a medium. For more on art activism see the introduction to this volume.

4. See for instance Rawlinson, Kevin (2015) 'Activists Occupy British Museum over BP Sponsorship'. *The Guardian.* https://www.theguardian.com/business/2015/sep/13/activists-occupy-british-museum-over-bp-sponsorship and Vartanian, Hrag (2016) 'Art Not Oil Coalition Issues Statement on BP's Sponsorship of UK Cultural Institutions'. *Hyperallergic.* http://hyperallergic.com/316161/art-not-oil-coalition-issues-statement-on-bps-sponsorship-of-uk-cultural-institutions/?ref=featured

5. Personal interview with Jess Worth, 15 July 2016.

6. For more on Gilberto's story see 'Gilberto Torres Survived Colombia's Death Squads. Now He Wants Justice', *The Guardian.* https://www.theguardian.com/world/2015/may/22/gilberto-torres-survived-colombias-death-squads-now-he-wants-justice.

7. It is worth noting that these statements were reproduced verbatim from BP's official website.

8. Script by BP or not BP?, October 2015.

9. As a Spanish speaker, I took on the role of the Spanish-English translation of Gilberto's story on-site.

10. Email interview with Gilberto Torres Martíncz, 14 July 2016. My own translation from Spanish.

11. While this chapter focuses on the construction of narratives rather than their role in facilitating participation and audience interaction, the themes of play and

humour are important to consider both in relation to relational aesthetics and to the collective identity of movements, two key themes in the study of art, labour and activism addressed in the introduction to this book.

12. There was a website built for the exhibition which holds information about the full list of objects, as well as testimonies by the people or groups who contributed them. Visit: historyofbp.org.

13. Personal interview with María de Vecchi on 18 July 2016. My own translation from Spanish.

14. Statement by Blacklist Support Group on the *A History of BP in 10 Objects* website. http://www.historyofbp.org/hard-hat/.

15. Clara Paillard, President of the PCS Culture Sector, has made this statement on several occasions. See for instance an article by Morgan Meaker for *Red Pepper* on oil sponsorship and privatisation: http://www.redpepper.org.uk/national-gallery-workers-strike/.

16. I refer here to the 2014 exhibition *Disobedient Objects* at the Victoria and Albert Museum. The exhibition brought together objects from a number of campaigns and protest movements into a major UK museum, contributing in this way to a wider conversation on the relationship between activism and cultural institutions. For more see: Flood, Catherine and Grindon, Gavin (eds.). (2014) *Disobedient Objects*. London: Victoria & Albert Museum.

17. In other actions, such as those made in response to BP's sponsorship of the exhibition *Indigenous Australia: Enduring Civilisation*, this strategy would be even more relevant as the group made direct reference to the institution's imperial origins and its stolen artefacts.

REFERENCES

Art Not Oil Coalition. 2016. *BP's Cultural Sponsorship: A Corrupting Influence*. Accessed 5 December 2016. http://www.artnotoil.org.uk/sites/default/files/BPs%20Corrupting%20Influence.pdf.pdf.

Bogad, L. M. 2016. *Tactical Performance: The Theory and Practice of Serious Play*. London and New York: Routledge.

Butler, Judith. 1995. 'Burning Acts – Injurious Speech'. In *Performativity and Performance*, edited by Andrew Parker and Eve Kosofsky Sedgwick, 197–227. London and New York: Routledge.

Cachia, Amanda. 2014. '"Disabling" the Museum: Curator as Infrastructural Activist', *Journal of Visual Art Practice 12*.3: 257–89.

Cutter, Susan L. 1995. 'Race, class and environmental justice', *Progress in Human Geography* 19.1: 111–22.

Dhaliwal, Suzanne 2015. 'Why Are Britain's Green Movements an All-White Affair?' *The Guardian*, 28 September 2015. Accessed 18 July 2016. https://www.theguardian.com/environment/2015/sep/28/why-are-britains-green-movements-an-all-white-affair

Eagleton, Terry. 2013. *How to Read Literature*. New Haven, CT: Yale University Press.

Evans, Mel. 2015. *Artwash: Big Oil and the Arts*. London: Pluto.

Farrar, Margaret and Jamie Warner. 2008. 'Spectacular Resistance: The Billionaires for Bush and the Art of Political Culture Jamming'. *Polity: the journal of the Northeastern Political Science Association* 40.3: 273–296.

Fremeaux, Isabelle and Hilary Ramsden. 'We Disobey to Love: Rebel Clowning for Social Justice'. Available at http://www.labofii.net/reflection/. Date N/A, accessed on 4 January 2013.

Godfrey, Rachel. 2012. 'The Political Aspects of Environmentalism in the UK'. *The Institution of Environmental Sciences*. Accessed 3 August 2016. https://www.the-ies.org/sites/default/files/documents/political_aspects_environmentalism.pdf.

Groys, Boris. 2013. *Art Power*. Cambridge, MA and London: The MIT Press.

Gudynas, Eduardo. 2009. 'Diez tesis urgentes sobre el nuevo extractivismo. Contextos y demandas bajo el progresismo sudamericano actual'. In: *Extractivismo, Política y Sociedad*, edited by CAAP (Centro Andino de Acción Popular) and CLAES (Centro Latino Americano de Ecología Social), 187–225. Quito.

Kershaw, Baz. 1992. *The Politics of Performance: Radical Theatre as Cultural Intervention*. London and New York: Routledge.

Kohler, Brian. 2010. 'Decent Jobs or Protection of the Environment? *International Union Rights,* Climate Change & Labour Standards 17.1: 12–13.

Lane, Jill. 2007 'Reverend Billy: Preaching, Protest and Post-Industrial Flanerie'. In *The Performance Studies Reader* (second edition), edited by Henry Bial, 357–68. London and New York: Routledge.

Martinon, Jean-Paul (ed). 2013. *The Curatorial: A Philosophy of Curating*. London and New York: Bloomsbury.

McNamara, Kim and Donald McNeill. 2012. 'The City Personified: The Geopolitical Narratives of Rudy Giuliani'. *Communication and Critical/Cultural Studies* 9.3: 259–78.

Pal, Swati. 2010. 'Theatre and Activism: The Agit Prop Theatre Way'. *Music and Arts in Action* 3.1: 48–64.

Polletta, Francesca. 1998. 'Contending Stories: Narrative in Social Movements'. *Qualitative Sociology* 21.4: 419–46.

Ravetz, Amanda, Alice Kettle and Helen Felcey (eds.). 2013. *Collaboration through Craft*. London and New York: Bloomsbury Academic.

Rimmon-Kenan, Shlomith. 2006. 'Concepts of Narrative'. In 'The Travelling Concept of Narrative', *Studies across Disciplines in the Humanities and Social Sciences 1,* edited by Matti Hyvärinen, Anu Korhonen and Juri Mykkänen: 10–19.

Serafini, Paula. 2014. 'Subversion through Performance: Performance Activism in London'. In *The Political Aesthetics of Global Protest: The Arab Spring and Beyond*, edited by Pnina Werbner, Kathryn Spellman-Poots and Martin Webb. Edinburgh: Edinburgh University Press.

Serafini, Paula. 2015. 'Prefiguring Performance: Participation and Transgression in Environmentalist Activism'. *Third Text* 29.3: 195–206.

Schlosberg, David. 2007. *Defining Environmental Justice: Theories, Movements and Nature*. Oxford: Oxford University Press.

Shepard, Benjamin. 2011. *Play, Creativity, and Social Movements: If I Can't Dance, It's Not My Revolution*. New York: Routledge.

Shepard, Benjamin; L. M. Bogad and Stephen Duncombe. 2008. 'Performing vs. the Insurmountable: Theatrics, Activism, and Social Movements'. *Liminalities: A Journal of Performance Studies* 4.3: 1–30.

Smith, Dave and Phil Chamberlain. 2015. *Blacklisted: The Secret War between Big Business and Union Activists*. Oxford: New Internationalist Publications Ltd.

Smith, Terry. 2015. *Talking Contemporary Curating*. New York: Independent Curators International.

Chapter 6

Working Dancers

Contemporary Dance Activism in Argentina

Konstantina Bousmpoura
and Julia Martinez Heimann

An enormous, empty room, only dimly lit. The first chords of 'Aurora'[1] ring out, evoking the Argentine national flag. The silhouettes of women and men, lit from behind, emerge from a small door at the end of the room. They form a compact group that moves forward timidly with the rhythm of the patriotic anthem while a sinister tone can be heard in the background. Panic takes over their young faces. They are trying to stop an inevitable path.[2]

The Argentine National Company of Contemporary Dance (Compañía Nacional de Danza Contemporánea or CNDC in Spanish) presented its first production, 'Oda a Nosotros mismos, la que sepamos todos'[3] (Ode to Ourselves, the One We All Know), to the public in March 2010, one year after this new artistic group was founded. The new national company emerged from a series of social and political demands made by a group of dancers that aimed to defend their labour rights. They created the Company as a self-managed space founded on the practice of collective leadership.

Awareness of dancers as cultural workers would become the central theme of their struggle and of their collective action with the larger dance community. This took place during the second phase of Kirchnerism, the predominant political movement that held power from 2003 to 2015, which was also the context in which we carried out our ethnographic-film research. 'Kirchnerism' spanned the governments of late President Nestor Kirchner (2003–2007) and former president Cristina Fernández de Kirchner (2007–2015) and was part of the new wave of electoral success of left-wing governments that emerged in Latin America after the crisis of the neoliberal consensus in the late 1990s.[4] Characterised by a marked politicisation of public space, the political cycle of Kirchnerism gave birth to increased discourse around expanding civil and human rights and ultimately enabled the State to respond to and accommodate diverse social demands made by the

Argentinian citizens. Kirchnerism was broadly supported by some key social sectors such as unions, human rights organisations and social movements that originated during the neoliberal crisis.

In this sociopolitical context, the dancers fought for their art to be recognised as labour, assuming their role as political subjects and cultural workers. This required a long struggle for the State to acknowledge their rights as workers. To bolster their demands, they created grassroots networks for collective action, mobilisation and political participation. Meanwhile, to emphasise their political stance as cultural workers they coined the term 'working dancers'.

After six years of essentially living alongside the Company doing ethnographic filming as researchers and filmmakers, we felt compelled to tell the story of the immense human and artistic effort made by this group of fierce, struggling dancers in an attempt to affirm dance as a professional occupation. Our aim is to address artists' labour and transformative role in society, and to reflect on local and global dimensions of this issue. In today's world, how can dancers fight for their labour rights? In order to create a digital archive, we collected material on film and in print between 2007 and 2014 while we were doing our fieldwork and participant observation. During this time we followed the Company throughout their social networks, during their public shows, on tours, and their national media coverage. In the same way that dance moves in and out of politics, the story of struggle that we tell is woven in and out of the visuals in the documentary 'Working dancers' that we produced as a result of our ethnographic film research.

This chapter combines insights from dance history and political theory to focus on the collective actions undertaken by dance groups in Argentina. It looks at how one particular dance group, the CNDC, called for the State to recognise their rights as cultural workers. It specifically addresses the ways in which they created proposals of joint action, aimed at creating a dynamic social movement, which enabled the group to continue their fight (on a larger social platform).

DANCE ACTIVISM AND POLITICS

An avenue cut off in the heart of Buenos Aires, traffic at a standstill alongside the City Congress. A crowd is gathering around a group of young dancers who perform a choreography, blindfolded, to the song 'La Maza', as interpreted by Mercedes Sosa[5] 'If I didn't believe in those who listen/If didn't believe in the things that hurt/If I didn't believe in the things that struggle/ What would a hammer be without a quarry?' When the song finishes the dancers embrace one another and sing in unison:

> Workers united, and if you don't like it, screw you, screw you.[6]

In 2007, the dancers of the San Martin Theater Contemporary Ballet (Ballet Contemporáneo del Teatro San Martín or BCTSM in Spanish)[7] in Buenos Aires found themselves in a fierce struggle against the very institution that employed them. Over the previous year, due to the extremely high physical demands of 'The Tempest',[8] a piece the Ballet had been rehearsing, four dancers suffered from meniscus injuries and were faced with a desperate situation: they had to stop training and dancing for long periods of time and had to cover medical and surgical expenses on their own. The event that finally brought the existing anxiety among the group to a head, and which represented a turning point for their professional futures, was the shocking accident suffered by Victoria, one of the dancers, during a rehearsal. Victoria broke the bridge of her nose, which affected her breathing capacity. The disdainful attitude of the BCTSM authorities, who did not take responsibility for the accident, made the dancers fully aware of the precarious conditions in which they were working: their lack of health coverage and labour rights.

In terms of artistic support and collective consciousness, Victoria's accident uncovered the need for workers to demand that the BCTSM create legal in-house positions for its workers in all areas of the Theatre, a shared sentiment of the working dancers that had been repressed for fear of reprisals. Since the Theatre's beginnings, dancers had 'service agreements' which, although renewable annually, left them vulnerable in the event of any political, economic or administrative change. In the interviews we held with the BCTSM dancers at the beginning of our ethnographic film research (2009), the dancers expressed this idea repeatedly. To begin with, the dancers asked for occupational risk insurance through a letter sent to all the relevant authorities, from the BCTSM Director up to the City Mayor of Buenos Aires. The letters were never answered. As accidents and surgeries went on without anyone listening to their demands, the dancers decided to join the State Employees Association (Asociación de Trabajadores del Estado or ATE in Spanish) and fight for their labour rights as cultural workers. The image of the dancer-activist fighting for their rights began to emerge in Argentina's socio-political scene by the end of 2007.

First, they decided to take the streets and make their demand visible. As cultural workers, they were asking the City Government[9] to provide them with better medical coverage for healthcare access and compensation insurance for injuries, maternity leave and the chance to pay into retirement savings funds. The occupation of public spaces led to the dancers being invited to TV and radio shows. For over two months, 'dance-protests' were held in the streets every Monday – the only day of the week the city's theatres are closed – and they captured the attention of TV cameras and newspaper reporters. *Perfil*, an Argentine biweekly newspaper, dedicated a whole section to the 'dance conflict' on 9 December 2007, with photographs of the protests and interviews with the dancers. Some of the headlines included:

'Why Contemporary Dance is Still in the Streets', 'Multiple and Renewed Issues in the Dance Sector' and 'The Explanation by the Ballet's Director; He Attempts to Make Peace with the Demand'.

Second, in order to organise their fight on the streets and to explain the cause of their struggle, they created the blog 'bailarinesorganizados.blogspot.nl' – still active, in which they reported the *new direction* of their future actions: 'To not give up and to start a collective project that advances the group's core values' – these values can be summarised as democracy, unity, respect, tolerance, sociability and collective work. People trying to cross the city centre stopped to enjoy the free performances by the Ballet while the street was taken over by dance and music performed by Argentine folk music legends. In this way, the dancers' demand became visible in the public sphere through media coverage of the dispute. The Theatre's directors responded to the demand by dismissing seven of the most important artists, including two trade union representatives – Bettina and Ernesto – and four members of another unionised cultural organisation. Dismissals took place due to alleged 'artistic differences' which, according to the BCTSM, 'were not in line with the type of company the Theatre was proposing'.

Some weeks after the dismissals, on 17 December 2007, at a national entertainment awards ceremony, the 'Premios Clarin 2007', all cameras were trained on the industry nominees, as chosen by a renowned and rigorous jury. Ernesto Chacón Oribe makes his way through the theatre to the stage. He takes his award and stands in front of the microphone:

> Ernesto: Thank you very much. The truth is I am deeply moved. This is a very special moment for me, and for the whole San Martin Theatre Ballet, which is turning 30 this year. Existing as it has for 30 years without ever having been legally or officially established. I brought something I wrote. This year, we, the dancers, took to the streets. We danced in the streets to claim our labour rights. Because it seems that there are some government officials who think that we, as working artists, should not have labour rights. All we were asking for was that the City Government provides us with better health conditions, access to medical coverage, to workers' compensation insurance, for the injuries, the accidents we suffer. The chance to pay into retirement funds. To have a regulatory framework and legally establish the company. Unfortunately and unjustly, the discriminatory attitude of the general management of the San Martin Theatre ... was to respond by firing seven of the best artists in the company, and I am one of them. Committing a true artistic genocide and, as a result, instilling a fear of making demands and a fear of speaking the truth, despite being in democracy. This award is not just recognition of my personal effort, but also a recognition of the effort and courage of all the members of the San Martin Contemporary Ballet. I dedicate this award to all the artists, and to all the people, who are not afraid to speak the truth and to fight for a fairer Argentina![10]

With this political-performative action, Ernesto amplified the dancers' demands within the public sphere and highlighted the country's historical context, in which the dancers demanded to be considered 'cultural workers'. Since the mid-1980s, dance scholarship has played a major role in situating dance and movement in the broader framework of politics and history as an interdisciplinary field of study. In his article 'Dance and the Political: States of Exception (2006)', Mark Franko states that dance can only be perceived through the lens of politics by resetting history. He asks us to consider that:

> On a micro-historical level, dance may perform protest, a direct and local way of upsetting a power balance. What the body itself, when given pride of place, can be thought of opposing also lends a definition as to how dance can cause the political to flare-up. (Franko, 2006: 6)

Ernesto finished his speech and the audience cheered loudly. He had taken the floor and denounced the historic conflict with the Theatre's directors and the Government of the City of Buenos Aires that was making dancers' jobs insecure and leaving them in a state of injustice and vulnerability. Susan Leigh Foster, when debating the dance studies discipline, suggests that the relationship between dance and history should be considered as a methodological shift from the moving body to the written word. In Foster's words:

> A body, whether sitting writing or standing thinking or walking talking or running screaming, is a bodily writing. Its habits and stances, gestures and demonstrations, every action of its various regions, areas, and parts – all these emerge out of cultural practices, verbal or not, that construct corporeal meaning. Each of the body's moves, as with all writings, traces the physical fact of movement and also an array of references to conceptual entities and events. (Foster, 2010: 291)

By encouraging people to 'fight for a fairer Argentina', Ernesto, with his gestures, voice, memory and words – which construct corporeal meaning – revealed some characteristics of the socio-political situation in which these demands took place and the significance of the recent historical events in Argentina. On the one hand, he mentioned the full democracy in which he is immersed, which clashed with the situation he had experienced, and which he depicted as a fear of making demands and a cultural genocide. Born in 1978, in the midst of the military dictatorship[11] in Argentina, Ernesto picked words like arrows in the political imagery of a country that has been a democracy for less than thirty years.

Under these terms, he first evoked the reality of the Ballet, created in 1977 during the dictatorship, establishing a link between the events he denounced and totalitarian expressions; then, the reason for his current situation as a jobless artist-advocate became evident. It is worth recalling that Ernesto had led the first demonstrations in the street and was a union delegate for ATE and one of the former dancers of the BCTSM with leading roles in the Ballet's productions. On the other hand, the resolve in his voice, like that of many 'historic' voices, calls for the recognition of dancers as cultural workers. Ernesto spoke as a mobilised, active, leading citizen, part of a democracy that necessarily enshrines the dancers' demands for labour rights. The dancers trusted in both the legitimacy of their demands and their chances of achieving a positive response – changes in government policy that acknowledge dancers as cultural workers. As we will see later, Ernesto's speech set the foundations for a series of performances and political mobilisations that would be held around the country to advocate for renewed labour policies for dancers. According to Franko:

> It is justifiable and necessary to speak of dance as political in circumstances that are conjunctural, that is, in circumstances where forms of movement and socio-political life take shape simultaneously if apparently independently. (Franko, 2006: 4)

In order to better understand contemporary performative protest, it is important to look further into the historical and political background of Argentina and address why, how and in what context such performative protests and artistic demands are possible.

Figure 6.1. CNDC, Ode to Ourselves, the One We All Know, 2010.
© Marcelo Raggone.

HISTORICAL BACKGROUND AND SOCIAL PROTESTS

Maristella Svampa, in her article 'Movimientos sociales, gobiernos, y nuevos escenarios de conflicto en América Latina (2010)' (Social Movements, Governments and New Scenarios of Conflict in Latin America), specifically looks into the link between existing social movements and the political matrix of governments in Latin America from 2000 onwards. The author acknowledges a change of era in the region, associated with a myriad of social and political processes, including a crisis of the neoliberal consensus, the emergence of so-called 'progressive' centre-left governments that value building a common Latin American identity and a stronger State presence. She suggests that these changes are accompanied by a new cycle of collective action by social movements that ultimately leads to 'the possibility of creatively thinking about the articulations between the State and society, between representative democracy and direct and participatory democracy, between institutional and non-institutional spaces, between the public State sphere and the public non-State sphere, among others' (Svampa, 2010: 27). Despite emergent issues and heterogeneous demands, collective actions and social movements are able to establish themselves successfully due to their actions as leading agents for that period. In turn, these collective actions legitimise other ways of conceiving politics.

In Argentina in particular, the path of social movements has laid out a new 'activist ethos'. Building on the human rights organisations that emerged after the last military dictatorship (H.I.J.O.S, Abuelas de Plaza de Mayo, Asociación de Madres Plaza de Mayo) and strong movements of the unemployed and 'piqueteros' (groups that temporarily block strategic roads as part of a bargaining technique), which emerged in the years leading up to the 2001 crisis[12] and period of unrest, 'a new generation of activists became established, bringing together ideas of territory, assembly activism, the demand for autonomy and horizontality in political bonds' (Svampa, 2009:18). In this period, many cultural collectives (visual artists, filmmakers, alternative journalists, social activists, poets) promoted new forms of intervention, linked to historical events,[13] which enabled them to move away from the known frames of action and routines of protest, and to create new forms of intervention: assemblies, factories taken over by workers, bartering, graphic intervention, 'escraches' (a type of demonstration in which a group of activists go to the homes or workplaces of those whom they want to condemn to publicly humiliate them) and other forms of action (Svampa, 2009).

Svampa (2009) recognises a second stage of the 'activist ethos' in Argentina from 2003 onwards, which coincides with Nestor Kirchner's government and the return of a patriotic and grassroots discourse. The strength and trust in collective actions and their new expressions born out of the new activism of 2001 were expressed in this new stage, even within grassroots trade unionism. Svampa states that, during the 'Kirchnerist' political cycle from 2003 to 2004, 'a new generation of young union delegates emerged after many years of apparent inaction and lack of faith in trade unions, who gave a new value to trade unionism as a tool for fighting for workers rights' (Svampa, 2009:18).

In his analysis of the political cycle known as 'Kirchnerism' (2003–2015) – a period following on from one of the worst economic, political and institutional crises in Argentina – Argentine political scientist Eduardo Rinesi reviews the ways in which the dominant discourses during this cycle furthered the concept of democracy as connected to rights within the context of a new relationship between State and society (Rinesi, 2013). He particularly analyses the changing meanings of the theoretical-political practice of democracy in that context. Rinesi points out that, just as democracy was thought of as a utopia in the 1980s, by the 1990s it was seen as routine, and around the 2001 upheaval as a convulsion; as of 2003 onwards, dominant discourses began using the term democratisation rather than democracy.

Today, in Argentina, democratisation is used to refer to the process of the full enjoyment of a vast set of rights: civil, economic, social and political rights (and to go even further: marital, identity, educational, labour and retirement rights) which make our society, in the terms in which we now tend to think about the world, more and more democratic (Rinesi, 2013: 24).

Rinesi concludes that, by introducing the question of rights in the exercise of politics, the Kirchnerist State moves from a focus on freedom to a focus on rights. In this regard, the development of conceptions of democracy during the 'Kirchnerism' political cycle is the equivalent of moving further in terms of acquiring rights.

In order to take a closer look at the complexity and heterogeneity of dancers' collective actions within Argentina's particular historical and political context, we propose incorporating the concept of 'demand' as developed by Ernesto Laclau in his text 'On Populist Reason' (Laclau, 2005). By analysing the structure of populism as a social logic and way of constructing political logic, the author introduces the use of this concept as an analytical category and moves towards the creation of what he calls 'chains of equivalences' within the context of social movements. According to Laclau, the internal characteristics of the demands, which could be either more precise or structured or more autonomous and specific, modify the ways in which they relate to other demands (Laclau, 2005). Thus, a very specific demand should be subjected to continuous negotiation processes to become equivalent with others. The logic of equivalences is achievable by overcoming the antagonisms in a plurality of demands and by converging the shared characteristics. One of the points where the demands converge is by identifying the *other* against whom a demand is being made.

Regarding that *other* against whom the dancers are making a demand, the importance of the following statement by Laclau should be borne in mind:

> At first, the social protest had a non-political bias – remember the chant 'they [the politicians] should all go'. The great achievement of 'Kirchnerism' in that regard was the creation of channels for those social demands to influence State policies, and thereby overcome their non-political nature. However, the new aspect that differs from classic populism is that the creation of grassroots chains of equivalence is verified through social agents whose original identity was established outside those chains and whose autonomy cannot be wavered. (Laclau, 2013: 16–17).

In this sociopolitical context in Argentina, the social demand by a group of dancers to be considered working dancers in defence of their rights is enshrined, from a semiotic point of view, in the cultural policy undertaken by the State. Although the struggle seems to emerge independently and with its own characteristics, as we will see later, it is connected to the political identity of dancers throughout history. The dancers demonstrated political awareness of their role as cultural workers within the policy framework of a State that capitalised upon the social demands of different stakeholders in relation to acquiring rights.

In Mark Franko's words:

> A contemporary art movement and a state apparatus have come face-to-face at a crucial moment in the development of each of them; something new is being created, both artistically and politically, that reveals the contradictory forces and tendencies at work. (Franko, 2006: 3)

'NUEVOS RUMBOS'

Ernesto's speech not only placed the working dancers' demand in the public sphere, but also set the ideological foundations for a series of actions that would take place immediately after. The dancer-advocate, assuming his transforming role, gained visibility in several public spaces by taking political as well as performance action. His premonitory statement of 'not giving up and starting a collective project that disseminates core values' had immediate effect.

In April 2008, six of the dancers who had been dismissed (Victoria Hidalgo, Bettina Quintá, Wanda Ramírez, Ernesto Chacón Oribe, Pablo Fermani and Jack Syzard) created an independent company *Nuevos Rumbos* ('New Directions') in order to get by financially and continue developing as dancers at the peak of their careers (most of them were around twenty-five years old), under a structure that they felt was in line with their principles. In their words, the founding goal was

> to bring back to dancing its cultural role and responsibility, to try to promote core values such as communication, democracy, unity, respect, tolerance, sociability, collective work, participation and freedom of expression; trying not only to evoke those issues through dancing, but also mainly to promote those values by working and operating collectively.

Nuevos Rumbos worked thanks to the efforts of its members: by giving one another training classes every day, by creating their own choreographies and by swapping roles as dancers, choreographers and directors. While they were striving to strengthen their project, the conflict with the Theatre's directors and the Government of the City of Buenos Aires turned into a legal dispute as the dancers had submitted a formal complaint specifying the link between their dismissal and their political participation in ATE and the Instituto Nacional contra la Discriminación, Xenofobia y el Racismo (INADI, the National Institute against Discrimination, Xenophobia and Racism). Although the situation was complex, 2008 was a very active year for *Nuevos Rumbos* and they consolidated as a group with an identity of their own, thanks to their collective effort and awareness of their role as cultural workers. In that year, they performed pieces with significant social and political commitment and collaborated with other groups, such as Madres de Plaza de Mayo (the association of Argentine mothers whose children were 'disappeared' by State terrorism during the military dictatorship between 1976 and 1983). The play *Madre e hijo* ('Mother and Son') was a milestone in this period. In this piece, a mother's search for her missing son is expressed through contemporary dance, until his *disappearance* becomes real when she decides to wear a white scarf – the symbol of the Madres – on her head. All the Company's plays were a declaration of their founding values and a clear statement of their intention to produce dance pieces that told Argentina's recent history from a critical perspective that had gained momentum during the Kirchernist period.

With the help of the labour union and the dancers from the Ballet Folklórico Nacional (National Folkloric Ballet), who had joined and supported them in the street demonstrations, the Company was offered a place to rehearse in the Ballet Folklórico Nacional's venue, an iconic building for Argentine culture: the original premises of the National Library. The decision was agreed to by authorities of the Secretaría de Cultura de la Nación (National Agency for Cultural Affairs), who let the Company use the space and also showed an interest in the project submitted by the group: the creation of a state-supported contemporary dance company under its own collective direction.

On 29 February 2009, the first National Company of Contemporary Dance (Compañía Nacional de Danza Contemporánea or CNDC in Spanish) was finally created with the same founding values as *Nuevo Rumbos* and under the collegiate direction of three of its members. Victoria, Bettina and Ernesto were the founders and the first directors of CNDC. The three co-directors of the collegiate leadership, based on the principles of participatory democracy and a horizontal decision-making structure, would be in charge of the difficult task of creating the Company and directing their fellow dancers and the technical team, while also advocating for their labour rights through their affiliation to ATE.

The imperative issues relating to civic and human rights which were finally gaining greater recognition through the movement's historical claims would be manifested through a production that commemorated Argentina's 200th anniversary. That commemorative piece was named *Retazos pequeños de nuestra historia más reciente* (Small Patchworks of our Most Recent History) (2010). This work, choreographed by Daniel Payero, one of the oldest members of the Company, marked the first period of the CNDC under the collective leadership of Bettina, Victoria and Ernesto (2009–2013).

Mark Franko holds that 'politics can also be internal to dance. . . . One can say by extension that in dance we read the relation of dancer to choreographer as a political relation' (Franko, 2006: 8). In this regard, he emphasises the political significance of both dancers and choreographers, and the ways in which their relationship – as a socio-political connection in itself – is made visible in public performances.

With *Retazos* the Company shared with Argentine society their desire to think about how to reconcile 'historical pain' without forgetting those painful events, in the context of full democracy. Ultimately, the piece also expressed the political relationship established among all the Company's dancers and made visible the performative language used to convey such relation. The dancers continued to play their roles as artist-activists in their performative dimension. The piece featured different fragmented performances representing some of the most important events in Argentine history, which have shaped the collective imagination: the struggle by the *Madres de Plaza de Mayo*, the military dictatorship and political persecution, the 1990s – characterised by the fierce emergence of neoliberalism – the regaining of consciousness and political debate, and the attainment of same-sex marriage, among others. Daniel Payero chose to end the piece with a group kiss, in which the embraces between several same-sex couples stand out. It is a celebration of having won the fight for same-sex marriage, approved by the National Senate in July 2010, a landmark that made Argentina the first country in Latin America to recognise this right. Although we are assuming that collective actions taking place at the same historical moment and on the same socio-political

Figure 6.2. CNDC, *Small Patchworks of Our Most Recent History*, 2010. An allegorical scene to celebrate the approval of the same-sex marriage law in Argentina.
© Marcelo Raggone.

stage are heterogeneous in their demands, we would suggest they have a unifying potential in their frames of action (Svampa 2010).

So far, we have seen how a group of dancers started the fight for their labour rights and the actions they carried out: street demonstrations; alliances with the dance community; public denouncements and political participation; the creation of *Nuevos Rumbos*, articulating dance and society; and finally, the birth of the CNDC, articulating dance with the National Government and the effect of dancers' work on the socio-political events of the country. The idea brought to the table by Svampa – to contextualise 'the new cycle of collective action' within an era of change in Latin America – is characterised by the link between State and society. This idea would go on to find its equivalent in the dance community's cycle of collective action toward fulfilling its demand for recognition of the cultural worker.

METHODOLOGICAL SHIFT: FROM FILMIC ETHNOGRAPHY TO AUDIOVISUAL PRODUCTION

The ethnographic film project began in 2009 with the observation and recording of a ten-member company. Just five years later, the number of dancers in the CNDC had risen to thirty and its internal dynamics had changed in response to the diversity of the new group. This re-configuration, as well as our own personal experiences, made us rethink the final aims of the research and the working methodology. As filmmakers with an academic background in Anthropology, from the very beginning we incorporated a camera as a tool for participant observation and for collecting and producing data. Filming was part of the research process and, as such, it organised the relationship with the subjects being filmed, to some extent.

Maria Julia Carozzi proposes focusing on the link between words and movement, between verbalisation and motor skills, in specific contexts rather than separating words from movement in research practices in dance anthropology (Carozzi, 2011). Therefore, we based our methodology for the ethnographic filming process on 'the words exchanged between the subjects studied and with the anthropologist before, during and after they dance or watch someone else dance' (Carozzi, 2011: 32). In particular, we considered it of utmost importance to observe and record the Company's spaces for collective thought – their assemblies and group discussions- and the discursive analysis of these consolidated spaces as part of their work.

At the same time we felt part of this historical process and identified with the core issue of 'socially and politically engaged artists'. The question of whether art should be considered as a job had become deeply sensitive to us due to the difficulties we had in finding ways to support our ethnographic film project without financial resources of our own. We decided to submit a project to the National Institute of Cinema and Visual Arts[14] (Instituto Nacional de Cine y Artes Audiovisuales or INCAA in Spanish) and, a couple of months later, they confirmed their support. We accessed a grant that allowed us to fully carry out our project and achieve our goals: the documentation and dissemination of a historical social movement.

BEING A STATE ARTIST: THE CHALLENGE OF UNITING IN TIMES OF DIVERSITY

Beginning in 2012, the CNDC had entered a period of crisis stemming from concerns regarding its organisational structure: at times, it was divided into different committees; at others, there were no directors, something that led to the need to rethink the feasibility of the model of collective direction. In order to overcome this crisis, the members of the Company decided to vote on a change in their organisational structure. As a result of the secret, direct vote by all the workers on the Company's artistic and technical teams, they chose to bring on an artistic director for a two-year term to streamline decision-making processes.

This was yet another pivotal moment in their political project, because the election of an artistic director was seen by many of the new members of the Company as a threat to their creative autonomy. On the one hand, the original proposal backed by the State had twelve dancers and the objective was to gain labour rights for the dancers as state employees. As the Company grew and came to have twenty dancers under contract who saw their demand for labour rights fulfilled, this objective changed. Since 2013, the question arose among the Company's members as to how to maintain creative autonomy whilst being State-sponsored artists and meeting their obligations as state workers.

The incorporation of new members from very different artistic backgrounds had also created an extremely tense atmosphere between the oldest members and founders of the Company and the new ones in meetings. Even if it seemed the core pillars on which the Company had been founded could be challenged in this new stage, as a result of frequent discussions and the lack of agreement in the assemblies, in the end, the multiple opinions came together in favour of unity. The Company stayed true to its policy of deciding and voting on all issues concerning their artistic and political work, and this strategy turned out to be a unifying element amongst the heterogeneous voices. As Diego, one of the first members of the Company, said, 'what characterises our Company is democracy and voting on everything. Voting is the dynamic. It is what bring us all together'.

The predominant discourses within the CNDC, evident through concrete and specific actions – the selection of teachers and choreographers, voting for union delegates, performing shows in prisons and in the Children's Hospital, their participation in the country's commemorative events, tours around the provinces, and the 'Partido-Compartido'[15] programs – were all aimed at the idea of democratising dance in the sense of extending the right to participate in the Company's projects to all of society.

Despite their questioning of the State, its mechanisms and the tendency of some members of the Company to challenge authorities by suggesting new alternatives, the discourses by the founders and the actions by the Company were still aligned with the State policy of that time. In fact, the policy of democratisation was always exerted in two spheres: the acquisition of labour rights and the right to 'dance for all.' However, this emphasis on permanent exchange and search for consensus led to difficulties in delegating and, as a result, the first artistic director of the Company would then be limited to managing the CNDC with little decision-making power over artistic activities.

Argentina's first national company of contemporary dance came into existence as a result of a growing demand for dancers to be recognised as cultural workers. This demand left a permanent mark on the company's genealogy. Nevertheless the dancers' collective efforts to create the CNDC and gain labour rights for State dancers cannot be seen as an autonomous attempt, isolated from the dance community as a whole. Since the beginning of their story, they considered themselves cultural workers belonging to a dance community. Many of the members of the Company had also joined the social movement in favour of the constitution of the National Dance Law, which had been under development since 2007 by another group of dancers.

ARTICULATIONS AND COLLECTIVE ACTIONS

29 April 2014. International Day of Dance. A big stage has been set up in front of the Argentine National Congress, and a banner reads: 'Dance is mobilising for its Law'. In spite of the increasing rain, the audience has gathered to watch the first performance. Forming a straight line, ten dancers move back and forth choreographically, swiping mops to dry away the water on the floor. They are preparing the space for the large amount of performances expected to take place that day.[16]

El 'Movimiento por la Ley nacional de Danza' (the Movement for the National Dance Law) had spent several years trying to get the National Dance Law passed in the National Congress. First led by the 'Grupo independiente por una ley nacional de danza' (the Independent Group for a National Dance Law), the movement had grown significantly as it expanded across the country, incorporating many dance companies that shared similar needs. The creation of a new, self-governing body, the 'Instituto Federal de Danza' (the Federal Institute of Dance), was central to the demands being made by the social movement, and, from the very start, it defined those who it regards as 'cultural workers', in terms of subjects who perform the body movement activity known as 'dance', whether in direct relation to an audience or not.

Figure 6.3. Street performance in the Congress Square of Buenos Aires in defence of the National Dance Law, 29 April 2014.
© Javier Fuentes.

In this way, working dancers are 'interpreters, choreographers, directors, teachers, rehearsers, researchers, managers, producers, critics and all other roles that may be created in the future'.[17] The 'Kirchnerist' State was being asked to allow for the possibility of creating a new law, *a new channel*, in Laclau's words, so that the demand for the creation of such an institute would be included in State public policies. The core idea of the demand is emphasised in the document written as a draft National Dance Law:

> [this new institution] will be directed by representatives of the Executive Power and representatives from the dance movement, in order to guarantee long-term strategic policies. Therefore, the cultural policy for dance is not subjected to the good will of authorities in power, while the dance community becomes an active party in the development of that process.[18]

At the time when the event took place, the CNDC's priority demands did not coincide with those being presented by the larger movement for a National Dance Law. Having made a space for itself within the State, the CNDC's new demands were oriented towards dancers' retirement benefits and the attempt to consolidate a new organisational structure for their Company. However, the new members' questioning of how cultural workers can exercise their artistic autonomy while working for the State allowed them to overcome the antagonisms (Laclau, 2005) and, within the particularities of their demands, identify commonalities with other dance groups. According to Ernesto Laclau, the social is built by tracing an *antagonistic border; s*pecifically, by 'partially backing down on the particularities [of the demand], highlighting what all the particularities have in common' (Laclau, 2005: 104). As Setién, one of the most recent additions to the Company, said: 'We all know what the State structure is like. . . . I don't think a Company should be an armoured space . . . nor an industrial space'.

By highlighting the autonomy of the artist within the CNDC, a door was opened to find similarities in the demands made by other dance groups that were fighting from outside the framework of the State. It is worth noting that, following Laclau, the presence of social actors whose identity had been modelled outside the 'State channel' – such as the new members of the CNDC – enabled the creation of 'chains of equivalency' (Laclau, 2005). That is why several members of the Company had been involved in the organisation of an event for debating the dance law in National Congress, where they connected with other non-State dance groups fighting for the federalisation of resources and recognition of the provinces. Moreover, within the logic of promoting unity in the face of adversity that characterised the Company, the vote in favour of supporting the group organising the event on 29 April (29A) was immediate and unanimous.

Fourteen dance collectives performed during the crowded event, which brought traffic to a standstill for several hours in the middle of downtown Buenos Aires. Among the groups performing were the current Contemporary Ballet of the San Martin Theater (still under the leadership of the same director who had been involved in firing the dancers), the Teatro Colón Ballet and the Folkloric Ballet of the University College of Arts-IUNA. Stars from the Argentine dance scene also participated in the event. The CNDC was represented by two dancers who, due to parenting responsibilities, had not gone on the Company's first Brazilian tour. Off stage, open classes and workshops were held throughout the day, culminating with a massive flashmob in front of the National Congress, choreographed in part by Laura Roatta, a teacher and choreographer at CNDC during its early years.

CONCLUSION

The fight for the National Dance Law in Argentina formed a link between the actions and activism led by different agents and groups, each of which was born out of specific claims that later converged in that specific sociohistorical moment. In the following years members of Congress failed to address the draft law introduced to Parliament in 2013, and as a consequence it lost parliamentary status. Nevertheless the movement gained a notable boost with the networking of national dance collectives. In 2016, the draft law was presented in Congress again and is currently being discussed in the Congressional Cultural Commission.

The initial demand for the recognition of the figure of 'cultural worker', as observed in the case of Argentina, can result in a powerful political demand that leads to transformations that exceed the granting of rights to the group initially involved. Despite the initial association between the CNDC and the Kirchernism movement, the Company's demands did not remain bound to the Kirchnerist political period ending in December 2015. Rather, to the contrary, the CNDC conciliated the many voices of its members and chose to invest its efforts in community participation and in continuing to support initiatives that affect the whole dance community in the long run, such as retirement for dancers. Nonetheless, the CNDC's institutional structure and nature continue to evolve.

Both the Argentine dance community's struggle and our own documentary serve as testimonies for other collective struggles led by civil society, and, in particular, for those addressing the role of the artist as a cultural worker in contemporary democratic societies.

NOTES

1. This refers to an aria *Alta in the sky* from the opera Aurora (composed by Héctor Panizza) which is used as tribute to the Argentinian flag.

2. All script quotations are from the feature-length documentary *Working Dancers* by Julia Martinez Heimann and Konstantina Bousmpoura, which is stored as an unpublished work in custody of Argentina's National Copyright Office, file number 5068238. Konstantina Bousmpoura and Julia Martinez Heimann, Greek and Argentine filmmakers and researchers, collaborated to create this documentary alongside Argentina's first National Company of Contemporary Dance, following their lives and their struggle for acknowledgement during the course of six years. The website for the project is: www.workingdancers.com.

3. Trailer for 'La que sepamos todos (Oda a nosotros mismos)' https://www.youtube.com/watch?v=MjRELalQFAw.

4. The aim of this chapter is not to analyse the political movement of Kirchnerism in the context of the rise of the contemporary left in Latin America after the neoliberal crisis. For further analysis of post-neoliberalism and the rise of left-wing governments in Latin America, please see Mitchelle A. Seligson (2007), Sarah Hunt (2012) and Christopher Wylde (2011).

5. Music by Cuban singer-songwriter and poet Silvio Rodriguez. Interpretation by Mercedes Sosa, an Argentinian folklore singer known as one of the leading voices in Latin American folk music.

6. Ibid., i.

7. The City of Buenos Aires is an autonomous district federalised and removed from the Buenos Aires Province in 1880. The General San Martin Municipal Theater (TGSM in Spanish) responds to the government of the City of Buenos Aires. Inaugurated in 1960, it is one of the most important theatres in Argentina. In recent years, it has suffered from an unrelenting decline. The City's 2013 Audit Report found anomalies in the use and management of public funds and weaknesses is operational management internal communication. The Contemporary Ballet of the San Martin Theater is the resident ensemble of the City of Buenos Aires, housed at TGSM and created in 1977 during Argentina's last military dictatorship (1977–1983).

8. Choreographic version of Shakespeare's *The Tempest*, directed by Mauricio Wainrot, Director of the San Martin Theater Contemporary Ballet from 1999 to 2016, with Ernesto Chacon Oribe as lead (solo) dancer in the role of Prospero.

9. The year 2007 was an intense year in terms of Argentine politics. Presidential, legislative, provincial and municipal elections were held. On 10 December, Cristina Fernández de Kirchner assumed the presidency and Mauricio Macri was inaugurated as mayor of the autonomous City of Buenos Aires. As leaders of markedly opposed political movements, these two figures became symbols of fierce opposition in the political realm – a tension that was further amplified by the media.

10. Video clip from the event: https://www.youtube.com/watch?v=-YTkq89Yqvo. All dance groups used Ernesto's speech widely during their subsequent struggles.

11. Argentina's last civic-military dictatorship began with a coup d'état that ousted then president María Estela Martínez de Perón on 24 March 1976. The so-called National Reorganisation Process, commanded by the then Lieutenant General Jorge

Rafael Videla, was characterised by the violent repression of oppositional political and social organisations, the systematic disappearance of people considered to be subversive (which reached 30,000 cases) and economic liberalisation with opening of imports, privatisation and debt accumulation.

12. The 2001 crisis was an economic, political and social crisis resulting from the neoliberal economic policies that were implemented starting in the last civic-military dictatorship and from the severe, ongoing economic recession that Argentina suffered in the 1990s. It led to an unprecedented social upheaval that took the lives of thirty-nine people in street protests and caused the resignation of the then-president Fernando De la Rúa.

13. Such as the devastating effects of the neoliberal overhaul of the economy during the 1990s, the upheaval in 2001 and the subsequent spread of institutional and police violence, including the murders of Dario Kosteki and Maximiliano Santillán.

14. Argentine documentary filmmakers struggled for recognition of their profession, which, in 2007, led the National Institute of Cinematography to create a specific funding mechanism that supports the production of digital documentaries and recognises the figure of 'Integral Documentary Filmmaker'.

15. 'Partido y compartido' (or 'Broken and shared' 24τη) was offered to independent dance groups as a space in which they could promote their activities, in an aim to unite state-supported dance with independent dance.

16. Ibid., i.
17. Website for National Dance Law: http://www.leynacionaldedanza.com/.
18. Ibid., xvi.

REFERENCES

Carozzi, Maria Julia. 2011. *Las palabras y los pasos. Etnografías de la danza en la ciudad*. Buenos Aires: Gorla, Editorial.

Foster, Susan Leigh. 2010. *Choreographing History*. In *The Routledge Dance Studies Reader*, edited by Alexandra Carter and Janet O'Shea, 291–302. Abingdon, Oxon: Routledge, 2010.

Franko, Mark. 2006. 'Dance and the Political: States of Exception', *Dance Research Journal*, 38(1/2): 3–18.

Laclau, Ernesto. 2005. *La razón Populista*. Buenos Aires: FCE.

Laclau, Ernesto. 2013. 'Argentina: anotaciones preliminares sobre los umbrales de la política'. *Debates y Combates*, 5: 16–17.

Rincsi, Eduardo. 2013. 'De la democracia a la democratización: notas para una agenda de discusión filosófico-política sobre los cambios en la Argentina actual. A tres décadas de 1983'. *Debates y Combates*, 5: 20–41.

Svampa, Maristella. 2009. 'Protesta, Movimientos Sociales y Dimensiones de la acción colectiva en América Latina'. Available online at: http://maristellasvampa.net/publicaciones-ensayos.shtml.

Svampa, Maristella. 2010. 'Movimientos sociales, matrices socio-políticas y nuevos escenarios en América Latina'. Available online at: www.social-globalization.uni-kassel.de/owp.php.

Chapter 7

Making Art Relevant in the Aftermath of the Egyptian Uprising

Rounwah Adly Riyadh Bseiso

In an article published on 17 December 2014, Surti Singh, an Assistant Professor of Philosophy at the American University in Cairo (AUC), wrote that 'a new set of questions is crystallising about the role of art in contemporary Egypt' and posed the following questions: 'Can art still preserve the revolutionary spirit that spilled out in the graffiti and murals that covered Egypt's streets? Should this even be art's focus?' (Singh, 2014). Singh's questions at the time were indicative of a growing debate in Egypt over what constitutes a legitimate 'art' and what its focus should be following the uprising of January 2011, given the emergence of new forms of art in public spaces. Street art is not necessarily a new phenomenon in Egypt – it has a less visible history prior to the uprising in Egypt (Abaza, 2016; Charbel, 2010; Hamdy et al., 2014; Jarbou, 2010). However, the increased visibility and prevalence of street art has brought to the fore new questions – what is the role of street art, or 'revolutionary' art as many have labelled it, in a post-uprising Egypt? Should street art incite the public to act against a repressive government, should it serve as a form of awareness, and/or should it document the uprisings 'real' history versus what is reported in state media? Is overtly 'political' art serving the 'revolution' or undermining it? Is aesthetically pleasing, but seemingly content deprived art, a disservice to the revolution? Ganzeer, one of the most well-known artists of the uprising, writes:

> There are a bunch of thirty-something artists in Egypt today who think of themselves as cutting edge for adopting a 1917 [citing Marcel Duchamp's 'Fountain' as the example] art form that most Egyptians do not relate to – they adopt it anyway out of an urge to appeal to art institutions centered in Europe and the USA. *Such an art form has no place in Egypt's revolutionary climate* [my emphasis]. Although Egyptians have obviously failed badly at achieving that

(for now), it does not mean that the effects of the revolution should not find their way into art and culture. Conceptual Art in Egypt, with its compass oriented to point north-west, proves itself to be *a rather anti-revolutionary art form* [my emphasis]. (Ganzeer, 2014)

Questions about the efficacy and appeal of Egyptian art during the uprising were also being addressed by other commentators; for example, Shehab Fakhry Ismail, a PhD Student at Columbia University, wrote a scathing article of the uprisings art as essentially another form of political propaganda:

Perhaps the biggest failing of Cairo's revolutionary art is that it fails to see itself as art. It fails to reflect on and experiment with its aesthetic vision as aesthetics. Rather, Egyptian revolutionary artists have succumbed to the temptation of seeing their art as subservient to a higher cause. . . . Instead of the facile aestheticization of the revolutionary moment . . . artists would do better to revolutionize the vocabulary of their art, which in no way precludes treating political themes in a more radical manner. Perhaps then will art do what it can actually do best – shake us away from the complacency of unthinking. (Ismail, 2013)

Such arguments are representative of the seemingly cyclical discourse of 'revolutionary art' revolving around what the 'right' equation is for finding the optimum form and content that best serves the revolution – that is, should art be more abstract, less direct and more conceptual, or should it be more realistic and life-like and contain clear 'revolutionary' tropes of justice, liberation, freedom and change that the public can easily digest. However, based on my PhD fieldwork (from November 2013 to August 2014) with twenty-five cultural producers (from various socioeconomic backgrounds) based largely on open-ended and semi-structured interviews, I found that the debate over what should (and should not) constitute revolutionary art is, however, reductive and largely focuses on art's revolutionary potential through its form and content.

Therefore, this chapter argues that there is more to producing art in the streets than the actual art works created – indeed, while the works are significant as the product of the revolutionary imaginary – the aestheticised and very visible 'face' of the revolution – the contemporary visual production of art on Cairo's streets during and after the uprising extends beyond its aesthetics. By making art 'relevant', that is, accessible and understood within a local context, and connected to the public through a dialogical form of communication, this chapter argues that cultural producers in Egypt are revolutionising art – that is, the *way* art is thought of and approached during a transforming society, in the aftermath of an uprising which affected the way we perceive and analyse power, politics and art and culture in a Middle Eastern context.

To make this argument, this chapter relies on my PhD fieldwork interviews, undertaken between November 2013 and August 2014, by artists and non-artists alike. However, prior to locating the research of this chapter, I emphasise that it is necessary to situate the uprising and its artistic movement within a broader history of artistic dissent within modern Egypt.

BRIEF HISTORY OF ARTISTIC MOVEMENTS AND MOMENTS OF CONTEMPORARY DISSENT

Indeed, although Egyptian cultural and artistic history is extensive, this section briefly makes note of the early twentieth-century art movements in Egypt which were roughly divided into the 'First Generation', 'Second Generation' and 'Third Generation' movements (Karnouk, 2005).

The First Generation represented a cultural renaissance (*al nahdah*) in the early twentieth century and was based on a more secular outlook which embraced a 'revival of classical Egyptian art' (the neo-Phaoronic style) in the light of centuries of foreign rule, and combined this with 'modern techniques and influences' (Mikdadi, 2004). The Second Generation was concerned with the larger political breakdown, primarily abroad (the Palestinian Arab Revolt of 1936, World War I and World War II and the rise of fascism and Nazism). In response, one of the major dissident art movement, the 'Art & Liberty' Movement (a chapter of the International Federation of Independent Revolutionary Art founded by André Breton in 1938 promoting unhindered cultural expression against the increasing cultural repression of the state), was established in 1939 by Egyptian surrealists George Henein, Ramsis Younan, Kamel el-Telmissany and brothers Anwar and Fuad Kamil (Berànek, 2005: 203).

Although the group's initial concerns were the rise of fascism and its war on alternative cultural expression, it moved on to address broader issues such as 'anti-imperialism, radical educational reform, Freudian theory and women's emancipation' (LaCoss, 2009–2010: 29). It also fought for local issues such as continuing British foreign domination; discontent with the monarchy; the bourgeoisie and elite academicism; and the rights of labourers, workers and Egyptian women (LaCoss, 2009–2010: 28).

In the 1940s, the 'Third Generation' of artists were represented by the 'Rejectionists', a combination of several groups founded by the students of Hussein Youssef Amin (a prominent Egyptian art scholar and painter). One of the most well-known groups they formed, The Group of Contemporary Art, advocated the use of art pedagogy in promoting societal activism (Russell, 2010: 256) and was dedicated to connecting art with ordinary Egyptians by grounding art in Egyptian culture.

In the aftermath of the 1967 Six-Day War, which ended with the crushing defeat of Egyptian forces through the almost complete destruction of its air force and the occupation of Sinai by Israel, an Islamic revival in the arts began to take hold in Egypt in the 1970s which reflected a change in the sociocultural landscape of the time (ibid., ch. 5). Sadat's *infitah* policies in the 1970s caused a massive blow to the cultural field and significantly reduced cultural funding and hindered artistic activities and curbed creative expression beyond formal avenues, which meant that 'artists working outside the mainstream, exploring controversial subjects or using unconventional techniques, found themselves isolated, and many emigrated to the West, returning to Egypt almost annually to participate in exhibitions' (Mikdadi, 2004).

It was not until Mubarak's rule in 1980 – in which 'the renewed active involvement in the cultural field' was reinstated as 'compared to . . . Sadat's marginalization of the field and its actors' (Mehrez, 2008: 3) – that the emergence of Youth Salons, sponsored by the Ministry of Culture in 1989, as well as the Nitaq Festival, sponsored by the Townhouse Gallery, began to emerge. However, after Mubarak's term as president was extended for another six years, as well as a growth in suspicions that he was grooming his son Gamal to be his successor, civil society and pro-democracy groups began to form. Within this charged atmosphere (in which Mubarak faced both local and international pressure to institute greater democratic reforms), the Writers and Artists for Change were formed in 2005 – a year which marked a 'historic mobilization civil society organizations and groups' (ibid., 4). In their founding statement, read by renowned Egyptian poet Ahmed Fouad Negm, the group argued for the emancipation of the political and cultural fields, and 'reaffirm[ed] the historic role and responsibility of Egypt's writers and artists . . . as the spearhead for change, since the nineteenth century *nahda*' (Mehrez, 2008: 1). The group provided a powerful reaffirmation that the cultural field was directly constitutive of the political field and that the lack of inclusion and participation in the latter meant restriction and exclusion in the former.

However, the Writers for Artists and Change, which initiated several protests calling for cultural and political reform (ibid., 2–7), eventually dissolved due to the precarious nature of the cultural field, which found cultural producers occupying positions in which they hold an 'ambiguous relationship that is at once their patron and persecutor' (ibid., 6):

> Yet regardless of the group's dissolution, artistic groups and acts of creative dissent continued, albeit sporadically. Representing an art group formed prior to the uprising was i-Catalyst (founded in 2007) which, although it was a short-lived initiative, still 'made an impact on the overall art scene in Cairo' (Jarbou, 2010) and represented the early beginnings of a more creative and informal use

of art that was found on the margins of the cultural field by indirectly questioning the dominant political and cultural hegemony of the state (ibid.). Another group, Graphics Against the System (GAS) (founded by artist and activist Mohamed Gaber) was a 'visual agitation project aimed at producing artworks and designs that agitate people and create political and social awareness'. (ibid.)

Movements and incidents such as these acted as significant precedents to the uprising and to the formation of contemporary movements such as the Revolution Artists Union (RAU) in the aftermath of the uprising, and although street art and graffiti that was prevalent during the uprising was not as prominent or visible due to the restrictive police apparatus of Mubarak's regime (Jarbou, 2010; Charbel, 2010), recognising their existence acts as a reminder that the alternative acts of cultural dissent that were celebrated in the aftermath of the uprising did not emerge within an isolated context, but were subsumed within decades of historic acts of political and cultural resistance against state domination and repression.

STREET ART IN EGYPT: LOCATING THE RESEARCH AND DEFINING THE CONTEXT

Prior to the uprising in Egypt there were fragmented writings on street art (which tended to be located in blogs and, much less frequently, newspaper articles), which indicates that street art was prevalent only in academic discourses in the aftermath of 25 January 2011. Since then, street art has been celebrated, analysed and documented through the proliferation of 'coffee-table' books (Gröndahl, 2012; Boraïe, 2012; Maslamani, 2013), surveys of street art with critical commentary and essays (Hamdy and Karl, 2014), newspaper and magazine articles and documentaries (e.g. 'Art War', 2014; 'Nefertiti's Daughters', 2014). Academic literature has also proliferated, which reflects a wide range of perspectives and multiple levels of analyses, from addressing street art trends in a post–January 25 Egypt (Abaza, 2016), to street art's representations of martyrs and its creation of a memorial space (Abaza 2012; Lau 2012, 2013), and graffiti as a form of protest and documentation (Sharaf, 2015). One of the most recurrent themes addressed in the literature is understanding street art as a form of dissent and a tool for political struggle (Khatib, 2013) and an 'aesthetic product of resistance' (Sanders IV, 2012: 143) which can reclaim and de-territorialise space to promote new understandings of power – as well as belonging – to that space (Tripp, 2013).

Bahia Shehab discusses the ways in which street art in Egypt can be seen as inscribing artists' emotions into the walls through a largely descriptive account of her own involvement in the uprisings (Shehab, 2016). John

Johnston looks at the Egyptian uprisings street art (in relation to street art in Northern Ireland) and argues that Egyptian artists need to see themselves as embracing the 'role of public educator' (Johnston, 2016: 178) in promoting a 'critical public pedagogy', which, he says, is currently missing in Egypt's street art as it only 'inform[s] rather than transform[s]' and that one of its main limitations is that it fails to adequately address certain issues such as gender inequality (Johnston, 2016: 191). Furthermore, he argues that street art in Egypt did not 'pay as much attention as it could have to . . . corrupt power structures of the political elite" and that street artists need to incorporate the 'universal principles of human rights and democracy . . . in the politics of revolution and strategies of political street art" (Johnston, 2016: 191). Yet this perspective, which measures the efficacy of street art through universalising discourses and a Western narratives which sees democracy as the ultimate measure of success, fails to take into account the critical ways in which cultural producers are negotiating with power within the restraints of their local context and that street art, based on my fieldwork, was not a one way conversation which revolved around 'teaching' the public, it was about learning from the public.

Christine Smith explores the ways in which public art during and after the uprising did not just act as a tool of documentation, pedagogy or protest, but more importantly, she argues, it acted as a 'diagnostic . . . in assessing social and political transformation' (2015: 22). In doing so, she looks at the effects of artistic interventions within public spaces and the ways in which art can act not only as an indicator of the political situation but also 'a tool to understand the complex social relationships that shape the politics of an era' (Smith, 2015: 39). However, while Smith concludes that art can unravel societal tensions, in the aftermath of the jubilation of the 2011 uprising she makes generalised claims on how public spaces have now become a place to define what is and is not acceptable in political discussions, and as a result how 'democratic possibilities become ever more narrow' (ibid., 39).

This is indicative of a constricted understanding of politics, one which denies the antagonism, passion and conflict that define "the political", according to Mouffe (2001), or which, as Rancière (2004) argues, is not a place for consensus but a place for conflict. Smith further argues that

> artists largely find themselves either in the role of opposition to the current government or in their old roles of being educators of the masses. Within these roles, the artists mentioned in this article have reproduced the relationships established for them by previous governments with regard to their responsibility to be modernizers and educators on behalf of the state. (Smith, 2015: 39)

An article which attempts to diverge from such a representational mode of analysis and present a more nuanced way of looking at street art is by

Yakein Abdelmagid (2013), in a special section by the *Review of Middle East Studies* entitled 'Cultural Production in the Arab Spring Part II', in which he acknowledges that despite the various ways in which street art has been addressed, it still largely focuses on being represented as 'as voices of dissent, modes of symbolic resistance, or expressive force of anger, solidarity, and commemoration' (Abdelmagid, 2013: 172). Beyond this 'politics of cultural representation' (ibid., 172) he proposes that we look at the ways in which these 'artistic expressions are usually grounded in the formations, expansions and contractions of social groups that keep on negotiating their identities, networks, capacities and limitations' (ibid., 172). Abdelmagid examines one such group, the Mona Lisa Brigades (an Egyptian street art collective which focuses primarily on social issues concerning women and children) and the ways in which they 'struggle to produce within varied constraints, their quest to find alternative spaces of production and performance and their continuous improvisations to create alternative aesthetics and public spheres', which, he argues, 'are inherently political acts and forms of struggle "from below"' (ibid., 172). By going beyond the politics of Tahrir Square or the events of the uprising, he argues that the political is continuously being produced and reproduced within the 'everyday life of the artists' (ibid., 172), a sentiment echoed by Mariz Kelada in her examination of alternative artistic and cultural groups and spaces in Egypt (Kelada 2015). What is important to note here is that in describing these decentralised acts and alternative forms of politics and political performances from below, they are not articulated in their resistance solely to the state – rather, they 'continually negotiate structures of power by crafting independent forms of collectivities and lifeworlds within the transitional contingencies of post-2011 Egypt, by focusing on establishing alternative public spaces and social imaginaries in the everyday life' (ibid., 182).

Hannah El Ansary (2014) also attempts to complicate the discourse on street art in Egypt by not only looking at the production and perception of art, that is, the way in which 'artists and activists think about their work as makers and shapes of aesthetic and political meaning' but also urging us to look at 'how this same art has been viewed by the broader Egyptian public' (El Ansary, 2014). Based on her study on the reception of street art, El Ansary concluded that most Egyptians did not feel they were being spoken to, but being spoken at. El Ansary interviewed about fifty-seven people on their opinion of graffiti and street art, and although that might be a miniscule number for the over nine million residents of the Governorate of Cairo, she makes a crucial point that the reception of street art and graffiti in Egypt is widely understudied and should be focused on now more than ever, in order to gain a more complex understanding of their possible effects and transformative potential.

While the uprising represents the central political figuration in which analyses of art and cultural production took place, these articles – published several years in the aftermath of the uprising – do indeed indicate the need (as Abdelmagid argues) to go beyond Tahrir and the political events of the uprising, and see the ways in which (in its aftermath) actors in dispersed spaces continue to displace normative subject-positions and constitute new ways of 'doing' art within the everyday. Furthermore, five years after the uprising, in the light of the continuous whitewashing of all traces of 'revolutionary art' on the streets and purging archive platforms of the uprising, the conversation has grown to now address the importance of the role of the artist and the archive in contemporary art in society (Downey, 2015; Pinther, 2016). Major projects such as Lara Baladi's 'Vox Populi: Tahrir Archives' (2016) – described as an 'index of online archives on the 2011 Egyptian Revolution and its aftermath' (Baladi, 2016) – are setting a significant precedent in the ways in which the notion of the archive can be considered as an act of resistance, commemoration and historical signification in preserving the events, acts, expressions of the uprising. The refusal to forget is a powerful instigator in archiving, with several Facebook pages dedicated solely to documenting street art not only in Cairo but in Egypt as a whole, the most active ones beings 'Graffiti in Egypt',[1] 'Street Art in Egypt'[2] and 'Walls of Freedom: Street Art of the Egyptian Revolution'.[3] Indeed, as Mark R. Westmoreland noted, five years in the aftermath of the Egyptian uprising 'the prohibition on public image-making has been forcefully reasserted' (Westmoreland, 2016: 257), which makes the process of archiving – and not forgetting – even more crucial.

THE (EXCLUSIONARY) CULTURAL FIELD IN EGYPT

While public art in Egypt existed in Egypt (see Karnouk, 2005; Winegar, 2006), what predominantly existed was not a public art by the *public*, but state-sanctioned art by state-sanctioned artists in state-sanctioned public spaces. As Nabil' Ashur, an Egyptian artist, argues:

> There was no such thing as public art in Egypt. What was called public art was actually 'public business', because everyone was just trying to make money. And because such business in the private sector was limited, everyone sought work with the government. What had happened, with the governor giving very little time to the artist to produce a work of blatant nationalism for purely political purposes, was par for the course when one mixed art, business, and government . . . in the end he artist wins financially and he can still put on an exhibition to redeem himself artistically. That was how the faulty system worked. (Ashur, quoted in Winegar, 2006: 210)

These powers regulated not only the parameters of the form and content of art works, but *who* was allowed to showcase them in public or in contemporary art institutions, governmental or private. Several artists I interviewed in Cairo during my PhD fieldwork between November 2013 and August 2014 referred to 'gallery art' or 'exhibition art' in derogatory terms – to describe a more abstract, sterile and out of touch work of art that is purposefully deprived of any meaningful content and produced by those who were privy to the government's nepotistic circle. Keizer, an anonymous street artist, emphasised that the power of a group of select individuals to define, create and promote this art – according to neoliberal and political interests – was the end of art in Egypt:

> The art scene before the revolution was extremely secluded to an exclusive club of people that had money to enter these places, sip a few wine bottles, and point and decide what art was. That's the problem, when they get to dictate what art is, that is a huge problem, I think that is when art died in this country, when they tried to define it and gave it value and turned it into an expensive commodity, when it could be just because that person is part of that exclusive circle. There was loads of nepotism. (Keizer, pers. comm., 2014)

Muralist, illustrator and music producer Sad Panda, the moniker he uses to hide his identity, expressed frustration at the marginalisation of young artists who have no connections to this 'exclusive circle' in the contemporary Egyptian art scene:

> First of all, they [private galleries] would say 'who are you? You are still in school or university and you want to showcase your work?' Secondly, this is a part of them from the beginning not even accepting your work. . . . . There are several reasons that lead you to say that you are going to revolt against the art institutions in that I am going to take my drawings and throw them in the street so that everyone can actually get to see it. (Sad Panda, pers. comm., 2014)

Indeed, this marginalisation of artists with no connections, or whose art works do not conform to predetermined standards of private or government cultural institutions, is the direct result of the totalising role the Egyptian state occupies in the cultural field:

> The [Egyptian] state – primarily through the Ministry of Culture – acted as legislator, patron, producer, distributor and controller of culture. In other words, the state set and enforced the rules for cultural activity, operated cultural facilities, produced or financed cultural and artistic works (books, plays, concerts, art exhibitions, etc.). It promoted and disseminated these works, screened and censored them to ensure that they did not fundamentally contradict the state's value system, and selected those that it deemed suited

for serving its interests by ensuring that they are made available at home and abroad. (El Husseiny, 2014)

The widespread emergence of visible creative expressions of the Egyptian uprisings disrupted this regulated cultural activity by eliminating the state and private cultural institutions as the 'middle men' mediators of culture, removing the barriers of artistic expression by simply becoming visible in public spaces and blurring the boundaries of the common-sense subject positions over who is allowed to 'produce' culture and occupy certain formal positions, thus rendering non-artists and unconventional spectators – whose access to the cultural field has been restricted due to socioeconomic conditions (Mousa, 2015) – to become legitimate producers and consumers of art, as will be discussed in the next section.

CULTURE FROM BELOW: FINDING ART'S PURPOSE AND POTENTIAL

The proliferation of street art in Egypt during and post-uprising has been a trendy topic to cover, with commentators using the oft-repeated phrase that Egyptian street art is a 'form of revolution' (Rashed, 2013) and applauding it as being a 'fiery visual reminder of Egypt's revolution' that 'packs a punch' (Sooke, 2013). Yet what lies behind the work of so-called revolutionary art? Beyond the aesthetics, how is art now being thought of and approached? In addressing these questions – regarding how current critical artistic practices, and its producers, are at the forefront of *revolutionising* art in the post-Mubarak era – we need to go beyond a consideration of what constitutes a legitimate 'revolutionary art' form or sensationalising the art of the uprisings as mere representations of the revolutions. By doing so, it is important to understand that works of art that tilt towards more 'universal', abstract and conceptual forms have been heavily promoted at the expense of critical local visualities and local narratives that had characterised the art field prior to the Egyptian uprising. As Mousa writes:

> While modernist art trends have subsided in many parts of the world and given way to post-modern or contemporary genres, they remain heavily promoted in Egypt by domestic and foreign art institutions. . . . . *The effect of this global modern art movement's influx into Egypt has been selective marginalisation of works with critical political or social meaning – meanings that are relevant to the realities of given localities within Egypt* [my emphasis]. (Mousa, 2015)

Most of the artists I spoke to seemed to retreat from adopting a conception of art as an ahistorical, universal idea towards an understanding of art as located in narratives constituted within relevant local socio-historical and cultural contexts. As artist and art professor Alaa Awad notes, one must use the symbols, context and language of society if one is attempting to meaningfully *address* society artistically:

> I am in Egypt, so I address the society through its culture and its political, cultural, and social situation. I have to express the society. Art that does not voice the whole society, politically and economically, does not exist. The artist cannot be separated from the world that they live in. Who will present the visualization that expresses the mechanisms of the Egyptian society? (Awad, pers. comm., 2014)

However, 'universal' versus 'local' does not necessarily mean authentic versus inauthentic, binaries that have been challenged by the uprising as cultural producers 'fuse the familiar and foreign, old and new' (Kraidy 2016: 16). The disillusionment with art in Egypt's cultural field does not only come from the promotion of Westernised, modern, universal art disconnected from local realities, it is also concerned with the Ministry of Culture's *control, regulation* and *promotion* of abstract; sterile art devoid of action; or what Radwa, an artist and the Head of the Media Unit in the Egyptian Center for Economic and Social Rights, characterises as art 'before the revolution [that] was about a state of numbness, people being tired and dragging themselves' (Radwa Fouda, pers. comm., 2014).

Furthermore, most of the artists interviewed agreed that the uprising was instrumental for the creation of art in public spaces (whether or not this was expressed in their initial motivations for becoming involved in art) as the uprising was the central framework from which to narrate, analyse, critically visualise and negotiate with the social and political context, either directly or indirectly. As such, the uprising could not be separated from the aesthetic dimension even if it was not addressed in the art on the streets as 'the revolution is what lead us to be able to draw on the walls' (Amr Nazeer, pers. comm., 2014).

The connection between art and the revolution is not one solely of revolutionary propaganda, though it may be the case in some of the more obvious 'political' art (with clear revolutionary tropes and themes) on the walls – it is one of context. The uprising attempted to deconstruct the idea that the political was the realm of the few, just as the massive participation in organic forms of cultural production in public spaces was also an attempt to deconstruct the idea that the cultural field belonged to the realm of the few. As Hanaa El Degham, an Egyptian visual artist who lives and works between Egypt and Germany, argued, the cultural moved away from a teleological understanding with an 'end result', that is, viewing or purchasing art in a gallery, gaining pleasure from looking at a painting at moving on, but as a continual social process which informs and is informed, by the public, in order to foster cultural participation and inclusion:

> The idea is that you don't just go down to the street and draw and that's it. You go down because you have an idea, and when you go down you will find that people will ask you what you are doing and 'what is that?' And you will find people disagree with you, and you will disagree back, and they will tell you something you never heard of, so there are nice conversations that occur between you and the people. (El Degham, pers. comm., 2013)

Several artists suggested that art was about *involving the public* in its very creation and fusing the artist and the public's everyday experiences into its creation. In this sense, social relations are constitutive of the creation of the work in the sense that the art (and the artist) were centrally involved in processes of mediation though the recognition of the street, not as a platform, but as *the* platform in which to meaningfully communicate with others and that initiated the premise of its cultural importance in the revolution. As Radwa noted, the power of the street (and street art) emanates not only as a cultural form, but as essentially the *only* legitimate media form:

> It is the only legitimate media form because of its interactivity. This is the power of street art. If it is not interactive it will be just like exhibition art, *nothing* [my emphasis]. *It says what the artist wants but it doesn't say what people think of what the artists think, this dialectic kind of conversation going on between the art piece and the people, it shows how diverse the country is, or the society is. If that dialogue kept going, and it kind of pushes forward it will change things . . . because we do not have an equivalent media, especially the media, we do not have a media that is interactive or intriguing* [my emphasis]. (Radwa, pers. comm., 2014)

This observation serves as a reminder of the largely unidirectional dialogue between the artist and the public that characterised the cultural field prior to the uprising and the attempt of artists and non-artists alike in the *aftermath* of the uprisings to create a counter-dialogue, one that is informed – and informs – by societal discourse, conflict and antagonism. As such, as El Zeft, an anonymous street artist who had no interest in either art or politics prior to the uprising, noted, street art becomes the medium through which to communicate and connect with the intended audience and create an interactive dialogue:

> Right now . . . it is much better for you to say what you want in the street, to tell the people I am with you I am sitting in the same place as you – not like the people who are sitting in the air-conditioned studios on a stage telling you something else. Street art creates question marks and discussions. This is what

you want. You don't want to put full stops you want to put question marks. (El Zeft, pers. comm., 2014)

Put differently, art is about being co-present with the public and therefore about being connected – either positively or negatively (in that the art is not necessarily intended to garner approval) – and stimulating engagement with other artists and between members of a community. In the aftermath of the uprising, art was viewed more as a social process in that it involved the interaction and dialogue of artists and non-artists alike between each other and the greater community in which they work. Therefore, creative practices are informed by practical, real-world considerations and are largely an outcome of societal interaction, dialogue and the need to communicate mutual experiences.

Mustafa El Husseiny, an artist and member of the Mona Lisa Brigades whose artistic projects and works are focused primarily in *ashwa?iyyat* (slums) and lower-income *sha'abi* (popular) areas in Cairo and Giza, argues that one of the most important lessons one can learn when drawing in the street is to not necessarily impose the art on the public as an gallery art does, but to produce it through an open and transparent dialogue:

We don't come and have an idea in our head that we are going to do it and that is it. We talk to people and what comes out of our conversation with people we try to translate it together so that we can produce an artwork from it. (El Husseiny, pers. comm., 2014)

This idea was echoed by Hanaa El Degham who said that "creativity has no location, you can go to the streets wherever you are. . . . This is how awareness will come about everywhere, if one person starts with himself and the people around him, he will also learn because he needs that awareness as well" (El Degham, pers. comm, 2013.)

Seen this way, the work of art is the product of a shared artistic-societal discourse, a merging of experiences and situations, that attempts to both construct and respond to the artist and the public needs and their wants, by enhancing the artists own realisations through the consciousness of the public, a consciousness which has been largely absent from the cultural field. This is pertinent to scholarly debates in the twenty-first-century approach to understandings of art within the backdrop of transnational concerns such as migration, environmental crises, conflict and global financial crises. In this setting, a greater emphasis was placed more on the social aspect of the work through participatory art.

Relational practices stems from the concept of 'relational aesthetics', the term Nicolas Bourriaud used to define a 'set of artistic practices which take as their theoretical and practical point of departure the whole of human relations and their social context, rather than an independent and private space' (2002: 14). This came under sharp criticism by writers such as Claire Bishop (2004; 2006) who argued that Bourriaud focused only on the production of social relationship and failed to take note of the conflictual and disruptive (the essence of the political) element of these artistic practices which force us to reflect upon and criticise society.

The emergence of relational aesthetics as part of the political mainstream of art discourse is indicative of the ways in which concepts of autonomous art and the individual artist are being renegotiated towards an understanding of the emergence (and legitimacy, in the art world) of the relationship between the works and the active spectator and that the ultimate form of a critical political art is a participatory, collaborative and performative art which emphasises the process of its creation with others. In the Egyptian context, however, I have found that the idea is focused not necessarily on participation and creating art with others, but on deconstructing the notion of art as an inaccessible cultural endeavour intended for a minority of the social-economic elite, and that art should be accessible – in its understanding, in its location, as well as in its participation. Art is not only for formal artists – or for art connoisseurs and academics who can understand its terminology – it is a realm in which the public necessarily belongs, a realm which should not be limited to formal circles, but rather be opened up to public discourse.

Ammar Abo Bakr, an artist who also used to teach arts at the Faculty of Fine Arts in Luxor, argued that Egypt's cultural institutions and the artists (and their 'inaccessible' gallery art) they promoted were concerned only with art as a commodity, that the artist was completely disconnected from producing any art which contained any relevance to society – for political and economic reasons – and that it was this type of artist that now had to be discouraged in the light of the uprising:

> the artist in Egypt that draws a nice portrait of a traditional Egyptian man in his *jjalabiyeh* or a nice typical looking Egyptian scenery in the countryside, and then sells it to some random person, that artist is a bastard and hopefully we will destroy and break him, because his role does not serve our society. (Abo Bakr, pers. comm., 2014)

Abo Bakr adds that this kind of artist and his works have no place in the cultural field after the revolution because art should no longer be a modernist, and neoliberal, endeavour:

> as we [artists] understood it, our role was not to draw portraits and rush off to sell them in galleries . . . the art I adopt is . . . from the motifs on the *koshari* food stalls and the art that the shoe shine man does on his shoe shine box, I adopt

this art that comes from a country which has been devastated over the years. It is impossible that you are going to reach the entire society if you don't reach his link, that is if you don't understand his tastes, you should be following his taste to see the material and the colors the regular Egyptian uses in his day to day life and how he uses it, such as what he uses to decorate tombstones. (Abo Bakr, pers. comm., 2014)

Indeed, through my fieldwork and my interviews I have found that in a revolutionary context art is created not necessarily in isolation to the revolutionary event but is constitutive of it, and the artist does not create in isolation of the social processes of the public sphere. Artist and non-artists alike are using art to mediate between themselves, the street and the people in it through interaction and dialogue and sometimes conflict, thus illustrating the potential for art to liberate hegemonic narratives of what constitutes cultural production. This may serve to liberate not only the consciousness of the audience in the process, but of the producer as well. The emphasis of liberating the artist and the audience's consciousness by connecting to society *through* society and by adapting to its circumstances comes across in the following comment by Radwa: 'As a graffiti artist it is not only about me as well, I am part of the big picture. You should not get yourself into the bubble of an artist, the world does not revolve around you and your opinion, so draw your opinion but bear in mind other peoples life' (Radwa, pers. comm., 2014).

The emphasis on collective understanding and cooperating with others suggests there is not only a desire, but a need, to connect with the public. Abo Bakr emphasises the importance of connecting art to the people in order to essentially 'return' art (and culture, more broadly) to its rightful location – to the public – echoing the demands for public participation in politics during the uprising. As he notes:

Art should be for the people. It should be everywhere for the people. It has to be for the people, it's not an option it's a necessity . . . look at the revolution. The meaning of revolution in its most essential meaning is groups of people going down in the street – it has no other meaning. A revolution is about a collective going down to the street, so that the street becomes the property of the public. (Abo Bakr, pers. comm., 2014)

In this sense, the concept of the 'people' extends beyond the immediate community, but refers to society at large. This implicates a greater role for the cultural which extends beyond the personal need to be creative or express some form of artistic genius, but to recognise that the potential of art lies in eliminating the normative understanding and location of art in Egypt as an elitist pastime by subverting the barriers between the private (art confined within state institutions and private galleries) and the public while simultaneously emphasising that the autonomy of art is essentially a reflection of the modernist (and outmoded) condition of the cultural field characteristic of a pre-uprising Egypt. During the uprising, the idea that politics was restricted to formal domains was – at the time – eliminated. This is also reflective of a challenge to the consideration of art as a formal discipline and the broadening of the understandings of culture – no longer seen as a privileged, restrictive domain – which locates the artist as a formal actor within a privileged, formal occupation (where validation is sought from the state) and the spectator (coming from a particular social and economic background) equipped with an understanding of art history and art terminologies. Artists and non-artists alike are articulating the importance of the public's participation, interactivity, dialogue and conflict in the process and production of street art highlight the importance of plurality as the *condition per quam* (Arendt, 1998: 7) not only of political life, but of cultural life, of which so many Egyptians are excluded from in their day-to-day life. The continued *existence* of this creative expression and discourse, in a historically heavily regulated political and cultural field, is emancipatory in and of itself for its ability to maintain its presence while subverting rigid boundaries of what art can be and who can make it, articulate different modes of thought and constitute alternative ways of thinking, seeing and producing art and culture. Furthermore, it is the artist who is the mediator between themselves, the art and the public, underlining the basis of understanding art as a non-exclusionary cultural form which can absorb, rather than negate, local narratives, visualities and sensibilities relevant to the public at large.

CONCLUSION

Through my PhD fieldwork, I have found that the work of art cannot be placed in isolation from its producer and the context of its production, and that the process of creating art – versus the actual art work itself – is what is of primary importance to the cultural producers interviewed. In this sense, therefore, the uprising did not simply add labels to subversive cultural forms (i.e. revolutionary art, revolutionary music, revolutionary film), its cultural producers altered the very way art was thought of an approached – that is, the *process* of their creation, thereby revolutionising – and liberating – the very practice of controlled cultural production which favoured modernist art that largely characterised the Egyptian cultural field prior to the uprising. Altering the process changed the dynamic of the creation of cultural forms, and cultural producers – be they formal or non-formal actors involved in the creation and distribution of cultural forms – emphasised the need to operate within, and through, society and its discourses.

Just as the uprising sought to make politics accessible and relevant, this is applicable to the cultural realm. There is no political revolution without a cultural revolution that follows the same emancipatory principles. In this sense, creative acts of the Arab uprisings 'may signal a reordering of the top-down state- and elite-led culture industry in the Arab world in favour of a model that allows for alternative aesthetic expressions and new cultural politics to emerge as forces of change' (Salih and Richter-Devroe 2014: 17). However, although the current political climate in Egypt has not been conducive (Amin, 2014; Chams, 2016; Kennedy, 2015; Tantawi and Rizk, 2016) to the independent cultural scene, creative manifestations of public expression and unconventional cultural acts still continue under increasingly difficult circumstances (Alfred, 2014; Jankowicz, 2016). The very existence – and resilience – of these creative acts presents a challenge to the normative function of art and the monopolisation of culture in Egypt by addressing broader, and pressing, questions regarding the role of art in a post-uprising Egypt, which touches upon crucial issues of control, relevance and accessibility in the cultural field.

NOTES

1. https://www.facebook.com/Graffiti.in.Egypt/?pnref=lhc
2. https://www.facebook.com/WallsOfFreedom/?fref=ts
3. https://www.facebook.com/StreetARTnEgypt/?fref=ts

REFERENCES

Abaza, Mona. 2012. 'An Emerging Memorial Space? In Praise of Mohammed Mahmoud Street'. *Jadaliyya*, 10 March. Available online at: http://www.jadaliyya.com/pages/index/4625/an-emerging-memorial-space-in-praise-of-mohammed-merging-memorial-space-in-praise-of-mohammed-m (Accessed 29 April 2013).

Abaza, Mona. 2013. 'Walls, Segregating Downtown Cairo and the Mohammed Mahmud Street Graffiti'. *Theory, Culture & Society*, 30(1): 122–39.

Abaza, Mona. 2016. 'The Field of Graffiti and Street art in Post-January 11 Egypt', in *Routledge Handbook of Graffiti and Street Art*, edited by Jeffrey Ian Ross, 318–33. London, New York: Routledge.

Abdelmagid, Yakein. 2013. 'The Emergence of the Mona Lisa Battalions: Graffiti Art Networks in Post-2011 Egypt'. *Review of Middle East Studies*, 47(2): 172–82.

Alfred, Charlotte. 2014. 'Street Art Just Got More Dangerous in Egypt, But Artists Are Getting More Creative'. *Huffington Post*, May 8, http://www.huffingtonpost.com/2014/05/08/egypt-street-%09artists_n_5148542.html.

Amin, Shahira. 2014. 'Egypt's Nascent Street Art Movement under Pressure'. Index, August 22, https://www.indexoncensorship.org/2014/08/egypts-nascent-graffiti-movement-threat/.

Arendt, Hannah. 1998. *The Human Condition*. Chicago, London: The University of Chicago Press.

Baladi, Lara, 2016. 'Archiving a Revolution in the Digital Age, Archiving as an Act of Resistance'. *IBRAAZ*, 28 July. Available online at: http://www.ibraaz.org/usr/library/documents/main/archiving-a-revolution-in-the-digital-age.pdf (accessed 12 August 2016).

Berànek, Ondřej. 2005. 'The Surrealist Movement in Egypt in the 1930s and the 1940s'. *ARCHIV ORIENTÁLNÍ*, 73:203–22.

Bishop, Claire. 2004. 'Antagonism and Relational Aesthetics'. October, 110:51–80.

Bishop, Claire. 2006. "The Social Turn: Collaboration and Its Discontents." *Artforum*, 44(6):178–83.

Boraïe, Sherief. 2012. *Wall Talk: Graffiti of the Egyptian Revolution*. Cairo: Zeitouna Press.

Chams, Dalia. 2016. 'Backed into a Corner: Egypt's Independent Culture Five Years after the Revolution'. AhramOnline. 26 January, http://english.ahram.org.eg/NewsContent/5/35/185941/Arts – Culture/Stage – Street/Backed-into-a-corner-Egypts-independent-culture-fi.aspx.

Charbel, Jano. 2010. 'A cry on the walls'. *Daily News Egypt*, March 3, http://www.dailynewsegypt.com/2010/03/03/a-cry-on-the-walls/.

Demerdash, Nancy. 2012. 'Consuming Revolution: Ethics, Art, and Ambivalence in the Arab Spring'. *New Middle Eastern Studies*, 2: 1–17.

Downey, Anthony (ed.). 2015. *Dissonant Archives: Contemporary Visual Culture and Contested Narratives in the Middle East*. London: I. B. Tauris.

El Ansary, Hannah. 2014. 'Revolutionary Street Art: Complicating the Discourse'. *Jadaliyya*, 1 September Available online at: http://www.jadaliyya.com/pages/index/19033/revolutionary-street-art_complicating-the-discours (accessed 26 November 2014).

El Husseiny, Basma. 2014. Culture, the State, and the Culture of the State. Mada Masr, January 7, http://www.madamasr.com/opinion/culture-state-and-culture-state.

Ganzeer. 2014. 'Concept Pop'. *The Cairo Review of Global Affairs*, Summer 2014, http://www.thecairoreview.com/essays/concept-pop/.

Gröndahl, Mia. 2012. *Revolution Graffiti: Street Art of the New Egypt*. The American University in Cairo Press: Cairo.

Hamdy, Basma and Don Stone. 2014. *Walls of Freedom: Street Art of the Egyptian Revolution*. Berlin: From Here to Fame Publishing.

Ismail, Shehab Fakhry. 2013. 'Revolutionizing Art'. Mada Masr, 15 October, http://www.madamasr.com/opinion/culture/revolutionizing-art.

Jankowicz, Mia. 2016. ' "Erase and I will Draw Again": The Struggle behind Cairo's Revolutionary Graffiti Wall'. *The Guardian*, Mar. 24, https://www.theguardian.com/cities/2016/mar/23/struggle-cairo-egypt-revolutionary-graffiti.

Jarbou, Rana. 2010. 'The Seeds of a Graffiti Revolution'. In: Hamdy and Stone, 2014: 9–12.
Johnston, John. 2016. 'Democratic Walls?: Street Art as Public Pedagogy'. In: Baker, M. (ed.), 2016. *Translating Dissent: Voices from and with the Egyptian Revolution*, pp. 178–96. New York: Routledge.
Karl, Don Stone, and Zoghbi, Pascal. 2011. *Arabic Graffiti*. Berlin, Germany: From Here to Fame Publishing.
Karnouk, Liliane. 2005. *Modern Egyptian Art: 1910–2003*. Cairo: American University in Cairo Press.
Kelada, Mariz. 2015. 'Social Change Between Potentiality and Actuality: Imagination in Cairo's Alternative Cultural Spaces'. *International Journal of Sociology*, 45(3): 23–233.
Kennedy, Merrit. 2015. 'Egypt Raids 2 Major Independent Cultural Institutions in 2 Days. National Public Radio (NPR), 29 December, http://www.npr.org/sections/the two-way/2015/12/29/461401135/egypt-raids-2-major-independent-cultural-institutions-in-2-days.
Khatib, Lina. 2013. *Image Politics in the Middle East: The Role of the Visual in Political Struggle*. London and New York: I. B. Tauris.
Kraidy, Marwan. 2016. *The Naked Blogger of Cairo: Creative Insurgency in the Arab World*. Cambridge, MA: Harvard University Press.
LaCoss, Don. 2009–2010. 'Art and Liberty: Surrealism in Egypt'. *Communicating Vessels*, 21:28–33.
Lau, Lisa. 2012. 'Mohamed Mahmoud Street: Reclaiming Narratives of Living History for the Egyptian People'. *WR: Journal of the CAS Writing Program*. 5. http://www.bu.edu/writingprogram/journal/past-issues/issue-5/lau/.
Maslamani, Maliha. 2013. *Graffiti of the Egyptian Revolution*. Beirut: Arab Centre for Research and Policy.
Mehrez, Samia. 2008. *Egypt's Culture Wars: Politics and Practice*. London, New York: Routledge.
Mikdadi, Salwa. 2004. 'Egyptian Modern Art'. *The Metropolitan Museum of Art*, October, http://www.metmuseum.org/toah/hd/egma/hd_egma.htm.
Mouffe, Chantal et al., 2001. 'Every Form of Art Has a Political Dimension'. *MIT Press Journals: Grey Room*, 2: 98–125.
Mousa, Sarah. 2015. 'Egypt: Making Art Public' Al Jazeera, 25 August, http://www.aljazeera.com/indepth/opinion/2015/08/egypt-making-art-public-150822104944575.html.
Naji, Ahmed. 2014. 'Learning to Walk after Crawling: Independent Cultural Institutions'. Mada Masr, 28 August, http://www.madamasr.com/sections/culture/learning-walk-after-crawling.
Nickolas, Mark. 2014. *Nefertiti's Daughters*. [film]. USA, EGYPT: Mosaic Films, NYC.
Pinther, Kerstin S. 2016. Artists' Archives and the Sites of Memory in Cairo and Algiers. *World Art*, 6(1): 169–85.
Quijano-Gonzalez, Yves. 2013. 'Rap, an Art of the Revolution or a Revolution in Art?' Orient-Institut Studies 2, 2013, http://www.perspectivia.net/publikationen/orient-institut-studies/2-2013/gonzalez-quijano_rap.

Rancière, Jacques. 2004. *The Politics of Aesthetics: The Distribution of the Sensible*, trans. Gabriel Rockhill. London and New York: Continuum.

Rashed, Waleed. 2013. 'Egypt's Murals Are More Than Just Art, They Are a Form of Revolution'. *Smithsonian Magazine*, May 2013, http://www.smithsonianmag.com/arts-culture/egypts-murals-are-more-than-just-art-they-are-a-form-of-revolution-36377865/?no-ist.

Russell, Mona L. (ed.). 2013. *Middle East in Focus: Egypt*, Santa Barbara, California: ABC-CLIO.

Salih, Ruba, Richter-Devroe, Sophie. 2014. 'Cultures of Resistance in Palestine and Beyond: On the Politics of Art, Aesthetics, and Affect'. *Arab Studies Journal*, 22(1):8–28.

Sanders IV, Lewis. 2012. 'Reclaiming the City: Street Art of the Revolution'. In *Translating Egypt's Revolution: The Language of Tahrir*, edited by Samia Mehrez, 143–82. Cairo: American University in Cairo Press.

Selim, Adham. 2014. 'Toward an Art That Hides Nothing behind'. Mada Masr, 3 August, http://www.madamasr.com/sections/culture/toward-art-hides-nothing-behind.

Sharaf, Radwa Othman. 2015. 'Graffiti as a Means of Protest and Documentation in the Egyptian Revolution'. *African Conflict and Peacebuilding Review,* 5(1): 152–61.

Shehab, Bahia. 2016. 'Translating Emotions: Graffiti as a Tool for Change'. In: Baker, M. (ed.), 2016. *Translating Dissent: Voices from and with the Egyptian Revolution*, pp. 163–77. New York: Routledge.

Singh, Surti. 2014. 'Historical Realities of Concept Pop: Debating Art in Egypt'. *Jadaliyya*, 17 December, http://reviews.jadaliyya.com/pages/index/20305/historical-realities-of-concept-pop_debating-art-i.

Smith, Christine. 2015. 'Art as a Diagnostic: Assessing Social and Political Transformation through Public Art in Cairo, Egypt'. *Social & Cultural Geography*, 16:1: 22–42.

Sooke, Alistair. 2013. 'Egypt's Powerful Street Art Packs a Punch'. BBC Culture, 9 May, http://www.bbc.com/culture/story/20130508-egypts-street-art-revolution.

Tantawi, Ghada, and Mariam Rizk. 2016. 'Egypt Takes Harsh Line towards Artists and Authors'. BBC News, 20 April, http://www.bbc.com/news/world-middle-east-36039529.

Tripp, Charles. 2013. *The Power and the People: Path of Resistance in the Middle East*. London: Cambridge University Press.

Westmoreland, Mark R. 2016. 'Street Scenes: The Politics of Revolutionary Video in Egypt'. *Visual Anthropology*, 29(3): 242–62.

Wilms, Marco. 2014. Art War. [film]. Germany: HELDEN FILM.

Winegar, Jessica. 2006. *Creative Reckonings: The Politics of Art and Culture in Contemporary Egypt*. Stanford, CA: Stanford University Press.

Chapter 8

Collective Art-Making to Agitate for Social Change

In and between Theatre, Live Art, Community Art and Protest Camps

Mel Evans

It is 10 pm on a midsummer Sunday evening in 2015 when Darren and I reach the final task in our tidy up from the latest Liberate Tate performance: emptying the loos. We exited the gallery nine hours ago, having spent twenty-five hours overnight, uninvited, in our performance *Time Piece* in which over a 100 performers transcribed texts on oil, art and climate change in a rising tide of objection to BP sponsorship of Tate up the polished concrete slope of the Tate Modern Turbine Hall. With all the other gear safely in storage, there is just this left. We've reached the sort of delirium you would expect on four hours' sleep; months of planning; and late nights spent sewing, sketching, discussing and rehearsing the performance. It's the sort of mission you can only achieve on the wave of intense emotion familiar to any performer after a show or any activist after an action: you're too exhilarated to mind too much that you're emptying out bucket loads of shit and piss.

The compost toilets, accessed during the performance inside their black cloth and bamboo cubicle, were central to the strategy to ensure we maintained our twenty-five-hour occupation of Tate and somehow offer an unlikely symbol to sum up our practice: both aesthetic and pragmatic, both steel-willed and gently cheeky. Liberate Tate has been an evolving act of perseverance, endurance, commitment and mutual trust and love. Over six years and sixteen performances made by over 500 people we created the conditions for continued BP sponsorship of Tate to seem untenable to the parties involved. At the beginning of our journey we were a loosely connected hub of artists and activists drawn together from visual and performance arts, community food growing networks, grassroots political organising and beyond.

By this signpost on our path as an art collective we were a widely known art-activist group with a recognisable aesthetic and a set of shared creative processes and methodologies.

Creative collaboration of this kind requires time, care and integrity. This kind of practice emerges out of a rich history of collective art-making such as the radical 'happenings' in New York in the 1960s (Schechner, 2002), non-hierarchical political organising ranging from protest camps to collective living and non-violent direct action (Feigenbaum, Frenzel and McCurdy, 2013), and community arts practice especially in marginalised communities (Braden, 1978), in Europe, North America and South America from the 1960s onwards. In this chapter I will examine several examples from each, to draw out the parallel ways of working together in some key groups of these kinds and offer a genealogical analysis of the practices that preceded and influenced the work of Liberate Tate. For all the work I will consider, a whole variety of analyses could be drawn around the content of the artwork/community work/protest; however, for the purposes of this particular study I wish to focus on the working methods – how the groups collaborate/d. Across all forms questions around collaboration will be understood through the lenses of Feigenbaum, Frenzel and McCurdy's notions of 'organic horizontality' and 'antagonistic spatial practice' (2013: 157–171) and Turner's concept of 'communitas' (1997).

In performance several key – and inspiring – collectives are The Wooster Group[1] (1975–present, New York) whose multimedia theatre shows reject the norms of the art form and incorporate competing texts and material; Forced Entertainment[2] (1984–present, Sheffield), again primarily based in theatres, their work is powerful in its heart-rendering and often pacey reckoning with the mundane hyperboles and muddied dreams of modern life; and La Pocha Nostra[3] (1993–present, California, United States; Mexico), a group who work between live art events and pedagogical processes, both over several days at a time, disordering borders through ritual, live art and hybrid archetypes. Each of these groups work experiments with media, duration, text sources and wider socio-political references from militarised border controls (La Pocha Nostra) to call centre capitalism (The Wooster Group); over considerable time each has developed a body of work that shares key aesthetic features at the same time as constantly exploring new dimensions; and, for each the collaboration between the contemporary company and the constant characters in it is the source of artistic expression.

Non-hierarchical, consensus-based organising is an immense and flexible tradition within social movements (Feigenbaum, Frenzel and McCurdy, 2013). In the UK, the working methods and styles of this kind of political organising are greatly shaped and informed by Greenham Common Women's

Peace Camp[4] (1981–2000, England), a site occupation establishing a possible utopia of cooperation and mutual support in direct confrontation with a U.S. nuclear base set up in southern England during the Cold War; the Peace Camp's creative protests and use of non-violent direct action[5] were echoed in the activities of Climate Camp[6] (2006–2011, England, Wales, Scotland) a national network holding annual or more frequent action camps at sites of high-carbon industry including power stations, airport runways and banks to envision a future of ecological justice; and Occupy Wall Street[7] (2011–present, New York) who, using the same camp-based tool, offered thousands of people a taste of direct democracy to develop practices of fair global wealth distribution. The parallels between these three events taking place in very different times and places are evident: a commitment to anarchist-communist, feminist, anti-oppression principles expressed and explored through experiments in lived utopias at sites of political conflict.

Glas(s) Performance (2004–present, Glasgow) and Common Wealth (2010–present, Bradford, Merthyr Tydfil, Yorkshire, Lancashire) both make performance work with and for regional or marginalised communities in Scotland, England and Wales. Unlike community arts practice that is shared within a limited audience only, both companies make professional theatre pieces shared with a much wider set of audiences. Where Glas(s) Performance explore a variety of themes drawn directly from performers experiences and stories discovered through the devising process, Common Wealth introduce a specific socio-political issue or campaign to the group of participant-actors and develop a piece of work responding personally to the content. Despite the narrative differences, both groups' work is highly collaborative, disrupting completely the idea of community arts as training for amateurs or of limited calibre, with their rich, powerful and skilled performance works.

Sitting within this wider, longer context of performance, protest and community arts practice, Liberate Tate[8] (2010–present, England) bear resemblances to each of the above groupings of examples of collaboration to make art. Liberate Tate formed in 2010 as a loose collective of artists, activists, academics, gallery workers and community food growers. In the following years it established itself as an art collective creating live art that is neither commissioned nor sanctioned by Tate, but which takes place only within Tate gallery spaces. From oily spills[9] to a 16.5-metre wind turbine blade,[10] from words and sounds[11] to overnight escapades[12] and permanent tattooing,[13] our artworks have disrupted norms of gallery behaviour and invited audiences on site and online to engage in critical debate. The project of Liberate Tate was fuelled by a clear strategic goal, a single aim targeted for its relation to a much wider set of politics. We wanted to end BP sponsorship of Tate to deny the company the benefits it sought from the gallery and undermine the longevity of the industry as a whole. The commitment and passion demonstrated by performers of each and every artwork were borne out of concern for the people and ecologies harmed by the oil industry and as an enactment of democracy within the public space of the gallery that BP invaded.

I will argue that Liberate Tate represent a new form on the spectrum of collective practice outlined, firmly fixed in neither art nor protest. The group works with a commitment to carefully crafted performance works, strategically developed campaign goals and participatory models of performance making. This new model is instructive for any protest group, set of arts practitioners or community organisers wanting to make social change, together. To establish and articulate the blending of these various forms, I will outline the various aforementioned groups and companies in greater depth to firmly establish the key strands groups like Liberate Tate might wish to draw on. Only through loyalty to the methods and principles each of art, protest and community participation can these new forms be born.

Creative collaboration is not easy. It is founded on the belief that we will make better things, if we make them together. For all the groups profiled, issues around space abound: rehearsal rooms, shelter, camps, sites of confrontation or antagonism and intervention in galleries. Time becomes another fundamental issue: labour and voluntarism, continuity and openness to new members or participants, longevity and timeliness of political action. Process is the third crucial tenet: what democracy looks like, what collective decision-making looks like, recognisable models meet anti-bureaucratic leanings and a desire for fun and informality and the foundation of trust in all group processes. By looking more intensely at these seven groups' processes I hope to reveal key learnings for others embarking on the journey of collaborative art and activism.

PERFORMANCE COLLECTIVES: THE WOOSTER GROUP, FORCED ENTERTAINMENT AND LA POCHA NOSTRA

Hot on the heels of 1960s attempts of non-hierarchy and revolution, The Wooster Group formed in 1975 in New York, emerging out of a series of politically motivated, experimental theatre and arts groups including The Performance Group and the Fluxus art movement (Higgins, 2002). Now after over thirty years of collaboration, the group has performed over twenty-one theatre, twelve film and five dance pieces. The company is constantly shifting in its membership of ten to twenty theatre, dance and media artists, with several continuing founding members including Elizabeth LeCompte, director of the Group.

The group works with company autobiography in their material as well as responding to existing texts, such as in *Route 1 & 9* or more journalistic investigations, like *To you, the Birdie!* Looking back, LeCompte and playwright and frequent Group collaborator Richard Foreman reflect on their roles and the practice of The Wooster Group in the wider context of defining art-making at the turn of the twentieth to twenty-first centuries:

> RF: You could make the case that this perverse historical period we're in produces serious art only if it's perverse. And I'd like to think that I am forced into what I know is a perverse strategy by the times. I'd like to think that in happier, healthier times maybe I wouldn't even be an artist.
>
> EL: You've said that a lot to me, but I haven't really understood it till recently. I've had this feeling of not being an artist. I don't know what it means to me ... Maybe it's age. I've had a vision of just doing landscape architecture. It has to do with figuring out how to replant the earth the way it was. Returning it. You know, some obsessive thing like that. Returning it to the way it might have been naturally.[14]

Here the two explore the role of the artist in relation to social politics and relate it metaphorically to environmentalism. The veins of this discussion run through all the groups' thinking and philosophies: how to make social change, how to relate to the land, what art is and what it might be. Their artistic or activist practice relates directly to how the individuals involved want to live in the world, in the same way that the activists design their activities or the community artists look to raise social consciousness.

The Wooster Group own and operate the Performing Garage as a shareholder of the Grand Street Artists Co-op. In their case, 1960s social politics laid an economic foundation for collective practice: owning the space as a co-op allows a sense of shared ownership to inform all the activities of the group. Shelter and co-existence reemerge as key themes in all the group's methods of working together. If you go to New York now and see the Performing Garage, you can see the special glow of decades of collective practice shimmering off and inside the building. Making work together means allowing each other to experiment, offer and test personal boundaries and a safe, familiar space to do that in can allow a more in-depth process together. The Wooster Group have been both lucky and dedicated enough to give themselves just that.

Commitment and longevity are equally key tenets of creative collaborative practice. In 1984 Forced Entertainment started making work from a performance base in Sheffield that they continue to call home to this day. They started out on the dole, and now they tour internationally to perform their work. Like the Wooster group, a few continuous members have formed part of a changing company directed by Tim Etchells. The group describes its own practice:

> The work we make tries to explore what theatre and performance can mean in contemporary life and is always a kind of conversation or negotiation, something that needs to be live. We're interested in making performances that excite, challenge, question and entertain other people. We're interested in confusion as well as laughter. We started working together in 1984; in the many projects we've created since then we've made lists, played games, spoken gibberish, stayed silent, made a mess, dressed up, stripped down, confessed to it all, performed magic tricks, told jokes, clowned around, played dead, got drunk, told stories and performed for six, twelve and even 24 hours at a stretch. We've worked on texts, we've danced and moved, we've fixed things meticulously, we've improvised. We've made serious work that turned out to be comical, and comical work that turned out to be deadly serious, digging deep into theatre and performance, thinking about what those things might be for us and what kinds of dialogue they can open with contemporary audiences.[15]

The group demonstrates that, like the Wooster Group, a lifetime of working together establishes a distinctive aesthetic practice born out of play and process, both of which are dependent on creative relationships built on trust and exploration. The picture the aforementioned quote paints of the collaborative process in the group is one rich with possibility and experimentation, with openness to spontaneous developments rather than a staunchly regulated stepladder to create work.

The depth of working relationships within Forced Entertainment has shaped the spaces they choose to work in and the process they embark on in those spaces. The group changes in composition for most works, centred by the continual presence of the founding members. Forced Entertainment note:

> Combining discussion, improvisation and writing, our rehearsal process is a creative laboratory that discovers unexpected and inspiring answers to questions of life and art. As six people who have worked together more or less continually for 30 years we share a big history and a lot of skills, conversations and ideas. We also share input into and responsibility for the work we produce.[16]

This sense of shared responsibility starts to resound with some of the values important to the protest groups: everyone works together to produce an outcome they are all happy with. In this way their practice starts to manifest an example of what Feigenbaum, Frenzel and McCurdy in their analysis of non-hierarchical organising structures in grassroots protest (2013) call 'organic horizontality'. Agreement is reached without formal procedures of consensus decision-making,[17] and everyone collectively shapes and holds responsibility for the final piece of work.

Victor Turner (1977) defines 'communitas' as a liminal space in which daily social and political structures ease away to allow for a deeper, looser form of communication and collaboration between people. Turner's concept is essential to Feigenbaum, Frenzel and MCurdy's notion of 'organic horizontality' which they analyse as emerging in protest camp conditions where living together facilitates 'communitas' and forms deeper senses of common understanding. Turner's concept has also been widely applied to art- and performance-making (Schechner, 2002) and various cultural settings for performance, therefore it is here that some of the shared aspects of protest and art methodologies meet. Forced Entertainment's description of their devising process to illuminate the inside of the rehearsal room and the dynamics of collective performance making reveals the creative potential in this liminal space in which communitas has been built:

> With a few exceptions we don't work with a ready-made text so making a show starts with us in a rehearsal room – discussing ideas, raiding the dressing-up box, trying a line of dialogue, playing a soundtrack, improvising a scene until something starts to stick. Then we keep developing the material – we experiment with it, debate it, videotape it, watch it, adapt and edit it before trying it on an audience which can open up a whole new set of questions.[18]

Their devising process is loose and discursive, and the focus on developing from improvisation will be familiar to community artists but much less so to activists and political organisers working in more rigid settings. This loose start to a creative process allows ideas to form from a broad range of channels, making the performance works complex, charged and fascinating, where some protest aesthetics can seem heavy handed.

In 1993 Guillermo Gomez-Peña, Nola Mariano and Roberto Sifuentes founded La Pocha Nostra: many others would soon join and rejoin these three artists to make up the current collective. The formation occurred in San Francisco, important because of its position and existence, like the group, always in and between the United States and Mexico. The group has co-produced numerous live art and performance events exploring borders, boundaries, global geopolitics, race, culture and the political function of art. I first experienced the group's methodology in 2006 in one of their regular five-day workshops held internationally. La Pocha Nostra, translated both as ' "our impurities" and "a cartel of cultural bastards" ', define their practice in relation to the art world and to political protest in their 'ever-evolving manifesto':

> La Pocha Nostra is neither an ensemble nor a troupe. We are more of a conceptual 'laboratory' – a loose association of rebel artists thinking together, exchanging ideas/aspirations, and jumping into 'the abyss' together. . . . La Pocha challenges the traditional art-world mythologies of the artiste as suffering bohemian and

misunderstood genius. La Pocha Nostra artists are social critics and chroniclers, intercultural diplomats, translators/mistranslators, informal ombudsmen, media pirates, information architects, reverse anthropologists, experimental linguists, and radical pedagogues. To us, the artist is, above all, an active citizen immersed in the great debates of our times. Our place is the world and not just the 'art world'. . . . La Pocha Nostra's performance pedagogy performs a major role in our political praxis. Why? It challenges authoritarian hierarchies and specialised knowledge by creating temporary utopian spaces where interdisciplinary dialogue and imagination can flourish. These utopian spaces are framed by, but not contained with, a pentagon-shape of radical ideas whose vertices are community, education, activist politics, new technologies, and experimental aesthetics. . . . La Pocha Nostra crosses dangerous aesthetic borders. We cede both our will and the stage to the audience. We invite them to co-create the piece and to participate in our 'extreme performance games' riddled with postcolonial implications. These games are integral aspects of our work.[19]

The mixing of political aspirations with creative process is self-evident in the group's writing. In a deliberate production of a counter-narrative to both the single artist as auteur found in much of the art world and the idea of politics as shaped by governments only, rather than the people whose personal experiences correspond with national and international policies. This intertwining of the personal and the political, a huge area of feminist critique (Hanisch, 1969) in art-making and activism, is fundamental to the group's approach.

There are notable parallels in La Pocha Nostra's working methods to those of The Wooster Group and Forced Entertainment, firstly in relation to the shape-shifting structure of the collective, steadied by the founding members to allow for a broad range of input and influence:

La Pocha Nostra is an ever-changing community. Depending on who is sitting at the table at any given moment, Pocha can be two people or fifty. We create regenerative sources of labour built from concentric and overlapping circles. The inner circle comprises six to eight artists and scholars whose membership is determined by their degree of commitment and time. The next circle includes performance artists, musicians, filmmakers, and designers working part-time on several Pocha projects. Members and associates can move from one circle to another. The constant change of membership inevitably alters the nature of the work and contributes to the permanent process of reinvention.[20]

As for the actual development of work, the similarities continue, with a parallel concentration on loose devising via different methods and techniques:

At a typical meeting or rehearsal, we'll have good food, some wine (and rum if we're lucky), and lots of strong coffee. Conversations about war, immigration, globalisation, and new technologies are interwoven with contemporary art theory and practice. Current affairs and politics are considered in nearly every aesthetic discussion and decision. There is always a lot of laughter. A strong feeling of community quickly develops. Rudeness and disrespect are simply not tolerated within the group. Our aim is to avoid, at all costs, the self-destructive existential malaise of the alternative art world – spiritual exhaustion, political quarrelling, and cannibalism.... Up to the rehearsal before opening, we continually ask ourselves: How can we make it more complex, more layered? At the same time, how can we make it more clear and succinct? How can we push the outer limits of the piece just 10 per cent more? Since it is an interactive performance, there are always more surprises, new juxtapositions, and unpredictable performative audience members who will charge the course of the performance.[21]

The flavour of this working process is equally refreshing for anyone familiar with dry political meetings or some formal script-based theatre rehearsals. Pocha's seamless weaving of political and aesthetic discussions challenge both activist notions of visuals as something to be considered 'after' the plan is made, and straight theatre's positioning of politics as source material to be weighed up objectively only. Again, the manifestation of Turner's communitas is richly evident, from the 'feeling of community' to the importance given to mutual respect, care and sustenance. Thereby it is easy to see that Feigenbaum, Frenzel and McCurdy's organic horizontality also arises to create the performance moments and experiments that are equally – and non-hierarchically – shaped by the audiences as well.

Together, these three groups reveal a collaborative creative process charged with political thinking. Now, let us consider the aspect of political organising that is also founded on collective processes.

UTOPIA IN CONFRONTATION: GREENHAM WOMEN'S PEACE CAMP, CLIMATE CAMP AND OCCUPY WALL STREET

In 1981 Greenham Common Women's Peace Camp began what would be a nineteen-year occupation of land directly outside a U.S. nuclear base in the south of England, strategically positioned by the U.S. government as a threat to the USSR during the Cold War. During the period of the camp, thousands of women across the country participated in the protest, developing collective methods of political organising that inform protest movements in the UK to this day (Holloway, 2002). In her telling of its story, Sarah Hipperson describes the impact of the camp on the campaign to end nuclear disarmament:

> The presence of women living outside an operational nuclear base 24 hours a day, brought a new perspective to the peace movement – giving it leadership and a continuous focus. At a time when the USA and the USSR were competing for

nuclear superiority in Europe, the Women's Peace Camp on Greenham Common was seen as an edifying influence. The commitment to non-violence and non-alignment gave the protest an authority that was difficult to dismiss – journalists from almost every corner of the globe found their way to the camp and reported on the happenings and events taking place there.[22]

The power of protest performed on one single site has imbued it with a legacy of hope for peace. Now on the map as New Greenham Park, Hipperson says that 'the site represents the four elements: earth, fire, water and air'.[23] Sculptor Michael Marriott created a flame sculpture symbolising the campfire and a stone and steel spiral sculpture alluding to the continuous outreach work of the camp. The spiral is engraved with the words 'You can't kill the spirit',[24] as testament to the motivations of the thousands of women involved that fuelled the importance and impact of the protest camp.

For Greenham Common Women's Peace Camp, the challenges of existing in that space were central to the act of protest: the women were bearing witness, by living beside the nuclear base; they were demonstrating the courage of their convictions by living in challenging conditions through all seasons; and they were creating a new space of their own to build community. Hipperson describes, 'It was a case of giving up comfort for commitment'.[25] Where the performance groups described in the previous section focus on togetherness over reasonable long durations in their working methods, performances and the continuity of their companies, the peace camp takes being together to a whole new level: the women lived together on the site, many for years and some for decades. This togetherness extends from a set of processes and working methods to a more utopian framework for a kind of political lifestyle that at the time was fairly new.

As Feigenbaum, Frenzel and McCurdy (2013) describe, this being together enabled organic horizontality to emerge in decision-making, a potential which the writers ascribe in this case and others to what they call 'antagonistic spatial practice': diverse people are brought together in a site of confrontation, and their collaboration depends not on signing up to an exact set of agreements but rather a clear single opponent they all share. This parallel will be useful when we discuss Liberate Tate's focus on BP sponsorship of Tate and is also highly instructive for the ways collaboration emerged in the following tow protest camps, Climate Camp and Occupy Wall Street.

Climate Camp started in the UK in 2006 and action camps or days of direct action on climate issues were held annually or more frequently until 2011. The group was organised nationally and non-hierarchically according to the following four central aims and objectives:

> Education: raising our own and wider public understanding of the problem, its root causes and how it might be solved; Sustainable living: exploring and experiencing in practice some of the ways in which a truly sustainable society

might function; Direct action: taking part in small and large group action to confront the root causes of climate change; Movement-building: acting in solidarity and forging links with people and groups with common or related interests, including workers and the communities or populations most acutely affected by climate change in Britain and throughout the world, to build a movement with the wisdom, diversity and strength to achieve true ecological and social justice.[26]

This four-pronged approach provided an entry point into climate activism for thousands of participants, and having joined the G8 protest camp which provided a working model for Climate Camp in Scotland in 2005, I first got involved in organising for Climate Camp in 2007. Its visionary approach enabled the aesthetic of the camps and actions to be rooted in a beautiful and powerful reimagining of what a future beyond fossil fuels might look like. This model of action camp organising has clear roots in the methods established by Greenham Women's Peace Camps and directly informed the practical application of the politics of Occupy Wall Street.

Occupy Wall Street kicked off on 17 September 2011 in New York, with the following resounding call to action:

> Today, we proudly remain in Liberty Square constituting ourselves as autonomous political beings engaged in non-violent civil disobedience and building solidarity based on mutual respect, acceptance, and love. It is from these reclaimed grounds that we say to all Americans and to the world, Enough! How many crises does it take? We are the 99% and we have moved to reclaim our mortgaged future. Through a direct democratic process, we have come together as individuals and crafted these principles of solidarity, which are points of unity that include but are not limited to:
>
> - Engaging in direct and transparent participatory democracy;
> - Exercising personal and collective responsibility;
> - Recognising individuals' inherent privilege and the influence it has on all interactions;
> - Empowering one another against all forms of oppression;
> - Redefining how labour is valued;
> - The sanctity of individual privacy;
> - The belief that education is human right; and
> - Making technologies, knowledge and culture open to all to freely access, create, modify and distribute.
>
> We are daring to imagine a new socio-political and economic alternative that offers greater possibility of equality. We are consolidating the other proposed principles of solidarity, after which demands will follow.[27]

With the site occupation akin to Greenham Common and the consensus-based action camp structure mirroring Climate Camp, Occupy Wall Street ignited a global movement seeking new ways of making change together.

Both Climate Camp and Occupy Wall Street share much more standardised organising methods than Greenham Common, both of which are structured around consensus decision-making using the same processes and hand-signals established across social movements around the world.[28] However where Occupy Wall Street was the first model of a now globally replicated form, Climate Camp was nationally organised with regional groups that participated in a centralised process:

> The only way in which the Camp for Climate Action exists is through neighbourhood meetings, UK Gatherings and direct actions that result from these meetings. Geographically organised neighbourhood meetings draw in activists from a particular area and normally meet in one or more towns or cities in their region. This system also operates during a Climate Camp, as camping areas and kitchens are arranged according to the neighbourhoods. Each neighbourhood and working group on the site sends a 'spoke' to daily hub meetings. Notes of each neighbourhood, working group and hub meeting were made available at meetings and on neighbourhood noticeboards.[29]

Climate Camps took place for time-limited periods of around a week in more rural sites, including power stations and airport runways. The Camp therefore was more like a planned event, rather than a long-term living site like Greenham Common or Occupy Wall Street:

> Working groups were set up to cover the logistics of preparing for, holding and deconstructing the Camp. The working groups networked with each other to enable the site to be occupied; site security, composting toilets, kitchens, camping areas, workshops and entertainments were all working [first]. Less obvious working groups were also in action, such as the welcome group welcoming activists and visitors, and the meetings group facilitating daily meetings and information flow between each neighbourhood and working group. The outreach group and media group were particularly active in the run-up to the event and during the event, inviting national and regional groups, local groups and people and explaining the camp to anyone who asked.[30]

Where Climate Camp met regularly through an organised process, Occupy Wall Street existed continually. Both exhibit 'antagonistic spatial practice', but where Climate camp as a pre-planned event followed consensus decision-making structures quite tightly, Occupy Wall Street mirrored Greenham Common's longevity and therefore might have been expected to show signs of 'organic horizontality' as was central to the women's peace camp. However as a city-based action camp, Occupy Wall Street encountered a much greater number of walk-ins than Climate Camp or Greenham Common. Consequently Occupy Wall Street established its processes by asking all participants to agree to a 'statement of intention on entering the space' and asked all new participants to attend trainings in consensus decision-making:

> We enter each Occupy Wall Street space with a commitment to:
> - mutual respect and support
> - anti-oppression
> - conflict resolution
> - nonviolence towards each other
> - direct democracy
>
> These agreements are in effect principles of social interaction, instilled into a terms of reference in an attempt to self-govern interpersonal behaviour as a fundamental practice of anti-oppression in collective organising. Where Climate Camp focussed on collective decision-making, Occupy Wall Street adopted perhaps a more deep-rooted redressing of power dynamics in the culture of its participants. This development reveals the limits to 'communitas' and 'organic horizontality', as Feigenbaum, Frenzel and McCurdy point out in reference to all three protest camps: 'campers faced difficulties figuring out how to balance issues of inclusivity, safety and well-being'.

Each protest group created an effective model of drawing global attention to a particular issue through a site-based protest activity that for participants engendered feelings of togetherness, equality and visions of possible utopias. These attempts to practice a kind of democratic politics that facilitates people's agency and genuine participation in affecting social change make interesting parallels with community arts projects seeking to engage in politics individuals and groups less readily vocal on their political objections than many of the activists that may have participated in each of the protest camps discussed.

FOR THE PEOPLE, OF THE PEOPLE: COMMUNITY-BASED PROFESSIONAL THEATRE MAKING BY GLAS(S) PERFORMANCE AND COMMON WEALTH

Glas(s) Performance was founded by Tashi Gore and Jess Thorpe in Glasgow in 2004. The artists describe their own practice:

> We make autobiographical theatre because we like meeting people and hearing stories. We hope that by sharing these stories with other people we might all learn a bit more about what it means to be human which might be a good thing. We deliver a socially engaged performance practice that collaborates with real people in the place of fictional characters to tell stories that resonate with audiences of all ages and experience. We aim to produce this type of

autobiographical performance work in Scotland and in doing so create a national platform for Scottish communities and individuals to tell their stories and share their histories in a professional and valued context.[31]

Their collaborative creative processes make the participants own stories the starting point for collective devising, placing immediate value on the sharing of non-professional storytelling. This participatory process focuses on the autobiography and creativity of all involved, rather than the outside expertise of scripts, documentary materials or political causes than have not arisen immediately form the group of individuals themselves.

Common Wealth was founded in 2010 by Aisha Zia, Evie Manning and Rhiannon White, who describe their practice as 'site-specific theatre events that encompass electronic sound, new writing, visual design and verbatim'. To place their work within a wider context of political and community theatre, the group says:

> We make work that is relevant and addresses concerns of our times. We seek out places to stage our work that are right in a community; a residential house, a boxing gym, places where people who might not go to the theatre might come to instead – we aim to make theatre for people who don't usually think it's for them, we're bored of theatre being for the middle classes and those that can afford it – we genuinely believe in theatre as an art form and the power it has. We think this should belong to everyone – as audience, participants and as protagonists. We're not necessarily interested in traditional story-telling but in creating memorable, unexpected experiences. Our ideas are rooted in socialist politics, working class backgrounds, a keen interest in contemporary music/ theatre/art/design, the people that we meet and an idealistic ambition to shift things. We see our plays as campaigns, as a way of bringing people together and making change feel possible.[32]

Their statements connect as much to La Pocha Nostra's method of political art-making as they do to Climate Camp's visioning of alternative futures.

Broadening participation in both the arts and politics is something the group practices as conscientiously as possible. Unlike political theatre made for discrete audiences or political events largely accessible to an already committed crowd, their working methods are designed to engage people who might often feel alienated both from politics and the arts. The group describes its techniques:

> Common Wealth are committed to non-theatre audiences and widening our audience from day one of our process on every project. We start with interviewing people and build a verbatim text, we ask about experiences, opinions, favourite songs. The sites we choose are as a result of us thinking about the cities/towns we're working in and how the site is placed within the

local community – who already uses it/has ownership of it and how we can include them in the making of the work. Because we're site-specific and work thoroughly with artists we start our set build/rehearsal process as early as we can and have an open door policy throughout so anyone can pop their head in. We knock on neighbours doors, introduce ourselves, put flyers and posters in places that people go, we find it more useful to put flyers in a GP surgery than an arts centre. Common Wealth work with cast and crews from all types of backgrounds – some have been working in theatre for years, others have never performed, others lend a hand with stage management or set design. In The Gurnos in Merthyr, we did one to one workshops, knowing we might lose people if they felt under pressure in a group. We always had something for people to do, to feel part of it – whether that was making signs, face painting or a quick writing exercise – just something to get on with so that next time we see them we could know them more.[33]

The practices proposed and employed by these two professional community theatre companies pose strong challenges to both the performance groups and the protest camps described, because their engagement with non-theatre and non-activist audiences expresses their politics of social change and real democracy on a fundamental level. The question can now be asked as to whether there is a route between these three schools of thought – protest, performance-making and community-based professional theatre – that can enable deeply developed aesthetics, effective political action and genuine broad political and artistic participation.

COLLECTIVE ART-MAKING FOR SOCIAL CHANGE: LIBERATE TATE

Liberate Tate bears resemblances with the three categories of groups in its collaborative practice, political organising and public participation. This is because the group takes inspiration and direction from all three, and, in doing so, it takes a step towards a new form of politically active, deeply participatory art.

Liberate Tate is an art collective nurtured by fifteen or so artists, but involving over 500 artists and activists in its regular performances. Since forming in 2010 it has become a hub of community building and exchange between artists and activists across disciplines and political concerns, and as such a blurring of identities has occurred: activists become involved in a deeper process of art-making, artists act politically in new and unfamiliar ways and each performance is shaped by all involved; therefore I will call them all performers, even if this is not an explicit identity every single participant personally assumes. For artists who have never experimented with direct action it has become a space to explore transgression and potentially illegal protest activity; for activists who ordinarily consider creativity as something to layer over the top of strategic plans it offers a more holistic practice of reinvigorating protest and opening up new possibilities to create change. In this sense it resembles the core-company with visiting artists' model of the performance groups the Wooster Group, Forced Entertainment and La Pocha Nostra, at the same time as utilising the tactics of antagonistic site-based protest camps Greenham Common, Climate Camp and Occupy Wall Street. By bringing participants from both artist and activist communities together in a collective creative process, the group draws on the participatory techniques of the community theatre companies Glas(s) Performance and Common Wealth.

As such, the group demonstrates practices of developing 'communitas' between the core and larger groups of artists, performers and participants and a form of 'organic horizontality' emerges in both the creative process and during the performances themselves. As was the case with the protest camps, 'antagonistic spatial practice' has been significant in coalescing creative collaboration around the particular target of BP sponsorship and inside the specific space of Tate galleries.

Process and product are one and the same, both in our art and when pushing for social change. Liberate Tate's artworks are collectively planned and rehearsed: the manifestation of each performance is dependent on the participation and varied creative instincts of all involved, including performers, visitors and staff. Staff reaction to our interventions becomes part of the material of the performance, enabling a spontaneous and responsive performance code to elicit surprising outcomes and maintain the urgency of confrontation. Whether writing on the ground or speaking aloud, visiting children playing a game in the performance or school groups explaining the politics of the performance to each other, it is the process of art-making with each and every one of these characters that creates the final piece, not merely a single object, image or moment.

Every time we make an intervention, we write a letter to the staff working in the gallery that day, articulating our confrontation with Tate's decision-makers rather than its workers. Our art-making is unpaid and all materials used in performances are paid for with income generated from print sales, performance lectures and writing commissions: the artwork pays for itself. Although we support the struggles of other artists to escape precarity in art-making, we find that to freely question the authority of the art establishment and one of the world's most powerful oil companies, we must be as unencumbered as possible from the constraints of funded creativity and campaigning.

Liberate Tate's 'art-making manifesto' bears resemblances to many of the aforementioned: the agreement of Occupy Wall Street, as well as the regular structure of Climate Camp, with a much looser, informal approach – like La Pocha Nostra's – focused on collective art-making initially rather than broad social movement organising:

- *We make together.* Everyone shares and carries the group's aesthetic and creative decisions. We will have disagreements and this is a healthy and valuable process, but everyone is invested in a shared outcome.
- *We question constructively.* Questions are necessary. However bald critique without a commitment to push the ideas further to reach a satisfactory place doesn't count as constructive questioning. We question as part of our collaborative search for a holistic, powerful art intervention.
- *We are 'in the room', except when we are 'not in the room'.* When we are in the room, we regularly participate in meetings and on email, and as such we know we are up to speed with the group conversation and creative process. When we are unable to participate regularly, we mindfully leave it to others to keep the fire burning, contributing when we can.
- *We are Liberate Tate but also ourselves.* We respect each other's boundaries outside (and inside) of the Liberate Tate 'room'.
- *Our creative process draws from artist and activist practices.* We build ideas loosely from concepts, shapes and visions, as artists. We hone ideas for political impact and strategic effectiveness, as activists.
- *We both hold and challenge our differences.* We each recognise the artistic, political and emotional significance of Liberate Tate for those involved.
- *We are patient.* With ourselves, with each other, with the art establishment, with Tate, with Nicholas Serota. *We are impatient.* With the art establishment, with Tate senior management, with the Board of the Tate Gallery.[34]

In March 2016 Liberate Tate celebrated the victory of its initial strategic aim and delivered the following artists' statement, from which this is a segment:

> We did this with our determination, commitment, stamina, tenacity, audacity, outrage, creativity, artistic craft, deep ecology and soulful collaboration. We did this with approximately 75 litres of molasses, 25 litres of sunflower oil, 20 helium balloons, 15 whispered hours of court transcripts, 1 tonne of arctic ice, 50 tubes of black paint, one 16.5 metre wind turbine blade, 1 portable toilet, 20 black sleeping sacks, 600 sticks of willow charcoal, 60 carefully selected texts, 60 millilitres of black tattooing ink, 600 black latex gloves, and 100 or so black veils – including one at 64 square metres. We did this together. We did this with Art. We did this as Art.[35]

The language of the group bears echoes of both the polemics of La Pocha Nostra and Forced Entertainment, as well as the pragmatics and political ambition of Climate Camp and Occupy Wall Street, alongside the acknowledgements of broad participation both in the production of the art/the campaign and in the much wider struggle to hold the oil industry to account. These parallels and crossovers open up a new form of creative practice that Liberate Tate signals towards: born out of careful artistic creation that remains embedded in strategic campaigning goals and dedicated to deepening engagement in both creative and political processes.

CONCLUSION

All the groups discussed here experiment with form, process and politics in attempts to reimagine and recreate the world we are living in, in some way. Liberate Tate tries to be guided by each of these methods in order that the process of aesthetic co-creation is made able to produce felt political outcomes. Our practice suggests that the very process of creatively pushing for change at Tate enacts in itself the political shifts necessary to remove power from oil companies and start to enable a vibrant living democracy. By challenging the oil industry with a democratic artistic practice, we seek to replace not only the sponsor logo on the door, but the wider politics that inform our cultures. As such, Liberate Tate is one experiment in the long history of how grassroots groups, artists and theatre-makers have experimented with ways of working and bringing people together as a method to facilitate social change. The process of learning and sharing these parallel tools and methods between artists and activists is a rich one, which will undoubtedly long continue.

NOTES

1. Theatre company, New York, 1975–present, thewoostergroup.org or see David Savran, *Breaking the Rules: The Wooster Group*. New York: Theatre Communications Group, 1986.

2. Theatre company, Sheffield, 1984–present, forcedentertainment.com or see Tim Etchells, *Certain Fragments: Contemporary Performance and Forced Entertainment*, London: Routledge, 1999.

3. Live art collective, California, 1991–present, pochanostra.com or see Guillermo Gomez-Peña, *Ethno-Techno: Writings on Performance, Activism and Pedagogy*, Oxon: Routledge, 2013.

4. Protest camp, see Alice Cook and Gwyn Kirk, *Greenham Women Everywhere: Dreams, Ideas and Actions from the Women's Peace Movement*. London: Pluto, 1983.

5. Non-violent direct action is a form of protest which usually involves physical blockade of industry or offices in order to halt production; people consciously choose to make themselves vulnerable to arrest, legal ramifications and sometimes physical injury in such activities.

6. Protest camp, see facebook.com/climatecamp or see Bibi van der Zee, *Climate Camp Disbanded. The Guardian*, 2 March 2011. Accessed 29 January 2017. https://www.theguardian.com/environment/2011/mar/02/climate-camp-disbanded.

7. Protest camp, see http://www.nycga.net or see Todd Gitlin, *Occupy Nation: The Roots, the Spirit and the promise of Occupy Wall Street*. New York: Harper Collins, 2012.

8. Art collective, see liberatetate.org.uk or see Liberate Tate in *Performance Research Journal: On Institutions* (2015) and *Performance Research Journal: On*

the *Maternal* (2017) or see Mel Evans, *Artwash: Big Oil and the Arts*. London: Pluto, 2015.

9. *Toni & Bobbi*, Liberate Tate, 2010; *Licence to Spill*, Liberate Tate, 2010; *Sunflower*, Liberate Tate, 2010.

10. *The Gift*, Liberate Tate, 2012.

11. *All Rise*, Liberate Tate, 2013; *Parts per Million*, Liberate Tate, 2013

12. *Time Piece*, Liberate Tate, 2015.

13. *Birthmark*, Liberate Tate, 2015.

14. Elizabeth LeCompte and Richard Foreman quoted in Bonnie Marranca 'The Wooster Group: A Dictionary of Ideas' in *PAJ: A Journal of Performance and Art* 25:2 (2003): 1–18.

15. Forced Entertainment website. Accessed 29 January 2017. forcedentertainment.com.

16. Ibid.

17. Consensus, that is, total agreement between all parties; consensus decision-making, that is, formal processes of making decisions by consensus as developed by activists groups starting with the Clamshell Alliance in the United States during the incarceration of over 1,500 activists in 1977 (see Anna Feigenbaum, Fabian Frenzel and Patrick McCurdy, *Protest Camps*, London: Zed, 2013, pp. 168–70).

18. Forced Entertainment website. Accessed 29 January 2017. forcedentertainment.com.

19. Guillermo Gomez Peña, *Ethno-Techno: Writings on Performance, Activism and Pedagogy*, Oxon: Routledge, 2013.

20. Ibid.

21. Ibid.

22. Greenham Common Women's Peace Camp. Accessed 29 January 2017. greenhamwpc.org.uk.

23. Ibid.

24. Ibid.

25. Ibid.

26. Climate Camp no longer has a public presence via the website it previously held. This description is taken from a British Science Association web page and used because from personal experience of participating in the organisation of the camp and presentation of it to the media, I confirm the accuracy of the description by British Science Association. Accessed 29 January 2017. collectivememory.britishscienceassociation.org/memory/camp-for-climate-action.

27. Occupy Wall Street website. Accessed 29 January 2017. nycga.net/resources/documents/principles-of-solidarity/.

28. See Seeds for Change website. Accessed 29 January 2017. seedsforchange.org.uk or Anna Feigenbaum, Fabian Frenzel and Patrick McCurdy, *Protest Camps*, London: Zed, 2013, p. 150.

29. Climate Camp descriptions documented by the British Science Association. Accessed 29 January 2017. collectivememory.britishscienceassociation.org/memory/camp-for-climate-action.

30. Ibid.

31. Glass Performance website. Accessed 29 January 2017. glassperformance.co.uk.
32. Common Wealth website. Accessed 29 January 2017. commonwealththeatre.co.uk.
33. Ibid.
34. Liberate Tate internal document, unpublished.
35. Liberate Tate website. Accessed 29 January 2017. liberatetate.org.uk.

REFERENCES

Climate Camp, facebook.com/climatecamp or see descriptions documented by the British Science Association. Accessed 29 January 2017. collectivememory.british-scienceassociation.org/memory/camp-for-climate-action.

Cook, Alice and Gwyn Kirk. 1983. *Greenham Women Everywhere: Dreams, Ideas and Actions from the Women's Peace Movement*. London: Pluto.

Common Wealth website. Accessed 29 January 2017. commonwealththeatre.co.uk

Etchells, Tim. 1999. *Certain Fragments: Contemporary Performance and Forced Entertainment*. London: Routledge.

Evans, Mel. 2015. *Artwash: Big Oil and the Arts*. London: Pluto.

Feigenbaum, Anna, Fabian Frenzel, and McCurdy Patrick. 2013. *Protest Camps*. London: Zed.

Forced Entertainment website. Accessed 29 January 2017. forcedentertainment.com

Gitlin, Todd. 2012. *Occupy Nation: The Roots, the Spirit and the promise of Occupy Wall Street*. New York: Harper Collins.

Glass Performance website. Accessed 29 January 2017. glassperformance.co.uk

Greenham Common Women's Peace Camp. Accessed 29 January 2017. greenham-wpc.org.uk.

Guillermo Gomez Peña. 2013. *Ethno-Techno: Writings on Performance, Activism and Pedagogy*. Oxon: Routledge.

Hanisch, Carol. *The Personal Is Political*. Written in 1969, first published in *Notes from the Second Year: Women's Liberation* in 1970. Accessed 29 January 2017. http://www.carolhanisch.org/CHwritings/PIP.html.

Higgins, Hannah. 2002. *The Fluxus Experience*. Berkeley, CA: University of California Press.

Holloway, John. 2002. *Change the World without Taking Power*. London: Pluto.

Liberate Tate in *Performance Research Journal: On the Maternal* (forthcoming 2017) Liberate Tate internal document, unpublished.

Liberate Tate website. Accessed 29 January 2017. liberatetate.org.uk.

Liberate Tate, 'Confronting the institution in performance: Liberate Tate's Hidden Figures' in *Performance Research Journal: On Institutions* 20:4 (2015): 78–84.

Marranca, Bonnie. 2003. 'The Wooster Group: A Dictionary of Ideas'. *PAJ: A Journal of Performance and Art* 25(2): 1–18.

Occupy Wall Street website. Accessed 29 January 2017. nycga.net/resources/documents/principles-of-solidarity/.

Savran, David. 1986. *Breaking the Rules: The Wooster Group*. New York: Theatre Communications Group.

Schechner, Richard. 2002. *Performance Studies*. London: Routledge.

Turner, Victor. 1982. *From Ritual to Theatre: The Human Seriousness of Play*. University of Michigan: PAJ Publications.

Wooster Group, The, website. Accessed 29 January 2017. thewoostergroup.org.

van der Zee, Bibi. *Climate Camp Disbanded. The Guardian,* 2 March 2011. Accessed 29 January 2017.

Chapter 9

Embracing Failure, Educating Hope
Some Arts Activist Educators' Concerns in Their Work for Social Justice

Jane Trowell

> Nothing is more repugnant to utopian conscience than utopia with unlimited travel; *endless striving is vertigo, hell*. (my italics, Bloch in Amsler, 2015: 108)

> The courage to hope comes not from confidence of doing something risky with a chance of success, but from cultivating a courageous "*attitude towards undecided material*" in the world. (my italics, Bloch in Amsler, 2015: 63)

> The idea of failure ... what is failure ... it is where we learn most deeply. (Peer W)

This chapter is written in the UK, specifically England, where we are living in neoliberal, materially and racially en-fortressed times. From a perspective of leftist social justice, increased oppressions are being meted out by a right-wing central government and media along racist, religious, xenophobic and protectionist lines. Post-Brexit, hate crimes are being emboldened in new sections of the white populace. People of colour, of diverse sexualities and identities, and others living here in diaspora are experiencing a spike in daily hostility and abuse (BBC, 2016). These conditions are prevalent in many countries across the world where neoliberalism and 'austerity' have wreaked economic chaos. The new Right is harnessing and racialising economic hardship, scapegoating 'others' rather than confronting a broken economic order. The times are volatile, old certainties are uprooted, the social fabric full of eruptive protest and counter-protest. However, this very volatility reminds us that the current situation is not set in stone as a permanent state: we must know that it remains, to use Ernst Bloch's term, 'undecided material' (Bloch in Amsler, 2015: 63). Hope in the undecidedness of the present and future is a tenet running through this chapter. Given the alarming yet undecided times we are in, it is essential that 'people can "learn hope" in order to reopen their relationship with political possibility' (Amsler, 2015: 6).

Many people on the spectrum of the Left feel fraught about failure. Many of us feel the pressure to redouble, treble or quadruple our activism. In this chapter I contend that now more than ever we need to make time to reflect, but not as a depressed act, but as part of an action/reflection cycle: we should become more strategic in the face of increased urgency. Now more than ever we must not be dazzled by political vertigo to become unstrategic in our actions or to grind ourselves down into Bloch's 'hell' of endless striving (Bloch, 1995: 315 in Amsler, 2015: 108). Our social movements do not benefit from a striving that leads to burn out, splits, heartbreak and guilt. For the forces that we are challenging, it would be a gift.

While 'failure' is my topic, I am refuting its negative associations. What would happen to the integrity of our pedagogical work with people, the power of the art produced, the impacts within wider movements for social justice, the sustainability of our practices if we, as arts activists and educators, were to reclaim and embrace 'failure' as, in fact, 'educating hope'? In other words, I will contend that to talk both internally and publicly about failure is part of building collective hope and action. I am aware that I am calling for reflection on failure from the position of a white, feminist, arts activist educator who gets to write a chapter in a book – my proposals are complicated by privileges afforded by coloniality, on which more later.

So far this may not seem a radical proposal to some readers. Within education, Donald Schön's influential theories around 'reflective practice' are already thirty years old (Schön, 1987) and there is much good practice within formal arts education. The issue at stake is within activist contexts: I am suggesting that the problem arises when arts activist educators operate with the main intention of activism and social change. Working as part of such networks for nearly three decades, I have frequently heard people (and sometimes myself) utter variants on 'It's a fail, it's an epic fail!' regarding the political impact of our own work or others'. In such a phrase, I often suspect a kind of scornful or ashamed shutdown, which can extinguish the future-generosity of learning. 'Failed' work is history, a distressing chapter best healed alone or an enraging memory to be suppressed. Yet a shutdown leaves all kinds of wounds that can fester, hindering our work.

Failure's bad reputation is understandable: in everyday speech, 'failing' is a negative. The derivation is from Latin 'to disappoint' and Old French 'to be weak' (Collins, 2000). So, in origin, the noun 'failure' indicates a judgement freighted with the emotion of the lost chance, of not rising to the challenge. Going deeper, the Latin and Old French definitions of 'failure' stem from the

Greek 'phelos' – 'deceitful'. I propose that 'failure' is deceitful only when it is buried or rejected by being made unspeakable of. Failing to discuss 'failure' is a form of deception to the self and to others, it suppresses both pain and complexity and, most importantly, it misses opportunities to advance the goals of our work. Finally, it disowns the failure and leaves discussion of it to others. This does not educate hope.

However, artists, creatives and arts educators should reclaim what we can offer in terms of embracing failure as educating hope. Novelist Toni Morrison speaks of the importance of 'stumbles along the way'.[1] Writer Samuel Beckett's 'Fail again, Fail better' is quoted far and wide, including in Silicon Valley.[2] Artists and creatives are taught that experimentation and the right to fail are integral to the artistic, creative and learning process. We are taught that it takes effort to reach the moment when we feel the work is ready or finished. We work through the grasping for form, the many experiments, the endless practice, those difficult rehearsals, the screwed-up pieces of paper and cutting room floor. These steps could be considered 'failures' in that they are not yet 'the final piece', but framed differently, they are also successive exercises in developing hope, through creativity, craft, criticality and endurance. Getting over disappointment, dealing with frustration, judging when work is going in the right or wrong direction, refining skills, picking up and carrying on: these are part of what artists learn to do. Educators in the arts foster these very skills with participants and students.

Given artists, educators and arts educators are brought up in these processes, why is it that when our work is done in an 'activist' mode, reflection is often squeezed out? How can embracing failure as educating hope help us to operate better in these extreme political times?

In this chapter, I will start by sharing some thoughts provoked through a vivid experience at a gathering of artists, arts activists and educators from nearly twenty years ago. Then I will introduce theories around 'educating hope' from sociologist and activist Sarah Amsler's recent book *The Education of Radical Democracy* (Amsler, 2015). I'm working with these theories as I see particular resonances for arts activists and educators.

Because I am interested in foregrounding arts activist educators' insights, I will share my peers' testimony on failure. These are nine diverse arts activist educators, whose views I invited in 2014. They work in live art, performance poetry, creative writing, art, film, music and dance. Some work in schools and universities; some in arts, environmental, social and health contexts; others work in social movements, protest campaigns and grassroots community projects and many work across contexts. However, what I primarily draw on here is their thoughts on embracing failure. In the main part of the chapter, I set peers' testimony on 'failure' in conversation with Amsler's theories. I will structure this through proposing three ways to 'embrace failure': cherishing *theory*, cherishing *courage* and cherishing *time*.

First, a snapshot from the past:

> *Picture the scene: it is 1998 and we are in Dun Laoghaire, Ireland at 'Critical Sites: Issues in Critical Art Practice and Pedagogy'. It is a three-day international artist–led conference organised by Projects Environment (now Littoral) in collaboration with Critical Access (Dublin).*[3]
>
> *On day two, my colleagues and I are offering 'True Confessions', a break-out workshop on when things 'fail'. Two of us are from arts activist group Platform (London), collaborating with our ally Lucy Milton from Helix Arts (Newcastle).*[4] *We've been feeling uneasy: while critics and theorists have been catching up with the rapidly expanding 'socially engaged arts' field, why aren't we practitioners creating and sustaining spaces for our own critique, and for mutual and self-development? Also, this conference has been full of high-energy presentations of 'successful' work by pioneering artists and arts educators including Suzanne Lacy, or deep theory sessions mainly delivered by scholars including Sarat Maharaj, Pitika Ntuli and Grant Kester. There's an air of inspirational exemplars but not much talk of failure or difficulty, something our session aims to make space for.*
>
> *We lay out fifteen chairs, which feels right. However, we are taken aback when minutes before the start, people flood in and we end up with over sixty, many sitting on the floor and tables. In my memory there was a hushed expectation: it felt strangely transgressive. We introduced our motivation, why we thought the session was needed, some ground rules on respect, anonymity and confidentiality and then shared vulnerable stories of when we felt things had failed in our work, for whom and tentative speculations as to why. People discussed in small groups and then came back together to draw out themes. With such a crowd, time was pressed, and when the session ended late, many people lingered in intense conversation. We sensed and people told us that 'True Confessions' had acted as a release, a rush of movement, an encouragement to face difficulty.*

Nearly twenty years later, I see this as an early experiment in what I mean now by 'embracing failure'. As arts activist educators we created a semi-public, thoughtful space where we framed the sharing of failure as a tender yet hopeful act, an act for which skills can be developed, an act towards making future change happen.

Between that memorable experiment in 1998 and a couple of years ago, I did not explicitly focus on 'failure'. I continued to embed 'reflective practices' into my individual work as an educator and continued to try to nurture it in collective transdisciplinary work with varying degrees of success. I vowed to speak openly and ethically about failure and difficulties (as well as successes) in public contexts because I had seen that honesty encourages people. As a specific example, I embedded it in the facilitation of Platform's experimental courses for artists and activists: 'The Body Politic – Social and Ecological Justice, Arts, Activism' (2004–2009).[5]

It was while reading Amsler's *The Education of Radical Democracy* (2015) that questions of failure came back to the forefront for me. Sarah Amsler, originally from the United States, has a background in sociology, politics and education. In her book, she works with theory from *The Principle of Hope* by German Jewish Marxist philosopher Ernst Bloch (1885–1977). Bloch's influential work comprises three volumes written in the United States between 1938 and 1947 while Bloch was in exile from the Third Reich – a dumbfounding exercise in hope in itself (Bloch, 1995).

While *The Education of Radical Democracy* gripped me throughout, I was surprised to find resonant themes that chimed with my experience as an *arts educator*, such as Bloch's and Amsler's philosophy on 'educating hope'. Although Amsler does not speak directly of failure, I took the book's theme of educating hope to be an antithesis to the *negative* framing of failure and found a place for failure in her grounded diagnosis of how educational practices of 'counter-capitalist radical democracy' against neoliberalism actually operate (Amsler, 2015: 19). Failure in political struggle, in arts activism, in education, can also be an opening.

Coming from the arts and education, Amsler and Bloch's lexicon is startlingly resonant. I will quote Amsler at length here:

> For Bloch, who was above all a critical theorist of revolutionary possibility, this *freedom of the counter-move* – of human beings *practising active self-determination* and *'forward dreaming'* in the concrete circumstances of their everyday lives – is accomplished not by attempting to transcend the extant limitations of the world or ourselves, but by throwing ourselves into *'what is becoming'*; seeking the *'open dimension'* in people, *where possibility articulates* and *the open dimension in things, 'on the leading edge, where becoming is still possible'*; and by gravitating towards wherever and whenever *the 'unbecome* is located and *seeks to articulate itself'*. (my italics, 2015: 3)

This relevance to the arts increased as I read on: the work of educating hope is for Amsler 'enlarging' (5), 'embodied' (19), 'refusing despair' (30), 'emergent' (53), 'freely experimental' (61), 'open to "surprise over bliss and fear"' (61), 'courageous' (63), 'knowing-daring' (103) and 'receptive' (111). Through it we can 'make a machine for fighting anxiety' (110), find and foster our 'militant optimism' (113), 'incit[e] an interest in freedom' (141), 'incubate insubordination' (146), 're-open the present' and 'unclose the future' (192). Most important for me, as an educator, is Bloch and Amsler's key tenet that we – people – are 'unfinished' (55) and, in terms of our creative and democratic potential, always 'unfinishable' (178).

Educating hope is holistic: it integrates the individual with social/societal possibility for change. In Bloch's words: 'Possibility here in fact means both internal, active capability, and external, passive capability-of-being-done; therefore, capability-of-being-other falls into capability-of-doing-other and capability-of-becoming-other' (Bloch, 1995: 232 in Amsler, 2015: 62). If we find ways to refuse to see ourselves as fixed and refuse to see others as fixed and refuse to see the wider situation as fixed, we can progress. We can *be* other, *do* other, *become* other than we currently are. This is hope in action, this can sustain us.

In 2014, I inadvertently reopened the question of 'failure'. After many years of work as an arts educator dedicated to social justice, mainly with Platform but also in art teacher education,[6] I started a PhD and was determined for the research to be of use to educators, a sort of 'service PhD' to our field. I sent my PhD proposal to a diverse group of twenty-seven arts activist educator peers whom I knew shared similar concerns. I invited people to tell me what they thought was important to them in it, what was missing or problematic. The peers reflect my networks and most are graduates, a point that some peers critique, as you will read.

The proposal was titled *Art, activism and liberatory pedagogies: an investigation into the potential, the dangers, and sometimes failure of art-activist pedagogies to analyse and undo inequalities and act as a powerful vehicle for social justice.*[7] Twenty-three people responded to me, with over 12,000 words of response. This I digested and searched by themes and keywords to see how different issues were arising among respondents.[8]

The keyword that most peers responded to (after 'arts' and 'activism') was 'failure'. Of course the question of difficulty arose without people using the exact words 'fail' or 'failure' and so on, and I will also refer to those responses. I was struck by the high level of interest. It recalled 'True Confessions' all those years previously. Peer T makes a very clear case: 'It's hard to come across critical accounts of these kinds of art activist educational practices (which would be really good so we can learn from each other!). By this I don't mean making it a negative and critical account, as the positive should of course be included' (Peer T).

Below, I work with nine peers' responses in the context of embracing failure as educating hope. Four peers are artists of colour based in England and six identify as women. I will work within three 'cherishings'. The word 'cherish' originates from the French 'chere' for 'dear' as in dear friend or 'expensive, valuable'. When you cherish, you protect, you value. Learning from peers, I propose that embracing failure to educate hope involves three acts of cherishing: cherishing theory, cherishing courage and cherishing time.

CHERISHING THEORY

Why can cherishing theory help us embrace failure, in order to educate hope? The theory needed is theory that helps us answer the biggest questions we have, theory that helps us live, create, confront abuses of power and be active for social justice. Peers suggest we cannot embrace failure unless we have identified the worldviews, theories and political standpoints that consciously or unconsciously underpin us and the work we are doing. We need to acknowledge how capitalism, secularism, religious faith, culture, domination of scholarly 'theory', economics and culture by European-descended peoples bear upon our goals and action. As artists, we need to question how our theories and cultural standpoints about aesthetics and the role of art impact on our work in a world where European norms in art remain dominant. But do we?

UNDERTHEORISED?

Peer U sets out some basic questions:

> I guess I'm asking, what is the endpoint art-activists are aiming in for? As educators, what is the ultimate aim? What is the future that is desired? What are the actions hoping to be inspired in others?

Peer P is troubled:

> The thing that worries me is that in the particular places where I struggle, there is not a robust analysis of exactly how and why things are going so badly wrong. I could go on.
>
> I think your quest to re-frame power and privilege in light of current theory is great, I hope you succeed because a lot of the stuff that is being said and processed is theoretically very, very weak. (Peer P)

Knowing the frontline grassroots contexts P mostly works in, 'theory' here is not defined as written texts that are associated with scholarly minded people, although these may be involved. Theory is a principle by which anyone organises their thinking and actions. So this is not about using potentially alienating or dense language in the contexts in which we work, but collectively sharing or creating a joint ethos, joint aims, immersing us in theory-making through discussion and practice. This theorising gives something to collectively refer to and hold on to. To answer Peer U's questions, it is also transparent, accountable and collectively revisable.

I believe Peer U and P's points are crucial and consider it a significant reason for why discussions of 'failure' fail to take place, or, fail to take place fruitfully. If the underlying theory has not been shared, terms unpicked and reselected, assumptions will be made which can sorely hinder the embrace of failure as educating hope.

The collective cherishing of theory is an ongoing process and helps 'enable the organization of human flourishing' (Amsler, 2015: 73) as 'people practis[e] "real" or "true" self-determination in common with one another' (Amsler, 2015: 74).

COLONIALITY

However, the best articulated social justice theory in the world can still fail to match up to actual behaviour of individuals and groups, our working and social processes, our art-making and decision-making, access to shared resources and wider structural inequalities. Even more challenging: an individual or group's *public espousal* of social justice aims and theory can actively conceal and perpetuate the colonial and power differentials within them. This is the unavoidability of 'coloniality', as distinct from colonialism, according to Nelson Maldonado-Torres:

> Coloniality survives colonialism. It is maintained alive in books, in the criteria for academic performance, in cultural patterns, in common sense, in the self-image of peoples, in aspirations of self, and so many other aspects of our modern experience. In a way, as modern subjects *we breathe coloniality all the time and everyday*. (*my italics*, Maldonado-Torres, 2007: 243)

Decolonial scholar Ramon Grosfoguel defines what coloniality does as follows:

> I use 'coloniality' to address 'colonial situations' in the present period. . . . I mean the cultural, political, sexual, spiritual, epistemic and economic oppression/exploitation of subordinate racialized/ethnic groups by dominant racialized/ethnic groups with or without the existence of colonial administrations. (Grosfoguel, 2007: 220)

Peers point to this. Peer E observes: 'I think the underlying power of the activist practitioner is really important to consider – it's almost harder to unpack ego, preconceptions, prejudices of the "activist" practitioner whose identity is framed around liberatory principles' (Peer E). Part of embracing failure is coming to terms with the mismatch between claims to liberatory theory and 'ego, preconceptions and prejudices' within each of us. For *white* arts activists and educators – who because of structural inequalities of coloniality still dominate the arts, education and NGO/campaigning in England – embracing our coloniality in why things fail is urgent work.

A U.S.-based white peer quotes her African-American colleague:

> Why are well-meaning white liberal artist/activist people wanting to do community arts? Why do middle-class college students getting community arts degrees get grants to want to 'help' or 'save' kids or adults in prisons or in afterschool programs, community based 'healing' projects (with mostly/all, people of color)? White people are getting jobs, making money off our misfortune, in our communities. They are in our city neighborhoods because of guilt. That's their problem, not ours. They should leave us alone and get out of our neighborhoods. . . . And shouldn't black people have opportunities to be trained, to be in charge, able to earn our livings off this work, since it's our community, our people? (Peer M)

While this example points to colonial, missionary behaviour in formal, paid contexts, the same concerns arise in unpaid arts activist work where white people dominate. Indeed, where white middle class arts activists work unpaid, there are often fraught questions of privilege in time and material circumstances.

So, embracing failure means confronting the conditions under which colonial, unjust and sometimes abusive power relations are reproduced or embodied by us, *even as we claim we are working for social justice*. This is where theory meets practice.

Here is the challenge: to consider who we are, our subjectivity and the nature of the earned and unearned privileges we have in relation to our theories and principles. How did we get to be the one(s) initiating a project/action, collaborating, getting the job or in charge? What structural processes enabled us, and not others, to have access to working in this way, to have access to resources, contacts, networks? Who comprises these networks, and who cannot be seen there, and why? What language, what knowledge base, what or whose processes and aesthetics do we choose, and who does it attract or repel? How is social justice in terms of gender identities, sexualities, ability/ disabilities, intergenerationality and all the intersections playing out in our groupings and in our work?

PROFESSIONALISATION

This relates to a question I asked peers: 'What does "liberatory pedagogy", "activist", "educator", "facilitator", "social justice", "arts", "creative" mean, and to whom?' Peer E commented: 'There is something about the professionalisation of these terms that speaks of privilege – i.e. people could embody all these terms but wouldn't label their work "grassroots". . . . Also who gains power in the name of speaking with/for the "oppressed"'. (Peer E) Peer R agrees: 'It's going to be important to seek out some of the art/activists outside those documented & known to academia i.e. after school arts programmes, community groups, prison work etc . . . thinking of people like El Crisis (poet) & Spoken Word education collectives etc who do political organising & work but maybe outside of being known to wider groups' (Peer R).

As our work gets known, we can be drawn into an inward conversation between 'professional radicals" or professional arts-activists on a 'circuit" – salaried, funded, or not. If we are involved in higher-stakes direct action arts activism we can all too easily become divorced from the systemic barriers that many oppressed groups feel to 'activism'. This can again reproduce 'professional-class' and often white domination. Another impact is that arts activists and arts educators of colour, those who are young, those who are from 'marginalised groups' find themselves spending precious time calling out or resisting cooption by professional or institutional forces – usually white-led – that want to gain radical kudos by association, or, at worst, who want to take over or disarm the work.

EMBODIMENT

The refusal of white arts activists and educators to want to see coloniality inside our work in social justice movements leads to multiple and sometimes jaw-dropping oppressions.[9] That this wilful blindness is most often occurring among white, privileged, educated individuals or groups puts the colonial finger in the wound of progressive politics. Talking the talk is not walking the walk.

It is not enough to cherish theory, we must, from whatever subjectivity or positionality, strive to embody it in practice, and then to monitor ourselves and check ourselves with others as an ongoing practice. Embodying theory and monitoring, checking with others involves 'voicing what is censured and visibilising what is obscured, moving between what has been fixed and expanding what is contracting, (Amsler, 2015: 177). Building such a practice may enable us to find what Nikolas Kompridis calls 'new tongues with which to say what cannot be said and new ears with which to hear that which cannot be heard' (Kompridis, 2006: 236 in Amsler, 2015: 162–3).

SCALE

Another aspect of cherishing theory is that it can help us address issues of scale of ambition in our work. Feelings of failure are often linked to the scale of change we were setting ourselves to achieve. Peer U points out: 'What responsibilities exist to manage expectations without depressing optimism and drive to uncover unimagined possibilities?'

Amsler provokes us:

> while attention to the big-A activist politics of the large-scale, globalized and publicly spectacular movements fires the public imagination, it can also diminish the importance of everyday spaces for counter-capitalist thinking and practice, deeper experiments in radical democracy, longer-term campaigns that chip away at power and build possibilities from the ground up. (Amsler, 2015: 198)

How are we theorising the scale of activity relative to people's capacity and how do we situate the work within macropolitics? Are we giving value to the range of tactics for confronting power, including the '*unspectacular politics of possibility* that people practise in places and areas of social life where *professional radicals* rarely tread and that most people take for granted as cultural furniture – education, cultural activity, social reproduction, community building and survival, and the '"behind-the-scenes" work' (my italics, Amsler, 2015: 22).

CAPITALISM AND THE STATE

Peer E suggests another risk of the under-embodied theory is the illusion of feeling that simply because we are critical we are 'outside' the system: 'Identifying privileges and ways in which our behaviours mirror the *practices and prejudices of capitalist societies* is a process that is often difficult/ unchallenged' (Peer E, my italics). Peer E asks us to consider how work and behaviour can end up re-inscribing capitalist approaches and values that we claim we're trying to delegitimise, negate and dismantle. From her I take that embracing failure also involves what Amsler calls the 'task of disrupting and unlearning the affective regimes of neoliberal capitalism' (Amsler, 2015: 112), in other words continually challenging how neoliberal capitalism produces our emotions and actions *even as we state we are against it.*

Take the case of the many micro-utopic arts activist projects/campaigns – many self-organised and some funded – that have erupted in recent years in the UK as a response to the 2008 crash and cuts to education and the arts. Many illustrate alternatives, prefigure or foreshadow positive futures, some claim to challenge capitalism, racism, privatisation, securitisation and so on. Many of these were inspirational, but how many could fall foul of an angry leftist outburst I witnessed at a social-political arts event a few years ago?[10] 'Fuck your micro-utopias!' came the shout from the floor, followed by a diatribe on the kind of 'arts activism' that does not intend to challenge or delegitimise power, but uses the language of protest as a fashionable aesthetic.

As Amsler points out, there is 'a common criticism that "prefigurative" forms of politics uncritically celebrate the *superficial performance* of new possibilities in "cracks" of domination without either seriously compromising or actually disengaging from institutionalised systems of power and structural relations of force (which are thus left intact)' (my italics, Amsler, 2015: 23).

CHERISHING COURAGE

With the complexities above in mind, it is not a surprise that talking privately or publicly about failure can feel and be difficult. We might fear that embracing failure could unveil deep difference, fierce critique and angry conflicts between us that we cannot get over or that could damage the wider movement. Where the critique is around coloniality, white arts activists and educators can find themselves avoiding or pushing back against these discussions: we can take offence, fear a loss of power or validity. Egos can crumple: but surely I'm a 'good ally'? Amsler suggests that we are in a moment where 'rather than embracing contradiction as constitutive of political life, there is a pull in popular politics towards feeling 'that conflict is bad' (2015: 183). This is a mistake. Embracing failure involves learning skills to be able to hear and say difficult things to each other. It does involve conflict, but is situated as educating hope. For white people, the task is continually to work on our own construction within coloniality, acknowledging how it operates within our choices as arts activist educators, and how we can counter it. 'Courage' derives from the French word 'coeur' or 'heart'; to encourage is to give heart or hearten. Embracing failure as educating hope is an act of enheartenment. If we don't at heart believe we can learn, what are we doing?

ALCHEMY

A peer offered me these thoughts:

> It looks to me that your work could begin to outline a series of successful strategies on how we can be truly effective and *this is gold dust*. But to get to the gold dust we need to really face the piles of shit and the failures, we all find that hard to do.... It takes a lot of courage to admit failure, anyway the funders don't like it either!! *I feel we have few safe contexts for facing up to our failures.* (my italics, Peer V)

If the discussion of failure arouses fears of personal, social, political or critical loss, then it clearly needs to be reclaimed as an act of becoming that can create the 'gold dust' of greater effectiveness in the undecided future. Framed as educating hope, courage becomes more attainable, and discussion could reopen the future. Amsler introduces the notion of alchemy, a process which turns base metal into gold: '[Alchemy] calls attention to how bringing ideas, people and materials together in freely experimental ways can have unpredictable and often inexplicable results. It also recognises both the "disaster character" and the "hope character" of possibility, privileging surprise over both bliss and fear' (Amsler, 2015: 30). If embracing failure is seen as genuine, experimental, non-formulaic and driven by cherishing the well-being and productiveness of individuals and the movement, then finding the courage to 'face up' to our failures becomes an act of alchemical creativity, turning the 'negative' into the gold of hope.

How are we going to become more courageous in embracing failure? I suggest we can be enheartened to discuss failure when we approach it thinking that, like success, failure is always 'unfinished', with many nuances and multiple viewpoints. We can shift from the shutdown of 'it's a fail!' to emphasise impermanence, its becomingness in the now and the future.

> The most potentially transformative kind of activity is that which can recognize 'undecided' and 'precarious' material in the present and work to shape its formation – including by creating such material through challenging that which appears as "decided" or 'fixed'. Indeed, [Bloch] argued that *the courage to hope comes not from confidence of doing something risky with a chance of success, but from cultivating a courageous 'attitude towards undecided material' in the world*. (my italics, Amsler, 2015: 63)

SKILLS

If we reframe 'failure' as 'undecided material' *in a world in which we are still learning*, then we can begin to cultivate methods and skills that can shape productive conversations about 'failure'. Amsler asks: 'What sort of practices heighten our receptivity to discomfort as a critical and creative emotion, and strengthen our capabilities to engage critically and generously in encounters with difference, ambiguity and unfamiliarity? Can we teach or learn to be radically open and discerning?' (2015: 184)

It takes courage and political commitment to listen to those coming from another standpoint. Our work is transdisciplinary and collaborative, and requires us to unlearn the fortress of disciplinary thinking, open our borders and relearn to hear from multiple perspectives, expertise, cultures and experiences. Peer G suggests using three lenses that challenge the dominance of political effectiveness as chief criterion for success: 'To my mind, the tension between "claims" and "failure" is especially interesting when it intersects with the 3D of . . . practice: art/education/activism. Something could be really successful from an educational perspective but unsuccessful from that of activism – or vice versa' (Peer G). If we take courage to 'step out of ourselves' and to share knowledges and to look at our work through these three and more lenses or standpoints, we begin to find the nuances in 'failure' and indeed success and begin the joint exercise in educating hope. Amsler links this to a previous point: 'With an aliveness to the importance of embodied theory, we can become people who have a courageous attitude, who are receptive to the practices of "engaging with troublesome knowledge and embracing uncomfortable encounters with otherness and critique"' (Amsler, 2015: 183).

CHERISHING TIME

However, the biggest block to embracing failure as educating hope is that of legitimising time spent on it. To cherish this time would be to frame the act of reflection as precious, as vital (literally life-giving), as a creative act of repair and deep nourishment.

URGENCY

Peer V speaks about the time pressures in urgent political struggles: 'I feel we . . . tend to just keep going and doing the same things because it's 'better to act' than not at all! Which is both true and not at all!' (Peer V)

With the pressure of political urgency and the rush of adrenalin, making time to reflect, to face up to difficulties, to understand the causes of conflicts can be sorely squeezed. Anything smacking of 'reflection' or 'evaluation' can be seen as an activity to make extra time for, only done when required by external partners, allies, funders – or worse, a meltdown between people – rather than anything more integrated, creative or political.

Our kind of work most often operates in restricted timeframes – a strategic date in a campaign, an urgent political moment or a set period that collaborators and/or external bodies have agreed is the project, action or campaign period. The first two in particular present challenges in terms of making time for reflection unless it is built into the fabric from the start.

But what would it be like if even the most responsive, urgent work was conceptually framed as part of a wider pedagogical movement-building process, part of: 'long periods of experimental work in educating autonomy – "a matter of digging a deep foundation, unostentatiously, patiently, and with a perseverance that is invulnerable to discouragement"' (Richard Hogue, 1924: 68 in Amsler, 2015: 137). How would such long-term framing impact on cherishing time for reflection and learning from failure? Flipping it over, how does time spent on reflection on failure encourage projects or actions to see themselves as part of long-term movement-building, thereby educating hope, and avoiding leaving people high and dry, or conflicted after projects end?

CAPITALISTIC TIME

I ask myself, can the pressure to 'act' and not reflect – even in the urgent service of anti-neoliberal, anti-oppression and social justice – conform in some ways and on some occasions to what could be called 'capitalistic thinking'?

Amsler suggests: 'When conceptualized as a critical resource, time does different things. Moving at alternative speeds – in non-capitalist time, counter-capitalist time, anti-authoritarian decision-making time – can be an act of defiance and intervention' (Amsler, 2015: 178).

Making time to discuss failure could be framed as an act of counter-capitalist 'defiance and intervention' that makes a real, generous opening:

> Claiming time (taking it, marking it, dedicating it, saving it, expanding it) is also a method for *cultivating possibilities of radical experience* – because time, in networked neoliberal societies of speed, in the frenzied anti-routines of high-stakes activism, in the compressed labour processes of advanced capitalism, and in the gendered divisions of labour in everyday life, is one thing that many people cannot imagine either having or claiming. (my italics: Amsler, 2015: 173)

Here time's preciousness and potency is acknowledged, as well as its unequal distribution across society. Are we building in recognition of differing capacities to make precious time to meet, to share, to reflect, who will be comfortable in different meeting settings, and how often, how long for, what times of day, day of week and so on? How much do we pack into our plans, influenced on some level by 'cost-benefit' thinking, putting pressure on participants, colleagues and ourselves? How much do we aerate the work, anti-capitalistically, with time to deeply think and deeply feel?

Peer U observes from the point of view of the educator:

> Many of the issues are complex and there are no easy answers, or it's the case that there are many levels and insufficient *time* to unpick the levels to get to the core ideas. There's a dual role of addressing the needs of the art forms, and developing technical skills, and adequately addressing the topic under exploration. . . . For the educator it is so easy to get caught up in the day-to-day practicalities over *time* that they could easily forget to stand back. (my italics, Peer U)

BECOMING

In relation to this, Amsler urges us to consider that 'learning to think, and to be radically democratic in everyday life, and to undertake radically democratic actions thus requires an education in becoming' (Amsler, 2015: 178). 'Becoming' is a continuous process and works against seeing ourselves or others as fixed. She elaborates that 'pedagogies of becoming concentrate on two types of work: creative and aesthetic ("art" in the broadest sense) and dialogical and relational ("conversation" in the broadest sense)' (2015: 178). Applying this to my theme, it suggests that embracing failure educates hope by cherishing it as creative time *and* relational/conversational time.

If political urgency is framed as a succession of imminent 'nows", pivoting around critical moments, critical periods, critical opportunities, then making time and spaces for 'becoming", for sustaining, for creatively nurturing will be sorely squeezed. If political urgency is reframed within a long becoming, a life's work, several generation's work, then time to embrace failure can be reconceived as part of building a steady, sustaining endeavour, in a pedagogy of becoming.

TIMING

In relation to this, there is also a cherishing of *timing and conditions*. Bloch speaks of the 'politics of possibility' and asks us to consider that there is a *range* of different temporalities of working towards change, some of which acknowledge everyday yet strategic labour: 'It is useful to know that the politics of possibility are often slow and plodding; that "not everything is possible or can be implemented at any time, *[as] absent conditions not only hinder they also block*"' (my italics, Bloch, 1995: 205 in Amsler, 2015: 108). This statement acknowledges that some political contexts close down space/time for active or dramatic change – consider the political situation in Germany during which Bloch, in exile, wrote *The Principle of Hope*. It points to the often quiet, unsung work of community-building, resistance and resilience. It also tells us that not all 'failure' is 'our fault': sometimes the forces at play violently shut down certain kinds of loud, public movement. As well as encouraging us in the 'slow and plodding' work, Bloch exhorts us, for the health of ourselves and the struggle, to periodically cease action. I want to repeat here the opening quotation: 'Nothing is more repugnant to utopian conscience than utopia with unlimited travel; *endless striving is vertigo, hell*' (my italics, Bloch, 1995: 315 in Amsler, 2015: 108).

ACTION/REFLECTION

The invitation is to cherish time to embrace failure as part of an action-reflection cycle, where we can share thoughts on failure and then continue better equipped with the work. Embracing failure makes an opportunity to heal the frenzied, angry, fragile and distressed soul or group and educates hope by acknowledging difficulty as part of our becoming in new futures. Many who are involved in political struggle feel anxious about stepping back. However, if this is seen through a creative cycle of action and reflection, periodically stepping back or more slowly is essential for the long-term goals of the work. It also works against giving the gift of burn out or splits between people/ groups to forces who would celebrate our collapse.

African-American lesbian feminist writer and activist Audre Lorde wrote: 'Caring for myself is not self-indulgence, it is self-preservation, and that is an act of political warfare' (Lorde, 1988: 131). Situating self-care as 'political warfare' is an arresting call, and it is key that it emerged from a writer and educator who was daily contending with racist, sexist and homophobic abuse within the brutalities of capitalism. Lorde's call also has universality. She demands we cherish our emotional, intellectual, political and physical bodies in order to better do the work over the long term. It takes a long time to recover from an abject sense of our own or others' failure if we are isolated. Sometimes people never recover and have to move away from activism. We need proper time built in to our process to consider 'failure'. Embracing failure is time spent on self- *and other-care*, as well as educating hope, skills and creativity for future work.

CONCLUSION

> Amongst grassroots political activists and communities of autonomy and struggle there is a tendency to forget . . . that every relationship of power and hierarchy that is legitimised through some form of participation and social formation *is necessarily an educational relationship*. (my italics, Amsler, 2015: 4)

In this chapter, I have attempted to bring together testimony on failure from arts activists and educators with theory on educating hope by Sarah Amsler and Ernst Bloch. I have explored how cherishing theory-making can put down roots for work that makes embracing failure a much more productive process. I have considered how and why courage is needed. I have looked at the role of coloniality and how it presents particular tasks for white arts activist educators. I have explored the dangers of the urgent 'activist' element in arts activist educators' work and how it can deprioritise reflective time to learn from failure. I have suggested ways to reframe our thinking about time to emphasise the 'becomingness' of our work.

I have suggested that embracing failure means acknowledging our different positions and subjectivities, but also recognising that these have been produced in colonial and capitalist frameworks. Living with these frameworks, but also acting to undo them and live beyond them, we can then take courage to examine how privilege, power and capitalism play out in our art, pedagogy and activism. We can begin to observe where strengths and weaknesses are, consider the contradictions, embrace the failures and frame such collective reflections on failure and success as central to the process of educating hope. In summary: Embracing failure educates hope because it is honest—it acknowledges that arts activist work for social justice is politically, socially and aesthetically complex and it shares that the work is difficult.

It educates hope because when all parties know in advance that there is a genuine, dedicated reflective process, 'failures' do not get bottled up.

It educates hope because immediate political urgency and practicalities are put aside for these processes, saying "we *can reclaim* time together. We *can* choose to step back, uncovering authentic, sometimes unwieldy feelings, and share lightly or deeply".

It educates hope because it develops the skills of collectively learning from failure: how shall we listen to each other across fragility and difference as artists, activist-educators, participants; how shall we make visible the workings of coloniality?

It educates hope because it encourages critical humility and undoes the convention of always 'bigging up' or defending the work and leaving the criticism to others.

It educates hope because it builds trust and confidence: people feel the humanity in the work, of each other with our faults and histories, because the goal is not to shut down each other or the past, but to learn together, creatively, to change the future.

NOTES

1. Write, Erase, Do It Over, interview with Toni Morrison https://www.arts.gov/NEARTS/2014v4-art-failure-importance-risk-and-experimentation/toni-morrison (accessed 30 August 2016).

2. 'Ever Tried. Ever Failed. No Matter. Try Again. Fail Again. Fail Better', extract from 'Worstward Ho', Samuel Beckett, 1983. http://www.slate.com/articles/arts/culturebox/2014/01/samuel_beckett_s_quote_fail_better_becomes_the_mantra_of_silicon_valley.html (accessed 31 August 2016).

3. http://www.littoral.org.uk/programme_littoral.htm (accessed 30 August 2016) Jane Trowell and Dan Gretton http://platformlondon.org; Lucy Fairley (then Milton)

4. https://www.helixarts.com (accessed 30 August 2016).

5. Six iterations of the course took place in London and Bristol 2004–2009, working with over 100 people. http://old.platformlondon.org/bodypolitic.asp (accessed 30 August 2016).

6. Since 1999, I have worked in various roles on the PGCE Art and Design, and MA Art and Design in Education at the Institute of Education, London.

7. Note: The current PhD title is ' "Real, honest colleagues?" White arts educators committed to social justice confront coloniality in our practices'.

8. The twenty-three peers are a diverse group of arts activist educators from my networks. A third are from majority world heritages, and the rest have white European heritages from wherever in the world. Sixteen identify as female, and seven as male. The majority are heterosexual. All see themselves as committed long-term to social justice.

9. An open letter from the 'Wretched of the Earth' bloc, 16 December 2015. https://blackdissidents.wordpress.com/2015/12/16/open-letter-from-the-wretched-of-the-earth-bloc-to-the-organisers-of-the-peoples-climate-march-of-justice-and-jobs/ (accessed 30 August 2016).

10. *Art: What's the Use?* Symposium at Whitechapel Art Gallery, organised by Dean Kenning and Gavin Grindon, University of Kingston, 2011.

REFERENCES

Amsler, S. Sarah. 2015. *The Education of Radical Democracy*. London: Taylor & Francis/Routledge.

BBC. Race and Religious Hate Crimes Rose 41 Percent after EU Vote. http://www.bbc.co.uk/news/uk-politics-37640982, 13.10.16. Accessed 19 January 2017.

Bloch, Ernst. 1995. *The Principle of Hope, Vols 1, 2 and 3*; trans. by Neville Plaice, Stephen Plaice and Paul Knight. Cambridge, MA: MIT Press.

Collins English Dictionary. London: Collins, 2006.

Grosfoguel, Ramòn. 2007. 'The Epistemic Decolonial Turn: Beyond Political-Economy Paradigms'. *Cultural Studies* 21(2–3): 211–23.

Hogue, W. Richard. 1924. 'A New Educational Movement'. *The Journal of Social Forces*, 3(1): 65–69.

Lorde, Audre. 1988. *A Burst of Light, Essays by Audre Lorde*. Ithaca, NY: Firebrand Books.

Kompridis, Nikolas. 2006. *Critique and disclosure. Critical Theory between Past and Future*. Cambridge, MA: MIT Press.

Maldonado-Torres, Nelson. 2007. 'On the Coloniality of Being: Contributions to the Development of a Concept'. *Cultural Studies* 21(2–3): 240–70.

Schön, Donald. 1987. *Educating the Reflective Practitioner*. San Francisco, CA: Jossey-Bass Publishers.

Chapter 10

In Case of Emergency Make Art
Exploring the (Non)function of Art in Response to Humanitarian Disasters

Jessica Holtaway

In 2015, art critic and Turner Prize judge Jonathan Jones wrote a newspaper article on an art exhibition taking part in the Fukushima exclusion zone. He said: 'But is art really capable of useful commentary on world events – or does it encourage fatuously emotional responses? . . . The artists showing in the Fukushima exclusion zone would do more good starting a discussion with science about the pros and cons of nuclear energy as a solution to global warming' (Jones, 2015). This raises an important question about the functional role of art, particularly as a response to a humanitarian disaster. Throughout time the purpose of art has been contested. In the face of a social and political crisis some writers and artists have renounced their work, declaring it insufficient. Nobel literature prize-winner (1947) André Gide said: 'For a long time now, works of art will be out of the question. . . . He who remains contemplative today demonstrates an inhuman philosophy, or monstrous blindness' (Gide, 1934).[1] Philosopher and sociologist Theodor Adorno famously stated, 'To write poetry after Auschwitz is barbaric' (Adorno, 1983: 34). These comments, interpreted and misinterpreted over time, outline a crucial issue at the heart of cultural practices: what do art and literature do? And why do they exist?

Drawing on the writings of philosophers Maurice Blanchot and Jean-Luc Nancy, the following pages explore the role of art in relation to what Blanchot calls 'the work of humanity'; the tasks we undertake to make the world a better place (Blanchot, 1982). It considers the idea that art, as a form of work, 'acts poorly and little' (Blanchot, 1982: 213) but that it exposes what Nancy calls 'general equivalence'; the quantification of human experience which leads to the idea that humans can be 'in charge' of the world (Nancy, 2015: 6,7). The aim of this chapter is to emphasise Nancy's idea of 'nonequivalence' above and beyond 'general equivalence'. In other words, it argues that to transcend processes of quantification requires us to acknowledge, and give priority to, the non-equivalence of each person, thing and experience. This chapter suggests that art suspends our inclination to quantify and reduce human existence – to create concrete goals that make assumptions regarding the needs of others. It asserts that creative processes, in failing to carry out the work of humanity, actually provide the conditions for humanity to be self-aware.

Here I reflect on my curatorial experience with the arts group Art Action UK, a collective that provides a 'respite residency' in London for artists living and working in East Japan following the earthquake, tsunami and nuclear meltdown in 2011. I joined the group in 2014 as a voluntary curatorial assistant. We acknowledge that Art Action UK does not generate a tangible political impact, but we nevertheless continue to provide a platform for artists who address complex global issues, particularly around nuclear energy production.

I seek to argue that, paradoxically, the failure of art to function 'effectively' gives it ethical significance. I suggest although art can, and does, create a material impact, it has an ethical role beyond that of immediate or tangible goals within society. Even though art may not be justifiable in terms of meeting concrete and immediate needs, it generates a consciousness through which to collectively question and articulate what is considered to be 'just'.

ART AND DISASTER

Art Action UK was set up following the earthquake and tsunami in East Japan in 2011. Founded by artist Kaori Homma, sociologist Yoshitaka Mouri and curator Meryl Doney, the group began to address ways in which to support individuals and communities affected by the disaster. As the extent of the damage became revealed and political dissent in Japan intensified, Art Action UK decided to focus on creating an ongoing, independent residency project. The residency aimed to offer a temporary respite to artists who live and work in Japan and who respond to events triggered by the disaster. It would provide an annual opportunity for artists to come to the UK to continue their art practice in a new environment, to share their experiences and to flag up the global implications of nuclear power production.

The first artist-in residence, Kaya Hanasaki, came to London in May 2012, fourteen months after the earthquake. Hanasaki responded to the political climate of Japan through criticising the way in which political decisions had been made and enforced in the year following the earthquake. Hanasaki's work created a sensory experience that reflected these political concerns. Her artworks also addressed the global political and social implications of the disaster.

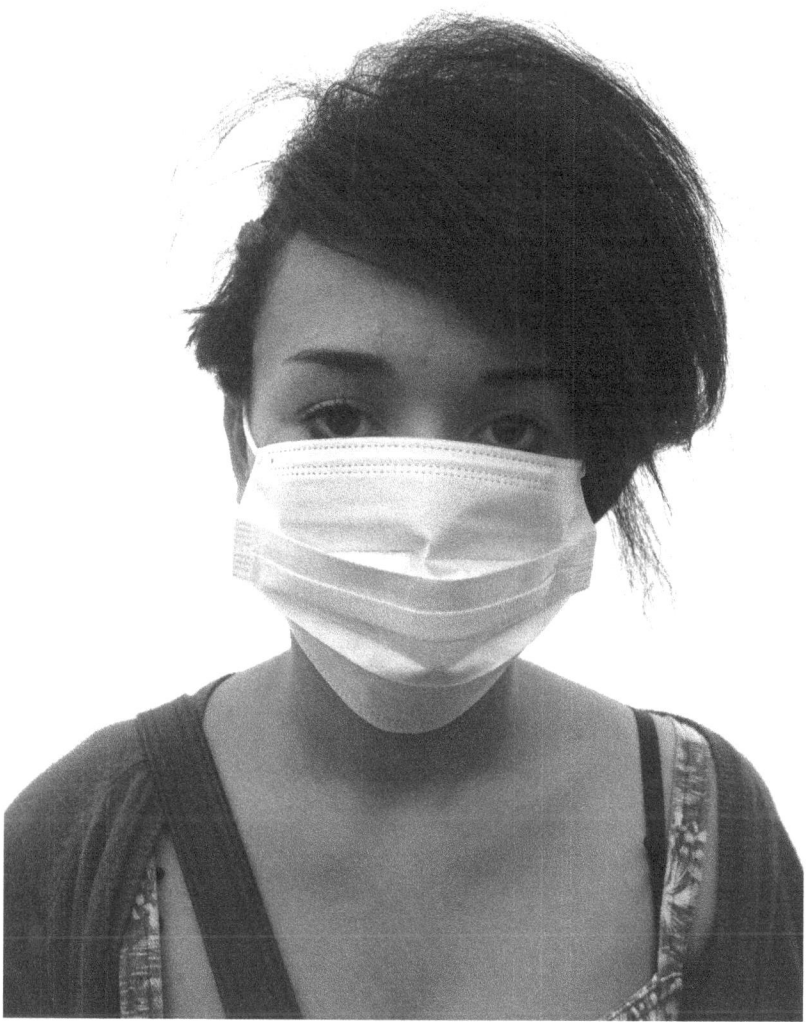

Figure 10.1. Image from *Portrait in Mask*, 2012
© Kaya Hanasaki.

Her residency work *Portrait in Mask* (Figure 10.1) was a performance and documentation project in which she asked participating members of the audience to each wear a surgical mask. The experience of wearing the mask amplified awareness of breathing and encouraged audience members to reflect on the anxiety and hyperconsciousness that pervades everyday life following a nuclear disaster. Hanasaki described wearing the masks as a socially divisive gesture. Wearing a mask demonstrated scepticism of the government's safety guidelines. This theme of mistrust in the decisions of the Japanese government carried a subversive message.

A month prior to Hanasaki's residency, new nuclear safety standards had been released. An earlier poll in July 2011 had shown that 74 per cent of Japanese people wanted Japan to become nuclear-free.[2] Despite this, the government instead proposed revised safety laws on the reactors, laws that specified that nuclear reactors would have a lifespan of forty years, with the possibility of extending that time. These laws potentially laid the foundations for future nuclear developments.

At the same time, the government had just begun to hand out free 'health books'[3] similar to the health books given to the survivors of Hiroshima and Nagasaki. Those with health books would receive free health care and would use the books to record and monitor their health. Additionally, government representatives were testing school lunches for traces of radioactive caesium.[4] The social and political climate of Japan was one of mistrust and anxiety. Although the government was keen to restore public confidence through increased testing, it was not willing to decommission nuclear plants that many people felt were unsafe.

Hanasaki is part of a vanguard of artists and writers who openly criticise governmental responses to what they feel is a crisis induced by capitalist technologies. For example, New York–based Japanese writer and translator Sabu Kohso describes this governmental approach as a programme of 'negative-commonization' in which radiation and debt have been 'nationally communized' (Kohso: Radiation and Revolution 2012: 7). Kohso states: 'All conduct of the Japanese government in the wake of 3/11 has proven that the state would choose continuation of capitalist operation and its own sovereignty over the well-being of the people. It has been constantly blurring information about present risks of radiation and critical conditions of the power plants' (Kohso: Turbulence of Radiation and Revolution: 2012). Like Hanasaki, Kohso feels that people and democracy are secondary to capitalist values. He says that the human body has become 'a battleground over the commons' or an 'informational front' in which concepts of commonisation/de-commonisation are under attack from capitalist ideologies (Radiation and Revolution: 2012: 11). Adapting to dangerous levels of radiation by creating greater 'transparency', altering safety guidelines and introducing new monitoring programmes, the government were able to reinforce and ratify the continued production of nuclear energy within an area of high tectonic disruption, despite widespread opposition.

As an ongoing curatorial project, Art Action UK forwards creative interventions, art practices and discourses that generate critical distance from the ideologies that drive, not only Japanese politics, but global capitalism. We foreground art practices that explore the way in which people are being subsumed and manipulated by political systems that translate human experience into a set of manageable and commensurate values. But even though Art

Action UK provides a platform for politically charged art practices, we try to steer clear of specific political affiliations and express a sense that we have little or no political effect. The group retains a distance from 'active' strategies. How, then, can Art Action UK facilitate social change? What kind of political engagement is activated through this 'ineffective' stance?

THE WORK OF HUMANITY

This idea of ineffectiveness was accentuated during the 2016 Art Action UK residency, which featured artist-duo Kyun-Chome (the collaborative name for artists Eri Homma and Nabuchi). The name 'Kyun-Chome' indicates a sense of doom and is comparable to the English metaphor 'butterflies in your stomach', used to describe the rush of adrenaline that increases the heart rate, causing a 'fluttering' sensation. Kyun-Chome's video installations explore the human experiences that culminate in what we think of as 'moral'. Unlike Kaya Hanasaki, whose residency works were more politically antagonistic, Kyun-Chome approach similar issues with a dark humour and sense of absurdity. Their work does not seek to make a direct political impact or encourage a particular form of dissent; it instead draws on existential concerns. It is ineffective, because rather than 'solving' existential concerns, it prevents us from thinking that they are solvable. It prevents us from collating the experience of disaster into a set of data.

Philosopher, writer and literary critic Maurice Blanchot has written extensively on the subject of creative labour and the ineffectiveness of art.[5] From the 1940s right up to his death in 2003, he published over thirty books and these writings influenced the work of other writers and thinkers such as Foucault, Deleuze and Derrida. For Blanchot, however much we may want art, or creative work, to 'act' in the world and be part of what he calls the 'work of humanity', it ultimately fails.[6]

Blanchot says that art and literature act 'poorly and little' and that 'as soon as art measures itself against action, immediate and pressing action can only put it in the wrong' (Blanchot, 1982: 213). But it is in this failure to be effective – in its failure to be a means-to-an-end – that we can find its significance and power.

A particular work in Kyun-Chome's exhibition, *Do Not Enter*, satirised the futile labour of human attempts to control the power of the sea. *Do Not Enter* (Figure 10.2) is a 2013 video piece in which the artists try to stop the sea sweeping onto the beach using barrier tape. Perhaps referencing the monumental efforts to raise the ground level in particular areas, as a precaution against future tsunamis, the piece also evokes a sense of desperation and futility. The artwork itself does nothing to endorse positive action, but instead

Figure 10.2. Film still from *Do Not Enter*, 2013
© Kyun-Chome.

it embodies a kind of compassionate critique. Similarly, in their 2015 piece *The Story of Making Lies*, the artists teach members of displaced communities to use Photoshop, so that they can figuratively remove the road barriers that prevent them from returning to their homes. Here, the artists restore social connections and give participants a new skill, but they cannot restore literal access to the homes. Although these works comment on and respond to the work of humanity, they are ineffective. And yet each work communicates a sense of the situation and a shared understanding of loss.

In his book *The Space of Literature*, speaking of what he calls 'the question of art', Blanchot writes about how art refuses to function effectively:

> Nothing is more important than this absolute autonomy which is refusal and that [sic] this refusal, which, through a change in sign, is also the most prodigious affirmation. For it is the gift, the creative gift, that dispenses without restraint and without justification, that never can be justified yet upon which justice can be founded. (Blanchot, 1982: 215)

Simply put, creative practices are important because they are not in service to a particular goal, or subject to a particular power. Blanchot thinks that although art may not be justifiable in terms of meeting concrete and immediate needs, it generates a consciousness through which we can collectively question and articulate what is considered to be 'just', In other words, if art is reducible to a moral goal, it serves a particular purpose within the work of humanity. It is 'within' a set of moral values that have been pre-decided and can become a tool for whoever has decided upon those values. Even if these appear to be positive goals, they are subjective and often rest upon particular ideals. Such an artwork would assume these goals were right for everyone and would close down space for reflection. Art, when used to deliberately carry out a social function, can become utilitarian rather than sustaining an open-ended critique.

It is true that creative practices can be appropriated by political powers and wielded to terrifying effect. But Blanchot reminds us of the speculative nature of art. Although art can be used to coerce, it is never entirely reducible to a straightforward function – it brings with it a shadow of ambiguity and is always subjective, referring to the unknowable experience of the other, of the artist.

To acknowledge the way in which art suspends our inclination to quantify and reduce human existence, to create concrete goals that assume the needs of others, generates an awareness of how creative processes, in failing to carry out the work of humanity, actually provide the conditions for us to be more self-aware. In other words, art creates a shared space for reflection and discussion – it fails to effectively take part in the 'work of humanity' but allows us to reflect on what we understand to be 'humanity'. This is particularly important in the aftermath of a disaster, when a focus on overall statistics and an increase in top down political processes, can lead to further disempowerment of many of those affected by the disaster.[7]

Blanchot refers to the inability to represent disasters with relation to literature that addresses the horrors of the Second World War. He says: 'We read books on Auschwitz. The wish of all, in the camps, the last wish: know what has happened, do not forget, and at the same time, never will you know' (Blanchot, 1995: 82). Knowledge is paradoxical – although we seek knowledge, the ethical significance is in the seeking rather than in the acquiring of knowledge. For Blanchot, to be ethical is to recognise the limitations of what we can know and to appreciate that knowledge can never be wholly acquired. He argues that no one can 'know' the experience of a disaster, it is beyond human comprehension, beyond language and beyond representation.

He says that creative practices such as art and literature maintain a sense of ambiguity, which prevents us from oversimplifying our perception of, and relation to, others. As such, we can never truly 'know' the experience of another person with certainty. This acknowledgement prevents us from reducing individuals and groups into 'ideas' or 'caricatures' that function within a preconceived political drama and generates an ethical consciousness. It is important to sustain this consciousness in order to provoke social changes in an ethical way.

Nevertheless Blanchot wants us to think about how the creation of this space for reflection itself requires work and needs maintaining. This is relevant for organisations such as Art Action UK, who want to generate a critical engagement with the issues at stake relating to global disasters, in particular the disaster in Fukushima, and to provoke further questioning within mainstream cultural discourses. The position of the group, as a catalyst and facilitator of open discourses, must be actively maintained. As support for the group grows, there is an increasing pressure for Art Action UK to define or deny specific stances with regard to political policies.

Although some of the members of the group campaign against nuclear power production, many of the residency artists do not share the same political views. Whilst some collaborating groups are keen for us to take a more hard-line political stance, other institutional connections are possible only through the ambiguity of our political affiliations. Although the purpose of the group is to sustain critical engagement with institutions, artists and researchers, audiences frequently demand a fixed response, a one-line affirmation of where Art Action UK stands with relation to the discourses we facilitate. But even though we elude a fixed political position, we do require functional strategies for sustaining the residency and its network. There is an important reciprocity between work and creativity.

TIPPING THE SCALES

So far this chapter has argued that to perpetuate human agency in the aftermath of a disaster requires a retreat from the certainty of political ideologies. As such it is crucial to sustain cultural practices that respond to political crises. Jean-Luc Nancy, in his 2015 book *After Fukushima: The Equivalence of Catastrophes*, addresses the incommensurability of singularities through a discussion of the Marxist idea of 'equivalence'. He situates creative processes at the heart of our ability to acknowledge 'nonequivalence'.

In the past century, nuclear power and weapons have introduced technologies that are capable of destruction beyond human conception. In *After Fukushima*, Nancy describes how nuclear technologies, in particular nuclear weapons, have introduced a 'balance of terror' – in which national security becomes symbolised by the level of threat that each nation has. For Nancy, this 'balance of terror' dissolves the link between the strong and the less strong in society and in doing so breaks down the relational structures that characterise and facilitate political engagement (Nancy, 2014: 21, 22).

After the disaster in Fukushima, the catastrophic impact caused by the breakdown of nuclear technologies in energy production plants quickly became evident. The use of nuclear weapons or breakdown of nuclear energy plants (and even the possibility of this breakdown) has caused a huge shift in the scale of political and social issues in the past century. But in the face of these global shifts, it is possible that cultural practices can tip the scales and create spaces of the 'in-common'; shared cultural spaces in which to acknowledge the increases in the scale of a given political issue, but allow for embodied exploration of human agency within these expanding frameworks of consciousness.

Nancy responds to Marx's theory of exchange – the idea that although 'value' is a dynamic concept, generated through social relations, it subsequently determines an 'exchange value', usually expressed in financial terms. In the context of global capitalism, Nancy argues that the systems that drive globalisation, the raw materials they require and the organisations that implement them, all depend on a 'general interconnection'; the idea that they must all lead to profit (Nancy, 2014: 5). He argues that this sense of 'general equivalence' is catastrophic. Social relations are increasingly demonstrated through 'exchange values', and because of this, people, things and experiences ultimately become reduced to predetermined values that can be constantly interchanged. The only way to resist this 'consumption' of reality is to acknowledge and support incommensurability – the distinctive particularities of each person, situation and experience.

Although every disaster is unique, Nancy says that each disaster connects 'with the totality of interdependences that make up general equivalence' and that over time this sense of general equivalence has given rise to the idea that humans can be 'in charge' of the world (Nancy, 2015: 6, 7). This idea of exchangeability, of everything having an ultimate value, has long characterised our experiences, actions and negotiations, but it is now escalating to a point at which the technologies we have created take on an independent significance and force over us and are beginning to define the conditions of humanity. The problem here is that the idea of humans being 'in charge' of the world immediately generates questions around power and control. Who implements and controls these technologies? And to what extent do technologies themselves reduce human choices?

When I first joined the Art Action UK in 2014, artists Haruka Komori and Natsumi Seo had just arrived in London for the residency programme. Komori and Seo are two young female artists who moved from Tokyo to East Japan in 2012 in order to help with the recovery process. Throughout the following years, they lived and worked in East Japan, documenting the lives of local citizens. Komori and Seo's short documentary films explore the emotional impact of the disaster. They are witnesses that testify for those who feel overlooked by the government. In documenting communities in East Japan, Komori and Seo aim to create new collective memories. They do not point a finger at individuals in political power, but they want people to ask more questions and to be more receptive to the concerns of the residents. They explore the scale of both the disaster and the government's response.

The issue is that for many of the survivors, the rapid and 'positive' actions of the government feel insensitive and have intensified the experience of trauma; the 'top-down' political process turns a blind eye and deaf ear to the people of the city. For example, the short film *Moving the Mountain* (Figure 10.3) asks us to reflect on the land reclamation process in Rikuzentakata. Here the tsunami was seventeen metres high, and following public meetings held very soon after the disaster (which many local people were unable to attend) it was decided that the ground was to be reclaimed and raised by twelve metres. Komori and Seo look at the human experience of this process, what it means for those affected and what hope, if any, it offers.

A later film – *I go to listen to the voices left behind* – follows Abe Hiromi as she returns to the site of her family home in Rikuzentakata. For Abe, remembrance is vital in coming to terms with the disaster and for rebuilding the future. In the film, she ignores the barriers around the site of her previous home and returns to tenderly lay out her parents' clothes in the warmth of the sunlight, in a gesture of honour and commemoration. Komori and Seo spotlight the significance of small acts such as this, acts that nevertheless require subversive interventions within the controlled boundaries of

Figure 10.3. *Moving the Mountain*, a film still from Komori and Seo's documentary film series *under the wave, on the ground*, 2014
© Haruka Komori and Natsumi Seo.

the redevelopment programme. In spite of an increasing sense of collective amnesia, these small interventions preserve a sense of individual agency that attests to the incommensurability of human experience.

In *After Fukushima*, Nancy urges us to 'think in terms other than regeneration or new generation. This should at least begin with a renewed understanding of what "technology" means' (Nancy, 2014: 36). Nancy suggests that technology, rather than having a functional role in carrying out human obligations, has become the very mode of our existence. It compels us to view everything as having 'a means and an end' and to reduce human experiences to an infinite set of 'general equivalences'. To actively resist this requires creative and critical approaches to cultural memories so as to renew our understanding of technology and the role it plays in the work of humanity. Komori and Seo, with their focus on a collective sense of loss and the need for processes of grieving and commemoration, provide insight into the social impact of the disaster. Their artworks prevent us from erasing this awareness by assimilating such a catastrophe in terms of statistics or exchangeable material values.

This leads us to the concept of 'nonequivalence', of the irreducibility of singularities. This is the idea that by acknowledging and reasserting the distinctive, incommensurable nature of each individual and situation, we can sustain a sense of human agency within everyday life and within crisis situations. This idea of non-equivalence does not annul or reverse equivalence, which is perhaps an unavoidable part of our social existence, but rather it shines a light on this dimension of human experience. Nancy says, 'Nonequivalence does not overturn equivalence; it makes it explicit. It says: All are equal in that no one is identical or commensurable with others' (Nancy, 2014: 60).

This awareness generates a critical consciousness of how we value, assess and determine our own relationships and actions. In turn, this prevents us from unthinkingly reinforcing 'general equivalencies' and sustains the possibility of tipping the scales back towards social interconnectivity, and away from the governance of profit-led technologies. Cultural practices do not present finite values or 'equivalent' representations to be exchanged and functionalised. Alternatively, they can help us engage with the ethical and social implications of expanding technologies by exposing hierarchies of power and reestablishing relational bonds between those with more power and those with less power.

WHAT CAN ART DO?

How can cultural organisations reestablish relational bonds that empower those who are vulnerable? Having considered Blanchot's ethical stance that art is important because it fails to be efficient, and Nancy's emphasis on non-equivalence, the following paragraphs consider ways in which art can nevertheless become a powerful tool in generating social change.

Art interrupts the familiar. It critiques and deconstructs situations that seem to be inevitable. In doing so, art reveals the fragility of the 'work of humanity'. But at the same time it brings to light the potential for modification and transformation. Curators can sustain the agency of such artworks by safeguarding its sense of ambiguity and inoperativity. This ambiguity prevents the artwork from having a particular function within a larger predetermined social project. The lack of immediate applicability demands that viewers and audiences pay close attention to the artwork and temporarily share in its evocation of an experience. Accordingly, these viewers affirm the incommensurability both of the artwork and the experience to which it refers. Close, empathetic attention evinces the non-equivalence of this experience, disengaging it from the 'general interconnections' that constitute globalisation as we know it and opening a fault line that can offer a new foundation for social evolution. Such attention and receptiveness can only arise from a state of becoming passive, from a temporary suspension of one's own opinions with an openness to change. It requires willingness on the part of the viewer.

This interruption is at the heart of the Art Action UK residency. The residency programme foregrounds artists who offer controversial and demanding creative engagement. Although this criticality is central to the group, its significance unfolds in the wider context of the residency. How might this criticality unfold within global cultural discourses?

The arresting nature of these interventions creates a space in which spectators are called forth to listen, bear witness to and share in the experience of the artwork. Appearing together with the artwork and with others in relation to the artwork generates speech and action. Nevertheless, for speech and action to advance and generate social changes depends on further interruptions of mainstream discourses. This often requires collaborative work to expand this informal space of speaking and acting together and to call forth a greater number of spectators. However, this collaborative work must still centre around the deconstruction of the familiar – its aim is to generate wider critical engagement, rather than a particular worldview.

Art Action UK develops critical discourses with institutions such as the Japan Foundation and the Daiwa Anglo-Japanese Foundation. Both these organisations are supported by government funding and financial corporations. They are embedded in established models that uphold capitalist systems of general equivalences. Art Action UK has a challenging relationship with such institutions. Whilst aiming to interrupt cultural discourses and sustain critical approaches to social issues in East Japan, we also want to keep the lines of communication open. Here there is a concurrent withdrawal from and engagement with these organisations. Subsequent collaborations therefore aim to sustain the kind of empathetic attention generated by the artwork in order to open up new discursive spaces that encompass those inside and outside the institutions. Here the aim is to extend the 'fault line' and increase the communicative potential of the artwork.

Even so, the incommensurable 'goal' – to restore relational bonds between the strong and the less strong, to allow for grassroots reform and 'a communism of nonequivalence' (Nancy, 2014: 41) – cannot be realised simply through empathy. New relational paradigms, based on non-equivalence, must be created. One way of doing this is to develop close networks and interdisciplinary alliances to bring about innovation. At the same time it is important not to let go of critical 'ineffective' engagement, because this is what will ensure true innovation. If, in the name of fulfilling a particular 'duty' of humanity, we lose sight of the ethical horizon of this duty, 'catastrophic equivalence' will ultimately be reinforced (Nancy, 2014: 41). However, powerful collaborations can arise from a shared criticality.

Alliances, held together through a shared critique of 'knowledge', can bridge disciplines. Art and science alliances, for example, can offer new experimental approaches to social issues. This is not the kind of functional collaboration that Jonathan Jones suggests – 'a discussion with science about the pros and cons of nuclear energy as a solution to global warming' – rather it refers to exploratory collaborations, such as art-science activisms, that forward critical engagement with the world around us. Art Action UK has begun to extend its network and collaborate with organisations such as Arts Catalyst, an arts and education charity that commissions artworks that critically engage with science. This kind of collective action can generate power. Unlike the violence that characterises top-down political processes and which is often rationalised in relation to a particular outcome, power can be generated through grassroots collectivity. Here power is not fully realised, but it sustains the possibility to achieve new relational networks, connecting and reconnecting the strong and the less strong.

CONCLUSION

Returning to Jonathan Jones's initial question – 'is art really capable of useful commentary on world events – or does it encourage fatuously emotional responses?' – I would like to underline the founding assumptions of this question, as demonstrated in his approach to both the disaster at Fukushima and the responding artworks. Despite the amplification of the disaster through flawed technologies, which have intensified the physical and social impact of the tsunami and earthquake, Jones describes the nuclear meltdown as 'well-managed and successfully contained' (Jones, 2015). In his call for 'rational debate', he dismisses art as too human and too emotional, ironically asking for a 'more open-minded debate' (Jones, 2015). Brushing aside the social impact of large-scale displacement, increased risks of cancer and unquantifiable psychological trauma, he sees the disaster in equivalential terms. His recommendation – that artists should collaborate with scientists to outline the pros and cons of nuclear energy – situates artists as servants of a wider social project to protect the mechanisms of global capitalism. As such, he wants to close down debate. Open debate brings with it the *possibility* of emotions and ideas that may be perceived as 'irrational'; if ideas and arguments are dismissed on these grounds, the debate is no longer an 'open' debate.

In contrast, Kyun-Chome explain their understanding of the relationship between art and disaster as one that necessitates indeterminacy:

> Throughout history, Japan has experienced many tragedies. Considering the area is geologically prone to major earthquakes and tsunami, from now on, Japan will continue to face more tragedies. However, if we treat this itself as a tragedy, these incidents can only exist as archived parts of history. In other words, it will only remain as a data for future generations, but will not communicate the human impact and experience of these disasters. Therefore, art needs to go beyond the polarity of tragedy or comedy. We believe that art is a language beyond verbal language, and we feel that we need to further develop its communicative potential. (from an interview on the Art Action UK blog, 19 May 2016)

Drawing from Maurice Blanchot, this chapter has developed the idea that, rather than being an effective tool that fulfils a predetermined programme of humanitarian work, art fundamentally hinders complete functionalisation. It has argued that this disturbance, this ineffectiveness, can paradoxically become a powerful way of critiquing and altering the social subconscious and can lead to new social paradigms. Developing this argument with reference to Nancy and the idea of non-equivalence, it suggested that art can create fractures in the chains of equivalence that characterise capitalism. Art 'malfunctions' within larger apparatuses of exchange, designed to produce profit for the few. As such, it creates glitches that can contagiously effect change and bring about paradigms, based not on the production of profit, but on sustaining relational networks that connect and support both the strong and the less strong. This argument provokes a rethinking of art activist practices – it implies that the effectiveness of these practices lies in their ability to deconstruct and create networks that are 'dysfunctional' within preconceived paradigms of global exchange.

This chapter has outlined a trajectory from individual artistic responses to disasters, through to collective responses and on to the formation of strong alliances that can power organic social changes. It has outlined the ethical responsibility of curators and cultural practitioners to sustain critical engagement with social and political concerns. It has argued that non-violent social change can take place through creative practices that develop carefully and collaboratively. Art can generate social change, but it does so through making us question our perceptions of the world and imaginatively engage with contemporary issues. This requires an active retreat from equivalential valuation and the foregrounding of emotional cultural practices.

NOTES

1. As referenced by Maurice Blanchot in *The Space of Literature*; 1982: 214–15.
2. Nagata Kazuaki, Fukushima meltdowns set nuclear energy debate on its ear, *The Japan Times*, 1 March 2012
3. (National Kyodo News post) Namie to seek medical fee exemption for all residents, *The Japan Times*, 15 April 2012.
4. (National news post) New safety standards for radioactive cesium in food products go into effect, *Japan Today*, 2 April 2012
5. Debates around the autonomy of art and reflections on the idea that art embodies a kind of freedom from utility can also be found within sociological approaches to art (entry points onto these debates could be through the writings of Pierre Bourdieu and Peter Bürger). Rather than wading into these discussions, which might perhaps lead to an analysis of the aesthetic essence of an artwork, this chapter focuses instead on the question, 'what can art and aesthetics *do*?' What is the social significance of the 'incommensurability' of an artwork?
6. Blanchot's translator Ann Smock also refers to the work of humanity ('travail') as 'purposeful activity' and 'effective or useful action' as opposed to the work of art (l'œuvre) (Smock, 1982: 13).
7. To read more about emergency planning, and the idea of undertaking a holistic analysis of disaster, David Alexander (UCL Institute for Risk and Disaster Reduction) offers extensive research into disaster recovery. For more on art and disaster: Majella Munro's research into Japanese art and the environment illuminates historical engagement with environmental disasters. Ele Carpenter's *The Nuclear Culture Sourcebook* highlights the global significance of the Fukushima disaster and provides a collection of incisive analyses of art and theory relating to the nuclear Anthropocene.

REFERENCES

Adorno, Theodor W. 1983. *Prisms*. Cambridge, MA: MIT Press.
Blanchot, Maurice. 1995, originally published in French in 1986. *The Writing of the Disaster*. Lincoln, USA: University of Nebraska Press.
Blanchot Maurice. 1982. (1986 paperback edition). originally published in French in 1955. *The Space of Literature*. Lincoln, USA: University of Nebraska Press.

Carpenter, Ele, ed. 2016. *The Nuclear Culture Source Book*. London, UK: Blackdog Publishing.

Holtaway, Jessica. 2016. 'Art as an antidote: artist duo Kyun-Chome discuss the fragility of the human condition and why we all need art', *Art Action UK blog*, http://artactionsupportforjapan.blogspot.co.uk.

Kohso, Sabu. 2012. 'Radiation and Revolution'. *Borderlands E-Journal* special issue: *Commons Class Struggle and The World*. Vol. 11, No. 2. http://www.borderlands.net.au/vol11no2_2012/kohso_radiation.htm.

Kohso, Sabu. 2012. 'Turbulence of Radiation and Revolution'. *Through Europe*. 3 March.

Nagata, Kazuaki. 2012. 'Fukushima meltdowns set nuclear energy debate on its ear'. *The Japan Times*. 3 January.

Nancy, Jean-Luc. 2014. *After Fukushima: The Equivalence of Catastrophes*. New York: Fordham University Press.

Jones, Jonathan. 2015. 'Apocalypse no! Why artists should not go into the Fukushima exclusion zone' in *The Guardian*. 20 July. https://www.theguardian.com/artanddesign/jonathanjonesblog/2015/jul/20/fukushima-exclusion-zone-art-politics.

Smock, Ann. 1982. in the Translator's Introduction to Blanchot's *The Space of Literature* (1982 (1986 paperback edition)).

ADDITIONAL ARTICLES

National Kyodo News post. 2012. 'Namie to seek medical fee exemption for all residents', *The Japan Times*. 15 April.

National news post. 2012. 'New safety standards for radioactive cesium in food products go into effect' *Japan Today*. 2 April.

Chapter 11

Post-Autonomous Art and Common People in Barcelona

Roger Sansi

The introduction to this volume argues that what is particular to the current cycle of art activism lies in a double movement, first acknowledging the relationality of artistic, social and political processes, and second, linking these newly articulated social relations to processes of economic production. In this chapter I will introduce art activism in Spain, in particular in Barcelona, where the first movement has been very explicit, while the second perhaps may not be so obvious, as I will explain. But what I wish to highlight here is the role of art in processes through which we generate discourse and knowledge, in particular the social sciences.

POST-AUTONOMY

In his recent book, *Art beyond Itself,* Néstor García Canclini argues that contemporary art has become 'post-autonomous'. Artistic practice does not result only or preferentially in art objects, but it is inserted in multiple contexts, from the media and urban spaces, to digital networks, the social sciences and forms of social participation. In these terms, art has become post-autonomous, it is no longer defined by the autonomy of the 'art world' or the 'artistic field'. Its practice is actually questioning the very division of social labour that autonomy implies and, by the same token, the sociology of art and the art history based on this notion, from Bourdieu and Becker to Foster and Bishop.

One could ask if the notion of 'post-autonomy' describes *the facts* of the international art world today – which, one could argue, still exists as an autonomous art world; but it certainly points out to a tendency and an aspiration of many different forms of artistic practice in the past decades. In these terms, it may be an interesting idea to think with. In this chapter I would like to interrogate this notion of post-autonomy further in two directions. First by pointing to how artistic practice is inserted in politics, in particular in reference to my own fieldwork in Barcelona.

For Canclini, modernist theories of the international artistic art world or the artistic field were based on a number of assumptions that may no longer be tenable. The artistic field, for Bourdieu (1993), would be a result of the process of division of labour in modern societies (like France, for example), in which art and cultural production would be given their own space, their autonomy. The art world, for Becker (1982), would be a network of specialists that collaborate with each other – again, a model based on the modern division of labour. The international art world would be a highly specialised, autonomous and elitist network (Thompson, 2008) organised as a market working back to back with financial markets, and hence its centres would be based in financial capitals like New York and London. The difference between the model of the 'field' and the 'international art world' is that the field presupposes a national frame (e.g. France) of public institutions that make the genesis of this field possible, while the international art world works as a global market. And yet both models, public national field of art and the international commercial art world, are based on the assumption that artistic practice in modern societies is highly specialised and differentiated, and autonomous from other forms of social practice, not just from other professions, but also from politics, religion and economy as different fields or worlds of practice. Hence the purpose of a social science of art would be to describe the autonomy of these worlds or fields and their internal structure.

García Canclini is proposing that this modernist model may not correspond to the situation of contemporary art and culture in the twenty-first century. For García Canclini, contemporary art is becoming *post-autonomous*: 'Art practices based on *objects* have increasingly been displaced in favour of practices based on *contexts*, to the point that works are now being *inserted in the media, urban spaces, digital networks, and forms of social participation where aesthetic differences seem to dissolve*' (2014: xviii). And that is partially a consequence of the fact that contemporary society is no longer based on the strong narratives of modernity, in which the division of social labour between fields made sense. For Garcia Canclini, contemporary society doesn't have a story line, a project, a vision of the future either in political and religious terms. In this situation, art appears as a possibility, not as an alternative politics or religion, but simply as a space that can provide with metaphors to address what Garcia Canclini calls 'imminence' – a sense of what is coming into being, this is not a mystical state, but 'the experience of perceiving in the existing reality other possible ways of being that make dissent, not escape, a necessity' (Garcia Canclini, 2014: 168). This formulation brings Garcia Canclini close to Rancière's notion of the politics of aesthetics as proposing new distributions of the sensible, and he certainly does make reference to Rancière, but Garcia Canclini does not want to reduce or circumscribe artistic practice to politics, as an already established narrative. For him what is interesting is precisely the 'post-autonomous' condition of art and its insertion in different circuits outside of art as an institution, like in the media, urban spaces, the social sciences, and in processes of social participation.

Still, there are a number of questions that are left open in this argument. To start with, do we really live in a society without a story line, or is this just the effect of a hegemonic story that becomes invisible – the story of uncertainty and crisis we live in? Why does art have this power of addressing imminence? And what are the consequences of this imminence? Why can't art result in new narratives, in new politics? Second, at a more critical level, this post-autonomy of art can be seen, in rather negative terms, simply as the subsumption of contemporary art in the society of the spectacle, where art becomes just one more commodity for mass consumption. This may be a rather simplistic argument, but also one that has to be addressed and explained if we want to discuss where art is if it loses its autonomous condition. This connects with a third point: in more ethnographic terms, the examples used by Garcia Canclini are highly successful artists (like Santiago Sierra or Gabriel Orozco), very well placed in the international art world, that in spite of any theories of post-autonomy, still exists and is growing. As a matter of fact, the international commercial art world has never been as powerful as today, and the pressure for artists to professionalise (or in other terms, to abide by its power) has never been stronger. This international art world coexists, in ambiguous and complex ways, with always growing peripheral, perhaps post-autonomous practices and spaces, we could call them 'third spaces', which do not necessarily respond either to market or public sector logics. And yet it would be important not to reduce these 'third spaces' to a 'third sector', as in the 'NGO-isation' of art practice. Fourth, and last, it would be necessary to think also about the consequences of this post-autonomisation for the social sciences, which is one of the social fields in which art has been inserted, according to Garcia Canclini.

To summarise, to understand this post-autonomous moment we have to consider at least four possible spheres of 'insertion', which at the same time are also losing their autonomy: politics, mass cultural production, the so-called third sector and the social sciences.

ART AND POLITICS IN BARCELONA

I will try to address this question by focusing on a specific case, the city of Barcelona. At the turn of the century, some art collectives in Barcelona were looking for alternatives to producing for the commercial art sector and/or public art institutions, working in collaboration with activist movements, applying different forms of visual and media production to specific political struggles. A very explicit example is the collective Enmedio, which means literally 'in between' formed by visual artists, film makers, photographers, graphic designers who in their own terms, decided to 'abandon their field of work' (*abandonar nuestra area habitual de trabajo*), to contribute with their skills to build tools for social protest. The tools they used were directly or indirectly inspired by situationism: the production of situations and interventions, performances, forms of public detournement and so on.[1]

Two of the key political issues in Spain at the turn of the century were the enduring unemployment and the precarisation of labour, as well as the housing crisis. In spite of the economic growth of Spain at the turn of the century, most of the jobs for young people in Spain were precarious and poorly paid and the access to housing was becoming increasingly difficult. From early 2000, the price of housing had been rising exponentially in Spain, creating a housing bubble that would eventually explode in 2008. But before the crash, a social movement emerged to ask for the right to decent housing (*vivienda digna*). An assembly in Barcelona, under the name V de Vivienda (*V for Housing*), organised a number of actions during 2006. Besides demonstrations, they organised all kinds of disruptive situations, like a pyjama party at IKEA,[2] and provoked disruption in several public events, with a character called Supervivienda, dressed like a superhero. Enmedio were actively involved in the organisation of these actions, this was the collective action of an assembly, formed by social activists from many different backgrounds. Some of them were in fact anthropologists. The IKEA occupation centred on the anthropologists rather than on the artists, if these distinctions did not make any sense. All these situations and events were not framed as works of art with an author, but as political acts organised by an assembly, constituted by people from different backgrounds.

All these events could appear like a rather colourful, if irrelevant, form of political protest, if it wasn't for the crash that finally happened in the following years. After 2008, the banking system collapsed in Spain like in many other countries and with it the mortgage crisis reached unprecedented levels. Spanish laws are particularly harsh on mortgages: the law determines that if a person borrows money to buy a home, they can be freed of the debt only when it is repaid. Even in the case of death, the debt is not cancelled. So many people were evicted and they still had to pay their mortgage. In that context, the number of the people affected by the housing crisis grew exponentially. As a result, the social movement for dignified housing became much larger, and what were relatively small movements, like V de Vivienda, became the Plataforma de Afectados por la Hipoteca (*Platform for People Affected by Mortgages*), a much larger and cross-cutting social movement, which was not just a bunch of activists, artists and anthropologists, but people of all social backgrounds and nationalities, among them many migrants.

But still, the strategy of the PAH was based on Direct Action. Through a number of public campaigns, like STOP deshaucios (*STOP evictions*), the PAH was able to make the media turn their attention to the housing situation as a national emergency in 2011. The tactics of the PAH were to organise a micro-mobilisation at the site where an eviction was taking place, to create a public outrage that would eventually stop the eviction, or in front of the banking institutions that ordered the evictions. Another technique used by the PAH, the *escrache*, was very polemical but it also gave them a lot of exposure in the media. The *escrache* is a type of demonstration in which a group of activists go to the homes or workplaces of those whom they want to condemn and publicly humiliate them, in order to influence the media and governments into a certain course of action.[3] In 2013, the PAH organised a petition for dignified housing, asking the Parliament of Spain to officially change the mortgage law, collecting 1,500,000 signatures. The initiative was discussed in Parliament, but it didn't pass. However, as a result of that initiative, the figure of one of the leaders of the PAH, Ada Colau, became extremely popular. Ada Colau was a former student of philosophy, actress, squatter and full-time activist since the early 2000. She was dressing up as Supervivienda. She exemplifies the trajectory of a generation that started to become politicised in the 1990s in the anti-war and anti-globalisation movements, then moved to more local, immediate struggles, like precarious housing and labour. Since 2006, she worked with the NGO Observatori DESC, a social rights watch organisation. It is interesting to note the change of image of Colau in her trajectory – from her performative impersonation of Supervivienda, to her image as representative of the PAH, a serious and righteous public speaker.

What was once a radical, small, situationist movement had become a movement of masses with a strong public approval. Part of its success was a result of a very effective use of the media. Art collectives like Enmedio actively collaborated in the media strategy of the PAH, from the demonstrations, helping build what Enmedio calls Visual Objects like in 'photographic actions' 'We are not numbers', or through the graphic campaign 'Si se puede, pero no quieren' in 2013 (*Yes it can be done, but they don't want to*). The campaign consisted of the massive reproduction of the message 'Yes it can be done', in a green circle, and 'but they don't want to', in a red circle. This campaign summarised in two sentences the political contestation to what had been the hegemonic political discourse in Spain after (and before the crisis): the notion that there was only one way out of the economic crisis, through the austerity laws enforced by the conservative Spanish government and ordered by the troika and that it wasn't possible to change the mortgage laws.

The success of the PAH and these campaigns eventually had larger political consequences. In 2014, a wave of new political formations and coalitions emerged, partially drawing on the new social movements of which the PAH was the leading example. One political party, *Podemos*, clearly connected with the *leitmotiv* of the PAH campaign (although arguably, also with the Obama campaign: 'Yes We can'. But that is a different story), extending it to political power itself: the core message was and still is, yes, it is possible: we can win the elections. The leaders of these new parties came from different backgrounds, but many of them came from academia, often from the social sciences, they are young political scientists, sociologists and anthropologists, artists and cultural producers, NGO workers, many of them with precarious jobs. They are not, in other terms, the usual politicians. One of the main and most successful accusations that these new formations levelled against the traditional political formations is that they are a 'caste': an endogamic network of power relations, not based on merit but on corruption and which didn't represent the interest of the people of Spain but their own. As opposed to this accusation, the traditional political parties accused the new political formations of precisely the opposite: of not being professional enough, but amateurs. In opposition to the 'caste' accusation, they have been described as the 'chusma', the rabble.

One of the new leaders that emerged in this wave of political transformation has been Ada Colau, who presented her candidacy to the city council of Barcelona leading the coalition Barcelona en Comú, Barcelona in Common. The people who formed this coalition were in their majority not professional politicians. In spite of that, they won the local elections in May 2015. A similar coalition, *Ahora Madrid* (Now Madrid) won the elections in the capital of Spain. This was unprecedented, challenging the hegemony of the traditional parties and also of the traditional media (newspapers and television) associated with them. During the campaign and after the criticisms to these new political formations were fierce and focused often in the unconventional backgrounds of the new politicians. Ada Colau's past was pointed at as scandalous: how could a former squatter become a mayor? Pictures of her as an activist, disguised as a superhero or as a fairy, were publicly mocked by adversarial media, as a proof of her lack of seriousness and professionalism. Several other members of her team were pointed at, in particular her communications secretary, Agueda Bañón, a visual artist who participated of what was called the 'postporno' activist movement, a feminist movement that produced queer media. Pictures of her pissing in the middle of an avenue caused a big uproar in the mainstream media. Little was said of her expertise precisely in the production of alternative digital media, starting with her engagement with the anti-globalisation network Indymedia since its foundation.

The success of this 'new politics' is interesting at several levels. At one level, the criticism of the caste of old politicians can be read in moral terms, as a discourse against corruption that proposes the necessity of a new politics lead by young 'normal people' (*gente corriente*) from the grassroots that are still in touch with the people (*el pueblo*). At a more deeply sociological level, however, what is interesting about this new politics is how it is reshuffling the division of labour and the division of power, established in Spain since the death of General Franco. To explain it in very quick and simplistic terms, one could say that the division of labour was based upon a clear separation of politics, which was partially professionalised, from other fields of intellectual labour, like the academic field and the field of art. At the end of the dictatorship, a young generation of activists had to decide if they became professional politicians or worked in other fields – like the social sciences, art, the media or the third sector. Some of these fields also became professionalised, and they became the ecological reserves of radical leftist thought, while the mainstream of politics and the media moved steadily towards neo liberalism. At the same time, however, the relation between economic power, political power and media became increasingly promiscuous. The accusations of the new politics against the 'caste' do not only impinge upon corruption but also on the revolving doors (*puertas giratorias*) between politics and corporate economic and media power: in other terms, the clear fact that the 'autonomy' of social fields is not respected in the promiscuous relations of economic power, media corporations and politics.

On the other hand, the leaders of this new politics are a younger generation that once believed in the division of social labour, in a modern democratic society, and tried to become professionalised in one of these fields – like art or academia, just to realise that these fields were closed to newcomers, because of the precarisation of labour conditions. The situation in politics was similar: the caste is, by definition, a gerontocratic system, in which new people and ideas are far from welcome, and the reproduction of the elite is based on very close personal or even familial ties. In these terms, the political involvement of a younger generation made them progressively aware that the social division of labour, the 'autonomy' of art and science from politics, didn't make sense. And that they themselves *could* become political leaders, they could take over the institutions; something that only ten years ago, they could never have thought of. But now we have new political organisations full of artists, activists and social scientists. Whether they will become 'professionalized' again is something that remains to be seen. But the surprising speed with which they have managed to upset a whole system of power, in spite of a manifest lack of resources, at least is interesting to look at, as a case study.

In these terms, 'post-autonomy', at least from the point of view of Barcelona, and Spain in general, can have a different meaning from what Garcia Canclini implied. Post-autonomy in this case means the questioning of an institutionalised division of social and intellectual labour that separated clearly between politics, art, social movements and the social sciences.

PARTICIPATION

What is the role of the social sciences in these processes? In my experience, social scientists in Barcelona have been involved in this new politics since its very beginning. Not only were they participating in many of the actions and movements I have described, but they see their work as militant research, strictly related to this political practice. Many of these social scientists were and are working on urban issues, gentrification, immigration, the housing crisis and so on. In many ways the anthropologist, the artist, the activist, were very difficult to distinguish, precisely because their forms of work were participative and based on assembly. Hence the 'authorship' of the actions as I mentioned, their status as art, or as anthropology, is quite irrelevant.

It could be argued, and it has been argued, that participation can turn against itself: it can become a policy, imposed from the top down, as a form of political expediency, a tyranny. In the wider sphere of social policy, development and management, participatory processes have become a common buzzword of neoliberal governmentality. The agents of this tyranny are often NGOs. The critique towards 'participation' policies follows the Foucauldian argument, by which the well-meaning projects of empowerment and participation are in fact institutional devices of discipline and control, instrumental to the construction of neoliberal subjectivities. In the field of cultural production, several critical voices have been raised against the 'nightmare of participation' (Bishop 2012; Miessen 2011), following similar arguments. Participatory art practices are often accused of building up devices of social control, and the art practices themselves, of reducing politics to a sort of applied 'social service', in the sense, again, that NGOs are used to provide social services and hide political problems. But we have seen in the case of Barcelona it is precisely the opposite: people coming from NGOs, the arts and the social sciences, are using participation not to neutralise politics, but precisely to organise a new politics.

CONCLUSION

To conclude, I want to start by making clear that this post-autonomous moment, as I have defined it in the case of Barcelona, is just a hint, or a possibility, of what it could be, a flash of 'imminence' in Garcia Canclini's terms. The reality, the sociological facts of most art, of most politics, of most anthropology even, around the world, is not post-autonomous. It seems to be the opposite: there is a growing pressure to professionalise, to specialise, to be competitive and to succeed in one's own professional field. And yet I would argue that this is not really a form of autonomy, since this growing pressure takes one particular form in all fields: neoliberal management. This may be called also a post-autonomous world, the 'new spirit of capitalism', in Boltanski's terms. This other post-autonomous, neocapitalist world is also a political project, an utopia (or a dystopia for most of its victims). What may change is that not so long ago, neoliberal management appeared as the only game in town. Perhaps, and I am saying it with a lot of caution, this is not the case anymore.

I have argued that key to understanding this new post-autonomous moment is the use of participation, as a crucial form of work in establishing new movements and relations between art, politics and the social sciences. This relation is not a trade or barter, what 'participation' implies is more than an equivalent value, but getting involved with, becoming part of, for example, a political practice. Participatory exchange is not a commodity but a gift (Sansi, 2015). The 'imperative to participate', that transforms art and anthropology, makes them be something more, and something else, than what they were before: it 'extends' them (Mauss, 1990; Strathern, 1990) it distributes their personhood to something larger. Some authors have talked about 'parasites' and 'para-ethnographies' (Holmes and Marcus, 2008, 2012), here I have talked directly about political movements.

We could understand it better perhaps in relation to Callon's arguments on new forms of politics. Callon called a new form of 'technical democracy' (Callon, Lascoumes and Barthe, 2011) constituted by 'hybrid forums' in which politics, science, art and all forms of knowledge are brought together (participate from each other) to address situations of uncertainty. This new form of democracy would be opposed to the conventional 'representative democracy' of the past, based on the separation of spheres (politics on the one hand, science on the other), and the 'representation' between them (citizens represented by politicians, laymen by scientists). The examples used by Callon are not just the worldwide web, but also other matters of concern, like nuclear waste, AIDS or climate change. These hybrid forums would overcome the 'double delegation' of citizens to politicians and to experts that characterises our current model of representative (or delegative) democracy, by proposing to bring together all the actors concerned in these matters, people *affected* and participating in this process. The PAH, in fact, as a collective of people *affected* by mortgages, is an excellent example of a collective where the distinction between citizens and experts, people and politicians is cancelled.

However, being based on the gift, as anthropologists know well, participation is not necessarily egalitarian, free and improvised. It can become hierarchical, obligatory and ritualised (Sansi, 2014). New hierarchies and forms of expertise and delegation can be produced by these processes. But what can still be argued is that the imperative to participate opens a space of possibility (maybe that is what Garcia Canclini means by 'imminence'); it generates new situations that, extending the range of its practice and placing it in a larger context may provoke an interesting rethinking of some of the basic tenets of Anthropology, precisely, as an 'autonomous' discipline, as a form of expertise. The 'post-autonomous' (Garcia Canclini, 2014) moment in Art and Anthropology, by compelling to participate, being part of larger experiments in 'technical democracy' can force us to question in larger terms, what does our work as anthropologists consist of?

AFTERWORD: THE DEMISE OF EXPERTS

Most of this chapter was written in reference to political events in Barcelona up to 2016. One of the points I am making, with a lot of caution, is that perhaps there are other games in town, different from neoliberal management. I have argued how in the context of the economic crisis, new political actors emerged in places like Spain. These actors are questioning the hegemony, the political system, the rules of engagement and the division of labour. They have bypassed the division between politicians, experts and lay people, generating experiments in democracy that eventually have been successful.

The world events of 2016 have given an uncanny twist to this tentative proposal. In the past few months we have lived through political processes that seem to have some elements in common with what I just described: the rejection of the 'elites', established institutions, and expertise, have been key factors in the so-called Brexit referendum of separation of the UK from the European Union, and the election of the Republican presidential candidate in the U.S. elections of 2016. Political commentators from the former establishment and the mainstream media in Spain were quickly drawing parallelisms between these political events and the 'new politics' in Spain. For them, all these movements were 'populist'. One rarely finds definitions of 'populism' in these media statements, but basically it has been argued that they reject the 'elites' and 'experts' and argue the need for the 'people' to take over the corrupt institutions that oppress them. The label 'populist' is misleading, since it is bringing together radically different political movements – from fascism on the Right to socialism on the Left. For good or bad these are the movements that are defining the current political moment internationally, and the critics of populism seem to offer no alternative but to return to the certainties of a model where the social division of labour was well defined, a model that may be finally collapsing. The very fact that we are talking about fascism as an actual, immediate danger in the United States and the EU in 2017 really is an unforeseen event, which few people would have considered a year ago. A form of imminence, to go back to Garcia Canclini, if probably not the kind of imminence he or I would be hoping for. In any case, in this situation, it is becoming even more obvious that for anthropology, there is no alternative but to take sides, to abandon its gilded autonomy, and plunge into new political experiments.

NOTES

1. See www.enmedio.info. (last accessed 2/10/2017).
2. https://www.youtube.com/watch?v=kO-fre2w6YI. (last accessed 2/10/2017).
3. Escraches are famously associated with activist groups in Argentina denouncing the involvement of members of the military in the countries 'dirty war' in the 1970s, which led to the disappearance of 30,000 people.

REFERENCES

Becker, Howard 1982. *Art worlds*. Berkeley: University of Claifornia Press.
Bishop, Claire. 2012. *Artificial Hells: Participatory Art and the Politics of Spectatorship*. London and New York: Verso.
Boltanski, Luc and Eve Chiapello. 2005. *The New Spirit of Capitalism* London: Verso.
Bourdieu, Pierre 1993. *The field of cultural production*. New York: Columbia University Press.
Callon, Michel, Pierre Lascoumes and Yannick Barthe, 2011. *Acting in an Uncertain World: An Essay on Technical Democracy*. Cambridge, MA: MIT Press.
Garcia Canclini, Nestor. 2014. *Art beyond Itself: Anthropology for a Society without a Story Line*. Durham, NC: Duke University Press.
Holmes, Douglas, and George E. Marcus. 2008. 'Collaboration Today and the Re-Imagination of the Classic Scene of Fieldwork Encounter'. *Collaborative Anthropologies* 1: 81–101.
Holmes, Douglas, and George E. Marcus. 2012. 'Collaborative *Imperatives: A Manifesto, of Sorts, for the Reimagination of the Classic Scene of Fieldwork Encounter*' in Konrad, M (ed.) *Collaborators Collaborating: Counterparts in Anthropological Knowledge and International Research Relations* edited by Monica Konrad. Oxford: Berghahn Books.
Mauss Marcel. 1990 [1925]. *The Gift. The Form and Reason for Exchange in Archaic Societies*. London and New York: Routledge.
Miessen, Marcus. 2011. *The Nightmare of Participation*. Berlin: Sternberg press.
Sansi, Roger. 2014. *Art, Anthropology and the Gift*. London: Bloomsbury.
Sansi 2015. Art, *Anthropology and the Gift*. London: Bloomsbury.
Strathern, Marilyn. 1990. *The Gender of the Gift. Problems with Women and Problems with Society in Melanesia*. Berkeley: University of California Press.

Conclusion

Jessica Holtaway, Alberto Cossu and Paula Serafini

As highlighted in the preface, *artWORK* began as a series of conversations and workshops that brought together artists, activists, writers and cultural practitioners from a variety of projects. The emergent discussions spotlighted a need to reframe engagement with the themes of art, labour and activism by focusing on how these are *praxes*, rather than simply delineated fields of study. Directing attention to art, activist and labour *praxes* caused us to look at how processes converge and connect. As our conversations developed into short texts for a self-published zine, we began to realise the complexity of these intersections and their significance within wider cultural discourses, both in the field of art and creative labour and in the field of activism and social movements. The need for extended analyses of how art, labour and activism intersect underpins this volume, as does an intention to explore new perspectives, emerging out of conversations between disciplines such as sociology, anthropology and art theory.

Each chapter in this book was written in 2016, a year that saw a series of significant political shifts, particularly in the West, where a majority of voters in Britain opted to leave the European Union and voters in the United States elected businessman Donald Trump as president. Alongside these shifts we have seen the side-lining of humanitarian imperatives, in particular the withdrawal of support for refugees, and an increased number of race-hate crimes. These political changes also have implications for cultural institutions, for example, through reductions in research funding for many academics and the breakdown of institutional affiliations, for example, those made possible through shared membership of the EU.

The chapters in *artWORK* have developed within these complex and shifting social contexts. Through close attention to grassroots creative projects they explore ways in which we can continue to maintain strong networks of communication, generate changes in labour conditions and create new forms of post-capitalist exchange. Although many intersections between art, labour and activism in this volume are micro-political, they contextualise grassroots projects within these larger global shifts. As such they do not suggest alternative generalisations about art, activism and labour, but instead advocate for a closer examination of the complexity of their intersections. At the same time, by focusing on particular issues, they show how grassroots projects can institute change within and outside of established institutions.

artWORK aims to be a resource for scholars and cultural practitioners from a number of fields. Although the projects in this volume are still developing, we hope that by magnifying and reflecting on the mechanisms and strategies that have characterised these projects to date, we can sustain critical and creative engagement that serves to strengthen both the internal structures and interconnections within and beyond each of these projects. At the same time, we intend this volume to provide stimulus for new projects and insight to sustain networks of support between developing cultural projects that are not included in this collection.

As outlined in the introduction, we began by addressing contemporary discourses on aesthetics, collective action, prefigurative politics and embodiment, to approach the intersections between art, labour and activism through two key enquiries. First, we wanted to explore how the organisational structures required for collective action can generate new ways of art-making and collaborating and resist co-option into capitalist frameworks. And second, we hoped to highlight ways in which practices at these intersections can reproduce or challenge ideas around the instrumentalisation of art and 'art for arts sake'. At stake in these two enquiries is the ability of art to generate social changes democratically[1] and without reliance on systems of exchange that reduce beings and cultural artefacts to a commodity value and the 'manner' of this ability; the way art conducts itself as it institutes change (as didactic/open/reflective). We were interested in how artistically inspired political projects can also harbour different forms of radicality that diverge from traditional democratic processes. As such, we aimed to develop these discourses through close attention to artistic experiments, deliberative decision-making processes and nuances within a variety of different creative practices, as well as their wider implications.

artWORK began by looking at selected organisational structures and their relationship to grassroots collective action. Chapter 1, 'Reimaging, Reimagining or Reimagineering: Rebranding Ulster', addressed current organisational structures and began to problematise some of their internal mechanisms and approaches. In their analysis of the cultural 'renaissance' unfolding in Belfast – involving the local government, traditional indigenous groups and arts professionals – researcher Sarah Feinstein and artist Sheelagh Colclough contrasted the concepts of 'reimaging' a city through public art commissions, 'reimagineering' through tourism and regeneration, and 'the reimagining' of community arts. This chapter championed the kind of community arts that nurture the agency of local communities in reimagining the urban space, looking to the future but without erasing the past. It suggested that when we allow public culture to reflect dissonance, conflict and tension, as opposed to using culture as a means for diffusing and erasing a conflictive past (and present), we open up spaces for participatory democracy.

The following chapter, 'Art, Activism and Addressing Sexual Assault in the UK: A Case Study', developed the idea of sustaining agency within grassroots community projects. Reflecting on her role as a cofounder of Clear Lines festival, writer and activist Winnie M Li addressed the challenges of working within an underfunded activist sphere. Referring specifically to the demands of labour and capital, she reflected on the emotional and psychological implications of working in an environment in which creative labour endeavours to transcend commodification. Li illuminated the need for stronger infrastructures of support between different creative groups. Calling for a cultural commons, sustained by collaborative networks, she argued that active affiliations can not only provide emotional support and prevent exhaustion, but they can also facilitate better media visibility.

These first two chapters began to bring to light ways in which existing frameworks can be subverted, altered and modified in order to sustain non-commodifiable creative practices. In this way, they led to the second part of our enquiry: by what means might modifications of existing frameworks generate new ways of art-making and collaborating? The following two chapters advanced an extended analysis of Macao, a creative activist agency based in Milan, Italy. These chapters traced the development of a project, from engineering interventions to subverting existing structures, to embodying radically new cultural possibilities.

Maria Murru and Alberto Cossu's chapter, 'Macao before and beyond Social Media: The Creation of the Unexpected as a Mobilisation Logic', explores the development of Macao – a new centre for arts, culture and research of Milan. This chapter highlighted the way in which Macao counters urban policy through discursive and performative practices. It focused particularly on the role of digital communications practices throughout Macao's actions and interventions. Murru and Cossu proposed the notion of 'eventful logic' as a new pragmatic concept through which the strategies and the logics of collective action through social media can be explained. Starting from an overview of the ongoing debate about the relationship between digital media and political protest, the contribution showed the eccentricity of Macao with respect to three already established analytical models: the logic of connective action by Bennett and Segerberg (2013), the concept of communicative cultures by Kavada (2012), the logic of aggregation by Juris (2012).

Extending the analysis of Macao to address its potentiality, Emanuele Braga's chapter, 'The Political Value of Techno-Future', explored new possibilities for the future of culture, based not on the accumulation of capital value through algorithms that gather and control behavioural data, but on technologies that work in synthesis with humans to generate decentralised political engagement. These emergent technologies (e.g. Freecoin) aim to restore power to collective, democratic decision-making processes. Braga addressed the relationship between humans and machines. He approached the social body as a desiring machine and looked at the labour that sustains this machine. Crucially, he asked us to imagine machines as prostheses for playful discovery of the world, rather than apparatuses of control.

Nevertheless, the precarity of emergent practices and the uncertainty of creative potential demanded a deeper analysis of how such practices can resist co-option into capitalist frameworks. Having reconsidered the role of machines within society, situating them as auxiliary rather than regulating, Braga's chapter ultimately centred on the role of the humans and their power to decide upon the social role of technology. Paula Serafini's chapter 'Changing the Narrative: Highlighting Workers' Rights in Environmental Art Activism' extended our perceptions of what it means to be human through close consideration of the relation between labour and narrative.

Serafini discussed the need for deeper connections between social justice and environmental campaigns. Drawing from her first-hand experience of actions by activist theatre group BP or not BP?, Serafini focused on how narrative frameworks in art activism can facilitate greater engagement with the ways in which issues of human and workers' rights, the environment, corporate power and neocolonialism all fold into each other. Departing from single-issue campaigns, these narrative approaches hail a decolonial approach to generating social change. These narratives, at times comedic, performative, metaphoric or shocking, encourage us to engage critically with underlying power structures that may not be spotlighted in single-issue campaigns.

Further developing the themes of 'humanity' and 'embodiment' in chapter 6, 'Working Dancers: Contemporary Dance Activism in Argentina', Konstantina Bousmpoura and Julia Martinez Heimann address the idea of workers' human rights. They discuss specific labour policies – and their dehumanising implications – that provoked activist dance performances in Argentina, alongside the initiative to create an artist-led dance company that would challenge the exploitative labour practices of state dance organisations. Through their analysis of the cultural work behind the performances themselves, as well as the process of documenting and circulating these performances beyond their immediate locale, Heimann and Bousmpoura amplify the significance of making a political demand through embodied performances. Reflecting on the writings of Argentine philosopher Eduardo Rinesi, who highlights a shift in focus away from freedom and on to rights, this chapter aims to build on a dynamic social movement and to further facilitate dance workers' rights *and* sustain creative freedom.

Chapters 1 to 6 therefore addressed the first research enquiry into existing organisational structures and the emergence of new, independent creative collaborations. The remaining chapters centred on discussions around the instrumentalisation of art and explored how it functions or malfunctions within social apparatuses.

In chapter 7, 'Making Art Relevant in the Aftermath of the Egyptian Uprising', writer and researcher Rounwah Bseiso examined emergent creative practices in Egypt that lie at the intersection of art and activism. Bseiso explored how street art in Egypt revolutionised cultural production through the process of intervening in and subverting cultural practices. These grassroots creative practices emerged informally, but in doing so, they began to alter their surrounding cultural framework, highlighting issues of control and receptivity within the wider art scene. This chapter highlighted ways in which intersectional practices begin to challenge assumptions regarding the 'function' of art and culture.

In the subsequent chapter, 'Collective Art-Making to Agitate for Social Change: Liberate Tate in Parallel with the Wooster Group, Greenham Common Women's Peace Camp, Forced Entertainment, La Pocha Nostra, Climate Camp and Occupy Wall Street', artist and activist Mel Evans traces historical and emergent intersections between art and activism, with emphasis on the creative tools and methods within protest movements, in particular the creative interventions of art group Liberate Tate. Drawing attention to the aesthetic processes of co-creation, she emphasised the way in which these processes can become models for democratic engagement, impact wider political discussions and trigger social changes. Here we began to see that art can sustain freedom of expression and recourse to platforms of social and political exchange.

In simple terms, it could be argued that art is instrumental in sustaining the freedom to create communicative bonds. Paradoxically, the apparent simplicity of art's instrumentality requires perpetual acknowledgement of the complexity of social interactions and creative practices. As Jane Trowell points out in her chapter 'Embracing Failure, Educating Hope: Some Arts Activist Educators' Concerns in Their Work for Social Justice', the success of projects for social change is bound up in the need to slow down, step back and embrace failure. Trowell argues that to embrace failure is simultaneously to educate hope. To acknowledge and work with a failed project allows active reflection and collective learning. To activate hope in this way emphasises the humanity of creative and educational projects for social change and underlines the need for supportive networks.

The idea of powerful 'ineffectiveness' is continued throughout Jessica Holtaway's chapter, 'In Case of Emergency Make Art: Exploring the (Non) function of Art in Response to Humanitarian Disasters'. Holtaway proposes that although art is ineffective as a mending tool in the face of humanitarian disasters, it can paradoxically become a powerful way of critiquing and altering the social subconscious and can lead to new social paradigms. Holtaway points to the current neoliberal context and argues that art 'malfunctions' within larger apparatuses of exchange, designed to produce profit for the few. By focusing on sustaining relational networks that support affected communities as well as addressing the general public, as opposed to working towards profit, non-commercial, relational art creates a glitch in the system.

Following the trajectory of this collection of chapters, we ultimately return to the idea of creating glitches, fissures or interruptions within established organisational structures that, through processes of regulation, serve to reinforce 'norms' and create marginalised social groups. However, the cyclical nature of this journey does not negate or undermine the potential of these analyses. Rather, in the light of Gregory Sholette's exhortation to 'occupy, organise and repeat', this cycle of creativity promises a perpetual renewal, opening practices again and again to new voices, ideas and sensibilities.

In the eleventh and final chapter of this volume, Roger Sansi-Roca reflects on the current 'cycle' through an anthropological analysis of art activism in Spain. Drawing on the experiences of the Enmedio collective, he explains that participatory exchange is a 'gift', rather than a commodity with an equivalential value. Understanding how the imperative to participate can be transformative leads on to his definition of a 'new post-autonomous moment' and emphasises the necessity for alternative political experiments.

If it is indeed true that art activist practices are perpetually renewed, we hope to highlight a common framework of reference that supports a deeper understanding of the current wave. French scholar Mathieu Gregoire also addresses this cyclical engagement by looking at the struggles of French artists during the past century. He stresses how each singular wave contained his own 'emancipatory horizon' (2013). Here, we attempt to frame such a horizon in relation to the wider socio-political climate in which artists/activists are situating their activities. It must be noted, however, that we do not approach such a task to generate a comparative view. We do not aim to universalise the different experiences we have gathered in this volume. Although, in certain situations, comparisons and generalisations can help to build a common framework, we insist more on a process of connecting facets to create a 'dice' which is constantly expanding and shape-shifting, a tool that facilitates playful engagement between different actors and that can perhaps lead to the expansion of common frameworks. The *Techniques of Art and Protest* conference that we organised in 2015 and which sparked the conversations that led to this volume aimed at mapping and bringing together actors who shared strategies and approaches to social change via artistic means. This book intends to reflect the complexity and heterogeneity of these shared facets. In this vein, we might understand our work, both in the conference and in this book, as an attempt to federate some of these facets and make them circulate through the movements, experiences and actors that the book speaks of (and to).

These actors emerge from contexts in which social, political and economic coordinates vary radically, from revolutionary Egypt, to European countries under neoliberal rule and Kirchnerist politics in Argentina. Although it is not the priority of this book to trace meaningful comparisons between different forms of art activism as they appear on the 'outside', a meaningful contribution might come from an overview of the relations they have on the 'inside'. In other words: how are art, labour and politics envisioned by the current wave of art activism?

Many of these initiatives struggle against dysfunctional art systems. Others have attempted to intervene in order to affect change and have failed, choosing to channel their energies in other ways. Often this calls for reflection on the antagonistic or non-antagonistic posture that different cases embody. This has to do with the belief (or the reasonable hope) that existing institutions can and must be changed, therefore consecrating energy to reform, even radically, existing art institutions (e.g. Tate). In other cases, the residual positive aura that the art systems still harbours is used to justify a struggle that strategically aims to build entirely new institutions (e.g. Macao). Here, a reflective critique is not necessarily linked with an antagonistic posture; it instead signals the emergence of an innovative movement with a repertoire of action that is not dependent on manifestations such as marches and rallies.

Local economic contexts also define the nature of the elements available to be recuperated or critiqued by art activism. Globally, we are witnessing an increasing 'uberisation' of the economy. In this context, platform capitalism and gig economies (Srnicek, 2016) are indeed phenomena that directly impact already precarious artists/activists and provide critical grounds for interventions. At the same time, however, we also find elements of digital culture and entrepreneurialism which can be *detourned* from the standpoint of a political subjectivity that guides its adoption to avoid the reproduction of self-exploitative elements (e.g. Macao). As Lacan might have said, the new creative worker exists between two deaths. For Shukaitis (2016) this is between the 'not yet' of being creative and the 'already' of being subsumed by capital. Therefore, the political work that art activists are putting forth revolves around this exact point: to reflexively tackle their subsumption by adopting politically the already non-neutral capitalistic dispositifs. This can be viewed as an active response to the growing inequality in the cultural industries under recent neoliberal trends. However, as Mark Banks points out 'inequity and inequality have *always* been present in cultural work' (Banks, 2017, 8).

This leads to the issue of economic sustainability of the current wave of art activism. Insofar as some of the experiences presented here indeed aim to build alternatives to precarity in a concrete way (e.g. through festivals, alternative organisational structures and embodied practices) they also deal with the widespread and substantial decline of public funding in arts and culture. As we know from social movements scholarship, activists often support particular causes through working as volunteers. This is why, as a number of chapters highlighted, it is important to imagine and implement different economic models starting from the organisational setting of a group, a community or a movement. It is here that art, labour and activism intersect, politicising relations in an attempt to redefine value in the last instance.

It is through organisational and aesthetic practices that many activists can explore new definitions of the notion of value, work and critique. Art activist practices demonstrate their ability to work as stitching mechanisms on imaginary and symbolic levels, also providing powerful network connections that can lead to the creation of political opportunities and implement change at a policy level – or create new organisations and practices that attempt to circumvent policy altogether. If the current wave of art activism has been interpreted as a dissolution of the artistic in the social in its various forms, we believe that this book illuminates a further step. That is, it throws light on ways in which these processes are now moving from an 'artistically politicised social' field into the economic field.

Considering this, and the aforementioned call to 'occupy, organise and repeat', it is necessary to ask: how can we sustain this cycle? Or more precisely, how can we create practices that are sustainable in an age of increasing cuts to welfare and the arts sector without falling into exploitative labour practices all too common to the fields of activism, community arts and art activism? The chapters in this book and the conclusions they offer suggest a number of issues that are key towards the development of sustainable creative political practices: strategic use of art and media tools; flexibility and embracing failure; strategic engagement with art organisations and state institutions and a rejection of definitions.

The first point, the strategic use of art and media tools, is developed by Cossu and Murru and by Braga in reference to Macao's use of social media and their development of cryptocurrency, but also stressed by Li in her analysis of Clear Lines festival and by Serafini in her account of BP or not BP? performances. These chapters put forward an idea of art activism as strategic and of media tools as tactical. This does not mean, however, that art is purely conceived of as an instrument or a means to an end, but rather that strategy is embedded in the creative process. Art and media are not tricks pulled out of a metaphorical hat, but they initiate language and form that characterise political action.

The second point is on flexibility and embracing failure. Evans's chapter provides a genealogy of participatory activist practice that clearly shows the kinds of compromises in organisational models for the sake of creating spaces that are conducive to collective creativity but also uphold activist values.

From the perspective of radical arts education, Trowell brings focus to the much neglected theme of failure and the need to embrace failure in order to move forward. These chapters act as a reminder that art activist practices need to be responsive to the contexts they are operating in and accept that creating those structures and processes is part of activist work. The tension between adapting to social and political events and taking the time to do reflective work on internal processes and the emotional labour of art activism is a key issue here, addressed also by Li's chapter.

Following from this is the issue of strategic engagement with art organisations and state institutions. The case of working dancers explored in Heimann and Bousmpoura's chapter demonstrates this approach in their creation of a new, artist-run dance company while still demanding labour rights from the state and engaging with key stakeholders in the dance world. In this sense this chapter also engages with issues of flexibility, as dancers developed a strategy that involved both engagement and negotiation with state entities and the withdrawal from state structures. But the strategic engagement we refer to here can also mean a hijacking of art organisations and state institutions. Braga's chapter for instance explained how Macao artists hijacked the Fashion Week social media accounts to bring attention to the underlying politics and economics of this high-profile event. Similarly, the rebel exhibition described in Serafini's chapter used the physical site of the British Museum to unveil a counter-exhibition that subverted the branding of the museum's famous *A History of the World in 100 objects* exhibition to tell a story of BP's role in environmental and human rights violations.

Finally, the chapters in this book adhere to a rejection of clear-cut definitions and categorisations on what constitutes art and what counts as activism. Through a rejection of the art world and its institutions, the artists presented in Bsesio's chapter reject the idea that art is what is found in gallery walls and move towards a kind of art that is instead rooted in social relations and an exploration of art as a social, public good. Holtaway's chapter also stands against definitions by challenging the idea of art as either instrumental or useless and exploring instead the significance of a non-instrumentality that can in fact lead to social and political change.

WHAT NEXT?

In the introduction to this book we discussed different ways in which art, labour and activism intersect in practices emerging from the field of art and culture as well as the field of social movements. While we proposed to frame this plethora of groups, artworks, practices and events under the umbrella of art activism, two questions still remain: what are the distinguishing elements among them? And what analytical tools might help us better understand the connections, similarities and differences between different kinds of practices that engage the aesthetic and the political, without setting rigid barriers? With this in mind, we propose a taxonomy that responds to the complexity of the contemporary scenario and offers a number of distinctions to help understand the ecology of art activism.

Subjects	Artists/non-artists/Non-professionally trained artists
Process	Extra-institutional (incl. constituent practices, social movements, grassroots)/Institutional
Main Arena	Political, Artistic, Social, Economic, Urban
Artistic Artefact/Medium	Events, Exhibitions, Protests, Performances, Visual, Sculpture and Installations
For example, Graffiti in Cairo: Non-professionally trained artists, extra-institutional process, political and urban arena, Visual.	

Figure 12.1. Four coordinates for the study of art activism and labour

This taxonomy suggests a process of plotting the preliminary coordinates of creative practices. 'Coordinating', from the Latin *coordinare* 'to place in the same rank', indicates processes of mapping or connecting. Although the table suggests categories – 'subjects', 'processes', 'arenas', and 'media' – these are interpreted in the light of the analyses throughout this volume – as dynamic placeholders, or starting points from which to engage with the multiple and entangled realities that constitute social relations. For example, approaching interventions and collaborations through the framework of this table might also allow us to further illuminate ways in which race, gender and class shape the trajectory of emergent practices and as such develop supportive collaborations and networks and ensure that the historic paradigms of control and power are not reproduced.

The first category, subjects, refers to the position as well as the identity of actors. Do they identify as artists, as cultural workers, as activists, or perhaps as all of the above? For example, sociologist Pierre-Michel Menger suggests that there are four kinds of 'artist': the generalised definition of 'those who make art, those deemed to be professionals by the state, those drawing an income from artistic work and famous geniuses throughout history. However, in a review of his book *The Economics of Creativity: Art and Achievement under Uncertainty*, Alison Gerber argues that none of these groups overlap well with the other and none appear 'to encompass the great variety of those we call "artists" on the ground' (Gerber, 2015: 1116).

With this in mind, it is important to note that this table does not mean to be exhaustive, nor to have a take on what can be qualified as 'proper' art; it is rather an attempt to render analytically manageable this complexity. In fact, the inclusion of art processes or artefacts by non-artists in a social movement context is entirely dependent on dominant aesthetic canons, on whether art gatekeepers can or should decide on their acceptability and on the divide between high and low culture. Issues of class and race again are paramount here, as access to artistic education, resources and positionality in creative-sector ecology will condition who gets to produce art and whose art is considered legitimate. In this book, we have sought to include examples of a wide number of combinations between these criteria whose commonality resides in actors' efforts to 'reframe creative work in more radical terms. . . . in order to differentiate it from both popular culture and the mainstream art world' (Sholette, 2016: 6). We hope that this approach speaks to artists who deliberately refuse to measure success using the terms and values of the art 'system' – embracing existing rationales that seek to negate uncertainty – but instead seek to adapt spaces for creative engagement, perhaps embracing 'post-autonomy' in new and unpredictable ways.

The second category, process, is divided into institutional and extra-institutional. As the lines between institutional and extra or non-institutional art can sometimes be blurred, one of the key objectives of this book was to examine the complexities of cultural and activist labour and the opportunities and challenges that emerge when operating within and outside the grey area between institutions and independent grassroots spaces. This categorisation is therefore not an invitation to simplify the position of a given practice, but to pay attention to the position of actors within an ecosystem of institutions, groups and loosely formed networks, in order to understand how this position and the power relations that come with it, inform a particular kind of artistic and/or political practice as labour.

Directly connected to the issue of process is the arena of action. Here we speak of physical, existing arenas such as the urban landscape or cultural institution, but also the wider frameworks a specific practice is operating within and/or attempting to intervene. The chapters in this book have for instance, covered projects that attempted to intervene in cultural policy, economics and mainstream media.

And finally, the last category, artistic artefact or medium, refers to the preferred medium of expression and action of a group. This question invites reflections on the politics of different mediums and practices such as the visual arts, social media and performance. How do different mediums allow or inhibit participation? What are the potentials of different forms of communication? How are different practices embodied by artists, activists and the public?

For instance, an analysis of Macao – a prominent example in this book – utilising the tools offered by this table, would invite us to consider the ways in which artists as subjects and actors intervene in the cultural, urban and economic spheres through the implementation of grassroots processes, the creation of a new institution that both engages with and counters the mainstream cultural sector of Milan and the use of social media and new digital technologies as tools of intervention.

This concluding suggestion – to initially approach creative practices through a temporal taxonomy – may seem to counter the intersectionality advocated throughout this volume. However, we believe that close attention to the arrangements of actors, processes, arenas and media can help plot the coordinates of emergent practices, bringing complex elements of activities into effective relationships. These coordinates will inevitably change and develop, but the initial process of 'coordinating' brings diverse projects into contact with each other, opening up possibilities for further intersections and affiliations.

NOTE

1. Furthermore, it is worth investigating how artistic-inspired projects can also harbour radical ideas that transcend traditional democratic processes. Sometimes both instances co-exist in the same movement, as they did in OWS, in which more radical projects were pursued outside of the consensus-based general assemblies (Roberts, 2012).

REFERENCES

Banks, Mark. 2017. *Creative Justice: Cultural Industries, Work and Inequality*. London: Rowman and Littlefield International.

Bennett, Lance and Alexandra Segerberg. 2013. *The Logic of Connective Action. Digital Media and the Personalization of Contentious Politics*. New York: Cambridge University Press.

Gerber, Alison. 2015. 'Book review *The Economics of Creativity*, by P.M. Menger' in *Organization Studies*, 36(8), 1115–17.

Kavada, Anastasia. 2013. *Internet Cultures and Protest Movements: The Cultural Links Between Strategy, Organizing and Online Communication*, in B. Cammerts, A. Mattoni and P. McCurdy (eds.), *Mediation and Protest Movements*. Chicago: The University of Chicago Press.

Juris, Jeffrey S. 2012. Reflections on #Occupy Everywhere: Social Media, Public Space, and Emerging Logics of Aggregation, in *American Ethnologist*, 39(2), pp. 259–79.

Menger, Pierre-Michelle. 2014. *The Economics of Creativity: Art and Achievement under Uncertainty*. Cambridge, MA: Harvard University Press.

Roberts, Alasdair. 2012. 'Why the Occupy Movement Failed', *Public Administration Review*, 72(5), 754–62.

Sholette, Gregory. 2016. 'Merciless Aesthetic: Activist Art as the Return of Institutional Critique. A Response to Boris Groys'. Field 4/2016. Available online at: http://field-journal.com/issue-4/merciless-aesthetic-activist-art-as-the-return-of-institutional-critique-a-response-to-boris-groys.

Shukaitis, Stevphen. 2016. *The Composition of Movements to Come: Aesthetics and Cultural Labour after the Avant-Garde*. London: Rowman and Littlefield.

Srnicek, Nick. 2016. *Platform Capitalism*. Cambridge: Polity Press.

Acknowledgements

There are several people and organisations that have directly and indirectly contributed to this book, and who we would like to thank for their support.

We are grateful to the Centre for Cultural Studies at Goldsmiths, the Goldsmiths Graduate School and the Department of Culture, Media & Creative Industries at King's College London for their support in planning PLANK's first event, *Techniques of Art and Protest*.

We thank our friend and colleague Marc Herbst with whom we have shared fantastic PLANK projects and events.

We would also like to thank Cecilia Serafini, The Common House and The London College of Communication for their support throughout the development of the PLANK network.

We also thank Rory Buckley for his assistance during the final stages of formatting and editing.

Above all, we would like to thank all of the contributors to this volume for sharing their experiences and insight.

Last, this would not have been possible without the guidance and support from Rowman and Littlefield International and the series editors Ruth Sanz Sabido and Stuart Price. We thank everyone who worked on this project with us.

Index

Abaza, Mona, 149, 151
Abdelmagid, Yakein, 153, 154
activism: activist work, 56 (*see also* labour: in art activism); art-science activisms, 221; environmental, 105, 169, 175, 177–80 (*see also* environmentalism). *See also* art activism
Adorno, Theodor, 209
aestheticisation of politics, 2, 3, 6, 238
affect, 6
Ahora Madrid (Now Madrid), 230
Alfred, Charlotte, 163
Amin, Hussein Youssef, 149
Amin, Shahira, 163
Amsler, Sarah, 189–207; advanced capitalism, 203; neoliberal capitalism, 199; neoliberalism, 199, 203
anthropologists, 228, 230, 232–34
anthropology, 138, 232–35; art and, 234; dance anthropology, 139
anti-imperialism, 149
archive/archiving, 154
Arendt, Hannah, 162
Argentina, 127–45; Argentine Congressional Cultural Commission, 143; Argentine culture, 127–45; Argentine dance community, 135–45; Argentine National Company of Contemporary Dance (CNDC), 127, 128, *132*, 137, *138*, 139, 140, 142; Argentine National Congress, 128, 141–43; Argentine society, 134, 137; National Senate of Argentina, 137
art: ineffectiveness, 242; as an institution, 91, 227, 243; instrumentalisation of, 5, 8, 28n5, 238, 241; and politics, 6; processes of, 6; radicality, 238; of social movements, 7; as a social science, 226
Art Action UK, 210, 212, 213, 216, 217
art activism, 106n3; in Italy, 65–66, 90; in Spain, 225; in United Kingdom, 168; waves, 3–4
artists: as activists, 137; as mediators, 162; mobilisation of, 1, 7, 8; as organisers, 10, 128; pressure to professionalise, 227, 233; state artists, 139; as workers, 8, 10, 66, 127, 128, 130
Art & Liberty Movement, 149
Art Not Oil, 107, 119
Arts Catalyst, 221
Art Work (exhibition), 9
Art Workers' Coalition, 9

art world: autonomous, 225 (*see also* politicisation of aesthetics: post-autonomy); commercial, 227; inequalities of, 10; international, 225–27
Ashur, Nabil, 154
Asociación de Trabajadores del Estado (ATE), 129, 136
ATE. *See* Asociación de Trabajadores del Estado (ATE)
audiovisual production, 138
Auschwitz, 209, 215
austerity, 189
automation, 87, 92, 240; algorithms and, 95
Awad, Alaa, 157

Bakr, Ammar Abo, 160, 161
Baladi, Lara, 154. *See also* Vox Populi: Tahrir Archives
Ballet Folklórico Nacional (National Folkloric Ballet), 136
Banks, Mark, 9, 47, 243
Bañón, Agueda, 230
Barcelona, 225–35; art collectives in, 227; city council of, 230
Barcelona en Comú (Barcelona in Common), 230
BCTSM. *See* San Martin Theater Contemporary Ballet (BCTSM)
Becker, Howard, 225, 226
Beckett, Samuel, 191
becoming, 200, 201; Amsler on, 193, 203, 204
Benjamin, Walter, 2, 3
Bennett, Lance and Segerberg, Alexandra, 11, 67–69, 80
Beránek, Ondře, 149
big data, 95
Bishop, Claire, 160, 225, 232
Bitcoin, 88
Blacklist Support Group, 118
Blanchot, Maurice, 209, 213–16, 219, 222
Bloch, Ernst, 189–207
blockchain, 88

Blurred Lines, 45
Boltanski, Luc and Chiapello, Eve, 14
Boraïe, Sherief, 151
Bourdieu, Pierre, 225, 226
Bourriaud, Nicolas, 4, 159–60
BP, 109, 110–11, 112, 113, 115, 117, 118, 167
BP or not BP?, 106, 107, 108, 109, 115, 119, 120
Breton, André, 149
Brexit, post-Brexit, 189, 234
Brison, Susan, 46, 49, 54
British Museum, 120, 121
Buenos Aires, 128, 129, 131, 136, 141, 143, 144n7, 144n9; Government of the City of, 131, 136
Building Peace through the Arts: Reimaging Communities, 27
Burrowes, Nina, 48–49, 54

Cairo, 147, 148, 150, 153–55, 159; Governorate of, 153
Callon, Michel, 233
capitalism, 195; anarcho-capitalism, 87; brutalities of, 205; capitalistic thinking, 203; counter-capitalist, 203; global, 212, 217, 222; machines and, 92–93, 97; pedagogy and, 206; the state and, 112, 199; subsumption, 243. *See also* Amsler, Sarah
Carozzi, Maria Julia, 139
Castels, Manuel, 11, 14
Chams, Dalia, 163
Charbel, Jano, 147, 151
choreography/choreographers, 128, 136, 137, 140, 142, 143
CIRCA, 114. *See also* Clandestine Insurgent Rebel Clown Army
civic rights, 137
Clandestine Insurgent Rebel Clown Army, 114. *See also* CIRCA
Clear Lines Festival, 45, 49, 52, 54–55, 58–59
Climate Camp (UK), 169, 176–80, 182–83, 241

CNDC. *See* Argentina, Argentine National Company of Contemporary Dance
Colau, Ada, 229, 230
Colclough, Sheelagh, 28, 238
Cold War, 175–76
collective identity, 12
colonialism, 108, 117, 196; (neo), 108, 117, 120. *See also* coloniality; decolonialism
coloniality, 196–98, 200, 205, 206; privileges afforded by, 190
comic books: *The Courage to Be Me*, 54
Common Wealth (Theatre), 169, 180
community arts, 29, 33, 168–69, 173–75, 179, 239. *See also* participatory art; socially engaged art
competition, 58–59
conferences: Critical Sites: Issues in Critical Practice and Pedagogy, Ireland, 192
connective action, 13. *See also* connective logic
connective logic, 11. *See also* connective action
Couldry, Nick, 71, 74
The Courage to Be Me, 54
creative city, 81
creative commons, 53, 55, 59
creative labour, 47, 51–52, 66
critical discourse analysis, 75
crowdfunding, 51, 55–56
crypto-currency, 88, 99
cultural and creative industries, 9
cultural capital, 51
cultural democracy, 40
cultural jamming, 76
cultural policy for dance, 127–45
cultural production, 226, 227, 232
culture: in Egypt, 149, 156, 157, 160–63; in Northern Ireland, 40; as resource, 25
Culture Night Belfast, 35–36, 38–40

curatorial practices, 121, 212, 220, 223; as activism, 119–20. *See also* Art Action UK

Daiwa Anglo-Japanese Foundation, 220
dance: as labour, 128, 131. *See also* working dancers
dance companies, 127–45; creation of a state-supported contemporary dance company, 136
dancers, 127–45; as activists, 129–30; as cultural workers, 127–36, 140, 141, 143
D-Cent, 88
decolonialism, 120, 196
decoloniality, 16
Deleuze, Gilles, 213
della Porta, Donatella, 79
democracy, 130–34, 136, 140, 150, 152, 233, 234; democratising dance, 140; experiments in, 234; participatory democracy, 133, 137; technical democracy, 233, 234
democratisation, 134
demonstration: *escrache*, 229, 235n3
Derrida, Jacques, 95, 213
dialogical art, 4, 5
dialogue, 49
Direct Action, 168, 229
Disobedient Objects, 119n16
distribution of the sensible, 227
Doney, Meryl, 210
Do What You Love (DWYL), 52
Downey, Anthony, 154
Duchamp, Marcel, 147
DWYL. *See* Do What You Love (DWYL)

Eagleton, Terry, 106
ECESR. *See* Media Unit in the Egyptian Center for Economic and Social Rights (ECESR)
economic production, 225
education: holistic, 194; of hope, 189–207; educational reform,

149; Spoken Word education collectives, 198
Egypt, 147–63, 241; cultural expression, 149; cultural renaissance, 149; cultural repression, 149; Ministry of Culture, 150, 155, 157; post-2011, 153; uprisings in, 148, 151–52, 156–58, 162–63. *See also* culture: in Egypt; Tahrir Square
El Ansary, Hannah, 153
El Degham, Hanaa, 157–59
El Husseiny, Basma, 156
El Husseiny, Mustafa, 159. *See also* Mona Lisa Brigades
El Zeft, 158, 159
embodied theory, 202; un-embodied theory, 199
embodiment, 15–16, 238, 240
emotional labour, 47, 52–53, 56
England: artists of colour based in, 194; campaigning in, 197; neoliberalism in, 189
Enmedio, 228, 229, 242
environmentalism, 105, 106; in the UK, 107, 117, 120, 122
ethics, 210, 215, 219, 221, 222; of oil sponsorship, 107, 167
Evaluate, 28, 29, 34, 40
event: economy, 66, 94; politics of, 80
eventful: logic, 80; protest, 79–80; temporality, 79
Everything's Normal, 48
exhibitions: *Disobedient Objects*, 119n16; *A History of BP in 10 Objects*, 115, 119, 121

Faculty of Fine Arts in Luxor, 160
failure, 189–207 (esp. 190–191), 241
Fairclough, Norman, 75
Faircoop, 88, 99
fascism, 149, 234; aesthetics of, 2
festivals, 36–37; Clear Lines Festival, 45, 49, 52, 54–55, 58–59; Nitaq Festival, 150; Unheard Festival, 47–48; Women of the World Festival (WOW), 48
filmic ethnography, 138, 139
finance : reprogramming, 98
financial crisis, 88, 89–90
financial markets, 226
flashmob, 143
Florida, Richard, 81
Folkloric Ballet of the University College of Arts-IUNA, 143
Forced Entertainment (Sheffield), 168, 241
Foster, Hal, 225
Foster, Susan Leigh, 131
Foucault, Michel, 213
Fouda, Radwa, 157, 158, 161
France: division of labour, 226
Franco, Francisco, 231
Franko, Mark, 131, 132, 135, 137
Fraser, Nancy, 46, 54. *See also* subaltern counter-publics
Freecoin, 88
freelance 'gig' economy, 52
Freudian theory, 149
Fukushima, 209, 216, 221

Gaber, Mohamed, 151
Ganzeer, 147, 148
García Canclini, Néstor, 225–27, 231, 232, 234, 235
GAS. *See* Graphics against the System (GAS)
gentrification, 232
Gerber Alison, 246
gerontocratic system, 231
Gide, André, 209
Giza, 159
Glas(s) Performance (Glasgow), 169, 179
Gleeson, Jessamy, 51
Gotham, Kevin, 37
graffiti, 147, 151, 153, 154, 161. *See also* street art
Graphics against the System (GAS), 151

Greenham Common Women's Peace Camp, 169, 175–80
Grégoire, Mathieu, 8, 242
Gröndahl, Mia, 151
Grosfoguel, Ramon, 196
Group of Contemporary Art, The, 149
Groys, Boris, 3, 6
Grupo independiente por una ley nacional de danza (the Independent Group for a National Dance Law), 141

hackers, 98
Halsall, Francis, 33–34
Hamdy, Basma and Stone, 147, 151
Hanasaki, Kaya, 210–13, *211*
Harvey, David, 37
hegemonic narratives: art and, 161
Helix Arts, 192
Henein, George, 149
Hesmondhalgh, David, 47
A History of BP in 10 Objects, 115, 119, 121
Hochschild, Arlie, 47
Hogue, Richard, 202
Holmes, Douglas, 233
Homma, Kaori, 210
hope: educating, 189–207
Hope, Sophie, 40
horizontal decision-making, 133, 137, 168
human-machine interaction, 89, 101
human rights, 128, 137, 240; human rights organisations, 133
humour, 114
hybrid forums, 233. See also Callon, Michel

i-Catalyst, 150
ICT. See information and communication technology (ICT)
IKEA: pyjama party at, 228
immigration, 232
imminence, 226, 227, 232, 234, 235. See also García Canclini, Néstor

improvisation, 173
INADI. See National Institute against Discrimination, Xenophobia and Racism (INADI)
INCAA. See National Institute of Cinema and Visual Arts (Instituto Nacional de Cine y Artes Audiovisuales or INCAA)
Indymedia, 230
information and communication technology (ICT), 10
Instituto Federal de Danza (the Federal Institute of Dance), 141
International Federation of Independent Revolutionary Art, 149. See also Breton, André
Ismail, Shehab Fakhry, 148

Jankowicz, Mia, 163
Japan, 210–12, 217, 220, 222
Japan Foundation, 220
Jarbou, Rana, 147, 150, 151
Jarman, Neil, 36
Johnston, David, 37
Johnston, John, 152
Jones, Jonathan, 209, 221, 222
Juris, Jeffrey, 70–71, 80

Kamil, Anwar and Fuad, 149
Karl, Don, 151
Karnouk, Liliane, 149, 154
Kavada, Anastasia, 69–70
Keizer, 155
Kelada Mariz, 153
Kelly, Owen, 40
Kennedy, Merrit, 163
Kester, Grant, 4, 192
Khatib, Lina, 151
Kirchnerism, 127, 128, 134, 135, 143, 144n4; Kirchnerist period, 134, 136, 143; Kirchnerist State, 134, 142
Kohso, Sabu, 212
Komori, Haruka, 217–19. See also Seo, Natsumi

Kompridis, Nikolas, 198
Kraidy, Marwan, 157
Kyun-Chome, 213, *214*, 222

labour: in art activism, 2, 47 (*see also* activist work); division of, 226, 231, 234 (*see also* labour: division of social labour); division of social labour, 225, 226, 231, 232; movement, 105, 113–14, 118–19; rights, 130; underpaid, 52–53, 59 (*see also* precarity); unpaid, 48, 51 (*see also* precarity)
Laclau, Ernesto, 134, 135, 142; antagonistic border, 142; equivalence/chains of equivalency, 134, 135, 142
LaCoss, Dan, 149
Lacy, Suzanne, 192
Latin America, 127, 133, 137, 138, 144n4
Lau, Lisa, 151
Lazzarato, Maurizio, 80
leadership: and anarchism, 14; in movements, 13
Lefebvre, Henri, 96
left-wing politics, 190, 199; the left, 234; radical leftist thought, 231; social justice and, 189
Liberate Tate, 167, 169, 181–82, 241
LMS, 16–17. See *also* London Mexico Solidarity
London, 226
London Mexico Solidarity, 117. See *also* LMS
Lorde, Audre, 205
luddites, 101

Macao, 65, 88, 239, 248
Madre e hijo ('Mother and Son'), 136
Madres de Plaza de Mayo, 133, 136, 137
Maharaj, Sarat, 192
mainstream media, 55–56; visibility, 57, 121–22
Maldonado-Torres, Nelson, 196
Marcus, George E., 233

Marx, Karl, 92, 216, 217
Maslamani, Maliha, 151
mass cultural production, 227
Mauss, Marcel, 233
McDonald, 15
McKee, Yates, 10
McRobbie, Angela, 39
media, 225–31, 234; alternative digital media, 230; media practices, 71, 74; queer media, 230
Media Unit in the Egyptian Center for Economic and Social Rights (ECESR), 157
Mehrez, Samia, 150
Melucci, Alberto, 71
meme (web), 77
Menger, Pierre-Michel, 246
micro-mobilisation, 229
Middle East, 148, 153; Middle Eastern context, 148; Six-Day War, 150
Mikdadi, Salwa, 149, 150
militant research, 232
military dictatorship, 131, 133, 136, 137, 144n7
modernity: narratives of, 226
Mona Lisa Brigades, 153, 159. See *also* El Husseiny, Mustafa
money, 98; social relations and, 100
Morrison, Toni, 191
Mouffe, Chantal, 153
Mouri, Yoshitaka, 210
Mousa, Sarah, 156
movement: reconsidering the notion of, 4
'Movimiento por la Ley nacional de Danza' (the Movement for the National Dance Law), 141
Mubarak, Gamal, 150
Mubarak, Hosni, 150, 151; post-Mubarak era
Murals, 147; in Northern Ireland, 29–30. See *also* street art

Nancy, Jean-Luc, 209, 216, 217, 219, 221, 222
narrative, 106–7, 109, 112–14, 117–18, 120–21, 240

National Dance Law, 140–43
National Institute against Discrimination, Xenophobia and Racism (INADI), 136
National Institute of Cinema and Visual Arts (Instituto Nacional de Cine y Artes Audiovisuales or INCAA), 139, 144n14
Nazeer, Amr, 157
Nazism, 149. *See also* Auschwitz
Negm, Ahmed Fouad, 150
neoliberalism, 137, 231; anti-neoliberalism, 203; neoliberal governmentality, 232; neoliberal management, 232–34; neoliberal subjectivities, 232; post-neoliberalism, 144n4; in the UK, 189, 203. *See also* Amsler, Sarah
New Social Movement theory, 12
New York, 226
NGOs, 232; 'NGO-isation' of arts practice, 229, 227; NGO Observatori DESC, 229; NGO workers, 230
Nitaq Festival, 150
nonequivalence, 209, 210, 216, 219, 220–22
Ntuli, Pitika, 192
nuclear safety standards, 211, 212
nuclear technologies, 216, 221
Nuevos Rumbos ('New Directions'), 135, 136, 138

Obama campaign, 230
Occupy Wall Street, 10–11, 13, 68, 70, 89, 169, 177–79, 241
One of Us, 50
Orange Order parade, 37. *See also* the Twelfth
organisation, 11
Orozco, Gabriel, 227

PAH: media strategy of, 229. *See also* Plataforma de Afectados por la Hipoteca (*Platform for People Affected by Mortgages*), (PAH)
Palestinian Arab revolt 1936, 149
Panzieri, Raniero, 93

para-ethnographies, 233
participation, 128, 136, 140, 143, 225, 227, 232, 233
participatory art, 5, 29, 55. *See also* dialogical art; relational aesthetics
Partido-Compartido programs, 140, 145n15
Payero, Daniel, 137
peace dividend, 31
peace washing, 27
pedagogy: of becoming, 203, 204; capitalism and, 206; conference on, 192; liberatory, 197; movement building processes and, 202; pedagogical work, 190
performance, 109, 110, 113, 167
performance action, 107, 112, 113
performative protest, 132, 176. *See also* performativity
performativity, 113, 117–18
petition for dignified housing, 229
photography, 54–55; *The Watchful Eyes*, 54–55
Pinther, Kerstin S. 154
Plataforma de Afectados por la Hipoteca (*Platform for People Affected by Mortgages*) (PAH), 228–30, 233
platform, 192, 193, 194
play, 114–15
Pocha Nostra (La), 168, 173, 241
Podemos, 230
political experiments, 235
political persecution, 137
political subjectivity, 12
politicisation of aesthetics, 2–3, 177; politics of aesthetics, 226; post-autonomy, 225–35, 242
populism, 134, 135, 234
'postporno' activist movement, 230
post-workerism, 101
precarity, 59, 60, 129, 243; precarisation of labour, 228, 231. *See also* labour: underpaid; labour: unpaid
prefiguration, 13, 238
pressure to professionalise, 233; artists and, 227, 233

public art programmes: in Northern Ireland, 31, 239. *See also* Building Peace through the Arts: Reimaging Communities; Re-Imaging Communities Programme
public policy: in Northern Ireland, 38

Queen, Bernadette, 36

Rancière, Jacques, 3, 12, 152, 226, 227
rape: representations of, 55; self-narratives of, 46. *See also* sexual assault
Rashed, Waleed, 156
RAU. *See* Revolution Artists Union (RAU)
Re:Evaluate, 28, 32, 34, 40
reimagineering culture, 25n1
Re-Imaging Communities Programme, 27, 30–31
relation, 11–12
relational aesthetics, 4, 159–60
religion, 226
religious faith, 195
Retazos pequeños de nuestra historia más reciente (Small Patchworks of Our Most Recent History), 137
Revolution Artists Union (RAU), 151
revolutionary art, 147–49, 154, 156, 162. *See also* street art: in Egypt
Richter-Devroe, Sophie, 163
right-wing politics: the new right, 189; UK central government and, 189
Rikuzentakata, 218
Rinesi, Eduardo, 134. *See also* democratisation
Rizk, Mariam, 163
On Road Media, 55–56
Roatta, Laura, 143
Robin Hood Minor Asset Management, 99
Russell, Mona L. 149

Sadat, Anwar, 150; *infitah* policies, 150
Sad Panda, 155
S.A.L.E. Docks (Venice), 97, 103
Salih, Ruba, 163

same-sex marriage, 137, 138
Sanders, IV, Lewis, 151
San Martin Theater Contemporary Ballet (BCTSM), 129, 130, 143, 144n7, 144n8
San Precario, 66
Schön, Donald, 190
science and art collaborations, 221
Secretaría de Cultura de la Nación (National Agency for Cultural Affairs), 136
secularism, 195
Seo, Natsumi, 217–19. *See also* Komori, Haruka
sexual assault: representations of, 55–56, 239. *See also* rape
Sharaf, Radwa Othman, 151
sharing economy, 87, 89
The Sheelagh Foundation, 28
Shehab, Bahia, 151
Sholette, Gregory, 3, 6, 10, 14, 242, 247
Shukaitis, Stevphen, 243
Sierra, Santiago, 227
Silicon Valley, 191
Singh, Surti, 147
situationism, 228; situationist movement, 229
Smith, Christine, 152
social capital, 51
socialism, 234
social justice, 189, 190, 194–98, 203, 206, 207n8
socially engaged art, 29. *See also* participatory art; relational aesthetics
social media, 11, 50, 54–56, 66
social movements: in Argentina, 133; collective action, 238; decision-making, 178; encampments, 168–70, 173, 175–79; non-hierarchical organisation, 172; organic horizontality, 173, 176; organisation, 90–91
social participation, 225, 227. *See also* participation
social sciences, 225, 227, 230–33
society of the spectacle, 227
sociologists, 230

Sooke, Alistair, 156
space: urban, 96
Spain: art activism in, 225–35; hegemonic political discourse in, 229; Parliament of, 229
spheres of 'insertion', 227
sponsorship: oil, 107, 109, 110, 115–16, 167
STOP deshaucios (STOP evictions), 229
Strathern, Marilyn, 233
street art: in Egypt, 147–63, 241; in Northern Ireland, 152
street demonstrations, 132, 136, 138
subaltern counter-publics, 46, 50, 54
Supervivienda, 228, 229
Svampa, Maristella, 133, 134, 138

tactical frivolity, 8
Tahrir Square, 153, 154. *See also* Vox Populi: Tahrir Archives
Tantawi, Ghada, 163
Tate Modern, 167
Teatro Colón Ballet, 143
Teatro Valle, 65–66
theatre, 112; *Madre e hijo* ('Mother and Son'), 136
Torres Martínez, Gilberto, 108–9, 110–13, 120–21
tourism, 37
Townhouse Gallery, 150
Tripp, Charles, 151
the Troubles, 25–26
Turner, Victor, 173
the Twelfth, 37–38. *See also* Orange Order parade

Unheard Festival, 47–48

value: exchange value, 217; Marx's value, 217
V de Vivienda (V for Housing), 228
Villani, Tiziana, 96
Virno, Paolo, 97
Vox Populi: Tahrir Archives, 154. *See also* Baladi, Lara

W.A.G.E. *See* Working Artists and the Greater Economy (W.A.G.E.)
Walls of Freedom: Street Art of the Egyptian Revolution, 154
The Watchful Eyes, 54–55
Westmoreland, Mark R. 154
Whybrow, Nicolas, 65
Winegar, Jessica, 154
Women of the World Festival (WOW), 48
Women's emancipation, 149. *See also* Mona Lisa Brigades
Wooster Group, 168, 170, 241
work: unpaid, 197. *See also* labour, unpaid
workers' rights: in Colombia, 112. *See also* labour, movement
Working Artists and the Greater Economy (W.A.G.E.), 9
working dancers, 128
World War I, 149
World War II, 149, 215
WOW. *See* Women of the World Festival (WOW)
Writers and Artists for Change, 150

Younan, Ramsis, 149
Youth Salons (Egypt), 150

Lightning Source UK Ltd.
Milton Keynes UK
UKHW010044090419
340716UK00001B/43/P